GW00686325

"Our Lord said to St. Faustina: 'It is a great thing to know how to make use of the present moment.' With Susan Tassone's new book, *Jesus Speaks to Faustina and You*, we have yet another addition to her wonderful collection of spiritual books with which we can daily immerse ourselves in the one thing truly necessary: Our Lord's Divine Mercy. This is a special title to immerse oneself in His graces, whereby we transform the ordinary, daily circumstances of life into praise and worship, and apostolate!"

—FATHER RAMIL E. FAJARDO, J.C.L., Judge of the Metropolitan Tribunal, Archdiocese of Chicago

"In *Jesus Speaks to Faustina and You*, it is nothing short of amazing how Susan Tassone has gleaned incredible insights into the Heart of Jesus and the heart of St. Faustina. Would one ever think that our merciful God was also speaking of His unfathomable love for each of us? It has been said, "Love does not measure, it just gives." Susan Tassone, inspired by the words of Jesus to Faustina, "just gives." In her day-by-day reflections, Susan shows us how to live the Divine Mercy, discern God's perfect will, heal the heartache in our families, comfort the dying, recognize the value of redemptive suffering, and how to pray the holy souls into heaven. In a dark world, Susan's book is a herald of true love, authentic happiness, and all the peace that a searching soul desires!"

—BARBARA MCGUIGAN, EWTN Host of *The Good Fight*

"Susan Tassone writes with sincere love for each of us and our Catholic faith. In *Jesus Speaks to Faustina and You*, journey with one of the most important 20th-century saints—St. Faustina—and draw daily strength from her spirituality and Our Lord. In a world that needs Jesus' mercy and love more than ever, learn from a saint who truly experienced it."

—PAUL MCKIBBEN, Managing Editor, *Catholic Digest*

"In *Jesus Speaks to Faustina and You*, each reflection is a nugget of wisdom from a cherished friend who constantly assures me that Jesus loves me much more than I am capable of accepting His love. Each day's words are deeply needed by a weary heart that has often been told lies contrary to what the Jesus of Holy Scripture says. Readers will owe a debt of gratitude to Susan Tassone for trusting that Jesus' words to St. Faustina are meant for each one of us and for relating His radiant love to me so well."

—FATHER DAN CAMBRA, M.I.C., Holy Souls Sodality at the National Shrine of The Divine Mercy

"Susan Tassone has once again brought to print the powerful message of Divine Mercy. By presenting the actual words of Our Lord to St. Faustina, *Jesus Speaks to Faustina and You* reveals how Almighty God yearns for us to perfect ourselves. He speaks to us with the love of a Father who wants His children home with Him in heaven. It is a great compliment to Susan's previous works."

—DAVID M. CAROLLO, Executive Director, World Apostolate of Fatima USA

"Susan Tassone has introduced many to the depth of St.Faustina's prayers and spiritual life. *In Jesus Speaks to Faustina and You*, she takes us even deeper into the message of Jesus and His mercy for the world. This book will help all who read and pray to live the spirituality of St. Faustina and Divine Mercy."

—FATHER EDWARD LOONEY, Author of *A Lenten Journey with Mother Mary*

# Jesus Speaks
## to
# Faustina and *You*

# JESUS SPEAKS
## TO
# FAUSTINA
## AND *YOU*

365 Reflections

SUSAN TASSONE

SOPHIA INSTITUTE PRESS
Manchester, New Hampshire

Sophia Institute Press
Box 5284, Manchester, NH 03108
1-800-888-9344
www.SophiaInstitute.com

Sophia Institute Press® is a registered trademark of Sophia Institute.

**Library of Congress Cataloging-in-Publication Data**

Names: Tassone, Susan, author.
Title: Jesus speaks to Faustina and you / Susan Tassone.
Description: Manchester : Sophia Institute Press, 2020. | Includes bibliographical references. | Summary: "Daily excerpts from the Diary of St. Faustina Kowalska with an accompanying reflection and prayer for each"— Provided by publisher.
Identifiers: LCCN 2019046139 | ISBN 9781644131015 (paperback) | ISBN 9781644131022 (ebook)
Subjects: LCSH: Faustina, Saint, 1905-1938. Dzienniczek. | Faustina, Saint, 1905-1938. | Catholic Church—Prayers and devotions.
Classification: LCC BX4700.F175 T37 2020 | DDC 282.092—dc23
LC record available at https://lccn.loc.gov/2019046139

First printing

This book is dedicated to the children of the world.

I beg You, Jesus, look not on our sins,
but on the tears of little children,
on the hunger and cold they suffer. . . .
At that moment, I saw the Lord Jesus,
His eyes filled with tears, and He said to me,
**"You see ... what great compassion
I have for them. Know that it is they
who uphold the world."** (Diary, 286)

# Contents

## Appendices

# Foreword

*Father Joseph Roesch, M.I.C.*
*Vicar General, Rome*

I have had the great privilege of living in the Eternal City of Rome for the last fourteen years. For the last seven years, I have been blessed to participate in a monthly meeting at our house in Rome with a few of our neighbors. We read over several pages from the *Diary* of St. Faustina Kowalska, *Divine Mercy in My Soul*, each month in advance and then we discuss the passages during the meeting. Each person brings his or her personal perspective, particular doubts and struggles. The words in the *Diary* never fail to speak to our hearts. Obviously, St. Faustina was a great mystic and she received extraordinary graces which most of us never will. So we might think that her holy life could shed very little light on our own, often mediocre existence.

However, apart from the extraordinary revelations, her lived experience was not terribly far from our own. She had doubts and fears, and she was often misunderstood and judged by the members of her community. She experienced all of the emotions and feelings that we all do. When we look at how God worked in her heart, we can catch a glimpse of how He wishes to work in each of our hearts.

In her beautiful new book, *Jesus Speaks to Faustina and You*, Susan Tassone demonstrates that Jesus wants to speak with each of us and to lead us to holiness. One of the ways that He does so is through the words in the *Diary* of St. Faustina. Susan has discovered many beautiful themes in the *Diary* that Jesus wants to convey to all humanity that she unpacks in her daily reflections. She shows how Jesus walks the path of holiness with us. Susan also explains many of the teachings of the Church through her reflections on the *Diary*. She includes key Scripture passages to help clarify the *Diary* message, references from the *Catechism of the Catholic Church*, the Church's teaching on purgatory, and quotes from many saintly ones.

St. John Paul II canonized St. Faustina on the Second Sunday of Easter in the Jubilee Year 2000. That day, he also gave a second name to that Sunday, the Sunday of the Divine Mercy. He said in his homily: "What will the years ahead bring us? What will man's future on earth be like? We are not given to know. However, it is certain that in addition to new progress, there will unfortunately be no lack of painful experiences. But the light of divine mercy, which the Lord in a way wished to return to the world through Sister Faustina's charism, will illumine the way for the men and women of the third millennium." St. John Paul II spoke prophetically that day of the problems that we would be facing today. However, he pointed out that our loving Father will never abandon us. Rather, He will always give us the "light of divine mercy" to show us the path to follow. St. Faustina had a special charism, or gift from God, to remind the world of God's great mercy.

St. John Paul went on to say in that homily: "Sister Faustina's canonization has a particular eloquence: by this act, I intend today to pass this message on to the new millennium. I pass it on to all people, so that they will learn to know ever better the true face of God and the true face of their brethren." Popes Benedict and Francis have echoed the words of St. John Paul II that the message of the Divine Mercy is essential for the world of today. It is the heart of the Gospel. We can only come to know ourselves and our true identity if we come to know God and His mercy.

God has used St. Faustina, a simple religious sister who only was able to attend school for three winters, as His secretary of mercy. God wanted her to remind us of the depths of His love and mercy. Through the centuries, many people have become confused about who God really is. They have an abstract concept of Him and many people think that God is out to get us. Nothing could be further from the truth. The *Diary* of St. Faustina reflects the Gospel and reveals the merciful face of God the Father in His Eternal Son, Jesus Christ. In *Jesus Speaks to Faustina and You*, Susan shows you the amazing depths of Jesus' infinite and unfathomable love for you that is available for you day by day, each day of the year.

Although Sister Faustina didn't have an extensive formal education, she was quite bright. Her teachers lamented the fact that she wasn't able to study longer in school. She had to return home to help her family on the farm. She read books and she often prayed for the grace to be able to understand what the Lord asked of her. She wrote her notebooks that became the *Diary* in obedience to Father Michael Sopocko, her confessor. When he came to hear the confessions of the Sisters, he couldn't spend hours offering spiritual direction to St. Faustina because of the extraordinary graces that she was receiving. So by reading her notebooks at his leisure, he had time to discern what the Lord was doing in her heart.

The *Diary* of St. Faustina has now been translated into over twenty languages. Our little group in Rome reads it in Italian. The Roman Breviary states that Sister Faustina's *Diary* is "among the outstanding works of mystical literature." There is a professor at Providence College in Rhode Island who uses the *Diary* as a manual to teach spiritual theology. There are examples in the *Diary* of everything that God could do to work in a soul and to assist it to grow in holiness. That spirituality professor states that St. Faustina covers the whole process of growing in sanctity using very simple language. There are many concrete examples in the *Diary* that demonstrate every stage of spiritual growth in the experiences of St. Faustina. Another author, Michael P. Riccards, writes that, "despite her meager education, her published *Diary* is a major work in mystical literature — rivaling even the works of St. John of the Cross. One can see the stages of the soul's ascent in these pages." God knew that not everyone would be able to understand the writings of St. John of the Cross. Since God desires the growth in holiness of everyone, He gave us the beautiful and simple *Diary* of St. Faustina.

When St. John Paul II first asked a famous theologian, Father Ignacy Rozycki to look over the *Diary* of St. Faustina to be certain that it was free from theological errors, the priest didn't want to bother. He thought for sure that it would be a waste of his time. He put the book on his desk, and then he never touched it for a long time. Finally, he picked up the *Diary* one day, with the intention of finding a theological error in it so that he wouldn't have to read any further. However, the first passage that he read touched him deeply. He felt drawn to read further. He then spent two years carefully analyzing the *Diary* and writing a 400-page analysis of it in French. He never came across a theological error. He asked pardon from God for having ignored his archbishop's request for so long. He then spent eight more years studying the *Diary* to gain deeper insights.

Having said all this, I have no doubt that you will grow in holiness by reflecting on the *Diary* of St. Faustina through this beautiful new book by Susan Tassone. As she did in her last book, she cites a passage from the *Diary* of St. Faustina on each day of the liturgical year. She then writes a beautiful reflection and a short prayer to help us to dwell on the "lesson of the day."

We can continue to reflect on what we have read throughout the day to help us to know God and His mercy better and to follow that path that He wishes to illuminate for us.

I loved Susan's last book, *Day by Day with St. Faustina: 365 Reflections*, and I love this one, *Jesus Speaks To Faustina and You*, as well. Her simple daily format allows us, in the midst of our busy lives, to dip into the spiritual treasure that is the *Diary* of St. Faustina.

May you each be blessed through your reading Susan's inspired reflections praying with her and St. Faustina to become the person God has called you to be!

# Personal Acknowledgments

There is a saying that goes: "If you ever see a turtle on a fence post, you know it did not get there by itself."

These outstanding people in my life helped me make this book what it was meant to be.

To Steven Jay Gross: You are the rock in my life.

To Bert Ghezzi: My esteemed friend and expert. You are always there. Always helpful. You always make a book shine. Without you this book would not be the gem it is today. I am blessed to have you as a friend. We are on our way to another best-seller. Thank you so much!

To Jackie Lindsey: Here we are again. Book #13. You are an incredible guide, support, and friend. All my works have your seal of approval which tells me I have a winner! So much thanks!

To Father Dan Cambra, M.I.C.: Your presence with its wisdom and insight about St. Faustina is invaluable. I owe you a debt of gratitude that only God can reward.

To Deacon Mike McCloskey and Father Scott Haynes: Thank you for your excellent theological consultation.

To Loyola University Chicago Library Head, Dr. Yolande Wersching, and her trusted longtime staff member, Vanessa Crouther: Both of you can find and uncover anything! Every book I have published was researched from your library, my alma mater. How often does an alumna have the privilege of her books being on the shelves of Loyola University Library? A truly great honor! My heartfelt thanks for your friendship and outstanding assistance for twenty years!

To Jean Studer: You seem to have an uncanny way to know when to call and check in! That meant a lot to me when I needed someone to bounce ideas off of and get a reader's view. You are a dear friend, and I thank you from the bottom of my heart!

To Maria Faber: Once again, you took an enormous work and made the beauty of Jesus' words flow in perfect harmony. This book has your mark on it, too! And I am forever grateful. Thank you!

To Molly Rublee, Digital Marketing Manager, Sophia Institute Press. You are a professional par excellence. You tackle a variety of tasks and responsibilities simultaneously and efficiently. You are a pillar and a dream come true for any author! Very special thanks!

# Jesus Speaks to *You!*

When I began reading St. Faustina's *Diary*, I was really surprised to learn that Jesus wasn't just speaking to St. Faustina. He was speaking directly to each of us. The more I entered into the *Diary*, the more I realized that Jesus was giving us a personal guide for life. I uncovered more than thirty major themes that He wants to share with us. They include mercy, trust, suffering, simplicity, fear, and faithfulness.

One key message that stands out from all the rest is Jesus' love for us. He chose us before time to be with Him for all eternity. It impressed me so much that at the end of each month I have included passages that Jesus shares with St. Faustina about His love for each of you!

As you explore each of these themes, you will discover how to be the best person God has called you to be. You will hear Jesus' words and learn to *live* by them.

Day by day you will learn:

- The amazing depths of Jesus' infinite and immeasurable love for you.

- Ways to heal your family through the mystery of God's mercy.

- Powerful weapons for spiritual warfare.

- How to overcome temptations—all of them!

- How purgatory is real, important ... *and a blessing.*

- How you can use the Divine Mercy Chaplet for all your material and spiritual needs including converting sinners, appeasing God's anger, comforting the dying, and finding solace in the midst of suffering.

- How to discern the will of God for your own personal life.

- How to become a saint by learning from the Saint of Mercy, a woman who spent her life—day by day—learning about the infinite love and the compassion of God, who is Divine Mercy.

May this book help you experience the unfathomable love Jesus has for you and your dear ones.

—Susan

CHAPTER ONE

# Reflections

FOR

*January*

# *January 1*

**Come to Me, all of you.** (*Diary*, 1485)

## *Reflection*

As we begin the New Year, Jesus invites us to come to Him. Our merciful Savior calls to all kinds of souls: the sinful, the despairing, a soul striving for perfection, and perfect souls. He has endless gifts of grace. But what do we offer in exchange? We bring the misery of sin. Yet, that's exactly what He wants from us—our sin. Why does He want this? So that we can be free. Whoever we are, whatever our sinful past may be, no one who comes with a humble heart is rejected. St. Faustina encourages us to appeal to His mercy by making a good confession. Afterwards, restored by God's grace, Jesus feeds us with the spiritual food that strengthens our souls, His Body and Blood. St. Faustina tells us the whole secret of the soul's sanctity is the Holy Eucharist. And so, with this New Year, Jesus opens wide His arms to you today. To saints and sinners alike He gives His invitation: "Come to Me, all of you" (1485).

## *Prayer*

Dear Lord, open my eyes to Your presence with the dawning of each new day. Jesus, have mercy on us and on the whole world.

# *January 2*
## LAW OF LOVE

**I have found My whole law on love....** (*Diary*, 1478)

## *Reflection*

Nowadays, "love" is a plastic word—twisted and shaped in many ways. Scripture says: "God is love" (1 Jn 4:8). When people contort "love" to defend actions contrary to God's law, we know that such a "love" is false—a poor counterfeit. St. Thomas Aquinas teaches: "To love is to will the good of another." We can't let lust, selfishness, or any kind of sin shape our definition of "love." Love involves more than the keeping of commandments, but it never involves anything less than keeping them. Love goes beyond the keeping of God's law, but it never goes around it. If we claim to be walking in love but fail to keep God's commandments, we come up short.

## *Prayer*

The love of God and neighbor is the greatest of Your commands. Strengthen me, O Lord, to follow Your holy law with all my heart.

Jesus, have mercy on us and on the whole world.

# *January 3*
## PLUNGED INTO THE ABYSS

**If I call creatures into being—that is the abyss of My mercy.** (*Diary*, 85)

### *Reflection*

Jesus urges souls to trust in the unfathomable abyss of His mercy. Because our God is a God who delights in showing mercy, even the greatest sinners should have no fear of approaching God. No one is excluded. On Calvary's Cross, the fountain of Mercy flowed from Jesus' Heart, and although there's a bottomless abyss separating God from His creatures, Jesus assures us that "this abyss is filled with My mercy" (1576). In the daily struggle of following Christ, we say with St. Faustina: "With one eye, I gaze on the abyss of my misery, and with the other, on the abyss of Your mercy" (1345). Jesus rescued us from eternal death and the abyss of hell. From the Throne of Mercy, God plunges us into the abyss—the abyss of His Mercy.

### *Prayer*

"Hail, Throne of Mercy, Lamb of God, / Who gave Your life in sacrifice for me, / Before whom my soul humbles itself daily, / Living in faith profound" (1321).

Jesus, have mercy on us and on the whole world.

# *January 4*
## CROWNED WITH MERCY

**Proclaim that mercy is the greatest attribute of God. All the works of My hands are crowned with mercy.** (*Diary*, 301)

### *Reflection*

Since mercy is such an indispensable aspect of God's very being, we would be most wise to plunge ourselves into its depths. We are far from perfect; in fact, try as we might, we all stumble quite often in our quest for holiness. It is such a great blessing that He is always willing to forgive us. Never for one second cease in your trust in His greatest attribute—*mercy*.

### *Prayer*

Your great mercy, Jesus, is the salvation of souls. Help me to shout out this life-giving message far and wide.

Jesus, have mercy on us and on the whole world.

# *January 5*
## CONTEMPLATING GOD'S ATTRIBUTES

**Get to know God by contemplating his attributes.** (*Diary*, 30)

### *Reflection*

St. Faustina wanted to know who God is. She shares her insight.

"My spirit rushed toward God with all its might. During that time, the Lord gave me much light to know His attributes.

"The first attribute which the Lord gave me to know is His holiness. His holiness is so great that all the Powers and Virtues tremble before Him. The pure spirits veil their faces and lose themselves in unending adoration.... The holiness of God is poured out upon the Church of God and upon every living soul in it....

"The second kind of knowledge which the Lord granted me concerns His justice. His justice is so great and penetrating that it reaches deep into the heart of things, and all things stand before Him in naked truth, and nothing can withstand Him.

"The third attribute is love and mercy. And I understood that the greatest attribute is love and mercy. It unites the creature with the Creator. This immense love and abyss of mercy are made known in the Incarnation of the Word and in the Redemption [of humanity], and it is here that I saw this as the greatest of all God's attributes" (180).

### *Prayer*

"May the greatest of all divine attributes, that of Your unfathomable mercy, pass through my heart and soul to my neighbor" (163).

Jesus, have mercy on us and on the whole world.

# *January 6*

**Look and see the human race in its present condition.** (*Diary*, 445)

## *Reflection*

St. Faustina's message was forward-thinking and perhaps intended more for our time than for her own. Her message seems perfectly suited to the issues roiling our country over matters that divide us: racism, immigration, politics and more. So many of us are angry, sadly often with the people we love because they don't see the world as we want them to see it. When we have this much anger, her message is very timely in this merciless age. St. Faustina gives us a path to follow. She says: Follow God's will. Be merciful with yourself and others. Forgive yourself and others. Share disagreements without becoming disagreeable. Turn to the Divine Mercy message for comfort and direction.

## *Prayer*

O Jesus, embrace the world and press it to Your Heart.
  Jesus, have mercy on us and on the whole world.

# *January 7*

## SPEAK TO SINNERS

**You are My Heart. Speak to sinners about My mercy.** (*Diary*, 1666)

### *Reflection*

Jesus would repeatedly tell St. Faustina that in addition to trusting in God, one needs to exercise mercy toward one's neighbor. She once said to her friend Sister Damiana Ziolek: "I have heard the Lord Jesus say that, on the Day of Judgment, He will be judging the world only in terms of mercy, because God is all Mercy. And acting out of mercy, or neglecting mercy, a person determines their own judgment."

### *Prayer*

Jesus, give me the grace to give mercy and receive mercy.

Jesus, have mercy on us and on the whole world.

# *January 8*
## MERCY FOR THE WORLD

> In convents too, there are souls that fill My Heart with joy.... They are a defense for the world before the justice of the Heavenly Father and a means of obtaining mercy for the world. The love and sacrifice of these souls sustain the world in existence. (*Diary*, 367)

## *Reflection*

Treasured in God's Heart are the saintly religious women of every age who've made sacrifices and showed mercy to sinners. These brides of Christ fill God with joy. When Americans dropped the atomic bomb on Hiroshima on August 6th, 1945, thousands of innocent civilians died instantly. Sister Julie and the other sisters had just attended Mass when the bomb exploded. Their convent was close to the epicenter. While 70,000 souls perished instantly, the priest and sisters were kept harmless. They helped the survivors suffering from radiation. They shared their suffering and tried to bring Christian joy to all they met. St. Faustina said, "[F]or it is precisely when when I suffer much that my joy is greater; and when I suffer less, my joy is also less" (303). The pure love and sacrifice of these saintly religious women obtain mercy for the world.

## *Prayer*

"The joy of others is my joy, and the suffering of others is my suffering, for otherwise I would not commune with the Lord Jesus" (633).

Jesus, have mercy on us and on the whole world.

# *January 9*

## MISSION NOT IMPOSSIBLE

**Give Me souls. Know that it is your mission to win souls for Me by prayer and sacrifice, and by encouraging them to trust in My mercy.** (*Diary*, 1690)

### *Reflection*

If you ever felt like you don't have much purpose in life, take a moment to think about what Jesus is saying to you. The only way that anyone can learn about Jesus is if someone tells them. Once in a while, a miracle happens, and Jesus may reveal himself directly, but most of the time, it's up to us to win souls for the Lord. While it is tempting to leave that responsibility to the "professionals" like priests, nuns, and missionaries, the fact is that Jesus wants each one of us to do our part. It's not as hard as we make it. We simply need to pray and offer small, regular sacrifices for the salvation of souls. When we do that, Jesus will do the rest.

### *Prayer*

Jesus, may both my words and my deeds reveal Your mercy to the world.

Jesus, have mercy on us and on the whole world.

# *January 10*
## YOUR GOD-COMMANDED PURPOSE

> **Why are you afraid to begin work which I have
> commanded you to carry out?** (*Diary*, 1181)

## *Reflection*

We all have a specific mission and purpose that was given to us at our creation.
YOU are the only one in the world that can fulfill it. No one else has your
mission. We did not just happen to be. We have a place in God's kingdom
to occupy. And a work to accomplish. However, we can become afraid. Turn
your fears about your work over to Jesus and allow Him to help. You don't
have to finish the work in a day. All you have to do is begin. You are important
to God and a part of His great plan and an integral part of salvation history!
Pope Emeritus Benedict XVI states: "Each of us is the result of a thought of
God. Each of us is willed. Each of us is loved. Each of us is necessary." Billions of possible human beings God saw, but He created YOU! There was
something about you that He wanted to be with for all eternity. Remember
that. Now get going!

## *Prayer*

Jesus, I'm ready to fulfill my mission.

   Jesus, have mercy on us and on the whole world.

# *January 11*

## GREATEST MIRACLE OF MERCY

**Tell souls where they are to look for solace; that is, in the Tribunal of Mercy** [The Sacrament of Reconciliation]. **There the greatest miracles take place** [and] **are incessantly repeated.** (*Diary*, 1448)

### *Reflection*

St. Faustina teaches us to be sincere, humble and obedient when we confess our sins in God's Tribunal of Mercy. Open your heart with complete sincerity when you confess your sins, so Jesus can bring His solace and richest graces. Don't be afraid to tell your sins. God knows everything already. Come to Confession with total confidence in your merciful Savior. When we confess our sins, we've got to strip ourselves of pride; otherwise, the soul "puts on a mask and avoids everything that might bring it recovery" (113). Avail yourself of the miracle soon.

### *Prayer*

Lord, give me a sincere, humble and obedient heart so that You can work in my soul a miracle of mercy.

Jesus, have mercy on us and on the whole world.

# *January 12*

**The prayer most pleasing to Me is prayer for the conversion of sinners. Know ... that this prayer is always heard and answered.** (*Diary*, 1397)

## *Reflection*

God is unwilling for anyone to perish and will go to extraordinary lengths to bring home the "lost sheep." Conversion is their only hope, and they desperately need our prayers. God is not giving up on people whom society may consider "incorrigible" and irredeemable. And neither should we—so keep praying for them to open their hearts! The following prayer is the one most pleasing to Jesus. He promises that it is "always answered." Pray it unceasingly!

## *Prayer*

"O Blood and Water, which gushed forth from the Heart of Jesus, as a fount of mercy for us, I trust in You" (187).

Jesus, have mercy on us and on the whole world.

# *January 13*

## LISTENING TO GOD

> Write, that I am speaking to them through their remorse of conscience, through their failures and sufferings, through thunderstorms, through the voice of the Church. And if they bring all My graces to naught, I begin to be angry with them, leaving them alone and giving them what they want. (*Diary*, 1728)

## *Reflection*

Jesus said to St. Faustina: "Oh, if souls would only want to listen to My voice when I am speaking in the depths of their hearts, they would reach the peak of holiness in a short time" (584). We hear God's voice best when we're quiet. Because we are proud, we want God to speak to us through our virtues; but He usually speaks to us in our vices, because when we are humbled by our sins, we fall on our knees and plead for His Mercy. When we're weak and vulnerable, we open our hearts to God. Jesus' words to St. Faustina come alive and speak to us best when we're at rock bottom: "The greater the sinner, the greater the right he has to My mercy" (723).

## *Prayer*

Father of Mercies, let me hear Your voice in my heart and follow it.

Jesus, have mercy on us and on the whole world.

# *January 14*

WHEN SUFFERINGS ARE GREAT

> **Know that if I allow you to feel and have a more profound knowledge of My sufferings, that is a grace from Me.** (*Diary*, 1697)

## *Reflection*

"As long as one can move about and work, everything is fine and dandy; but when God sends illness, somehow or other, there are fewer friends about. Yet there are some. They still take interest in our suffering and all that, but if God sends a longer illness, even those faithful friends slowly begin to desert us.... And so the soul, like Job, is alone; but fortunately, it is not alone, because Jesus-Host is with it. After having tasted the above sufferings and spent a whole night in bitterness, the next morning, when the chaplain [Father Theodore] brought me Holy Communion, I had to control myself by sheer effort of will to keep from crying out at the top of my voice, 'Welcome, my true and only Friend.' Holy Communion gives me strength to suffer and fight" (1509).

## *Prayer*

Lord Jesus, when things get rough and I'm fatigued, my mind is dimmed, and the sufferings are great, it's then that I take an active part in Your Passion.

Jesus, have mercy on us and on the whole world.

# *January 15*

## CASTING STONES

When I complained to the Lord Jesus about a certain person [saying], "Jesus, how can this person pass judgment like that, even about an intention?" the Lord answered, **Do not be surprised. That soul does not even know her own self, so how could she pass a fair judgment on another soul?** (*Diary*, 1528)

### *Reflection*

As He did when He said, "Let the one who is without sin cast the first stone," Jesus here points out how wrong it is to focus our attention on other people, and especially their shortcomings, while neglecting to take a hard look at ourselves. Maybe that's why we have so many negative, judgmental things to say about other people; it takes the spotlight off of us and our own failings, and therefore makes us feel less guilty. As Jesus wisely counsels, get to know your own soul (and do some "housekeeping" with it) before worrying about how awful the actions of some other person might be, as if God can't deal with that all by Himself. He can.

### *Prayer*

Lord, keep my concentration squarely on my own faults, and how to correct them, and not on what I perceive as the shortcomings of others.

Jesus, have mercy on us and on the whole world.

# January 16
## THERE IS NO "BUT" IN TRUST

Let souls who are striving for perfection particularly adore My mercy, because the abundance of graces which I grant them flows from My mercy. I desire that these souls distinguish themselves by boundless trust in My mercy. I myself will attend to the sanctification of such souls. I will provide them with everything they will need to attain sanctity. (*Diary*, 1578)

## Reflection

Trust can be as difficult or as easy as we make it. "Jesus, I trust You" is all we need. The minute we start saying, "I do trust God, but …" trust is lost. God loves it when we come to Him with no reservations. Do you honestly believe He would ever let you down? Bolster your faith with the irrefutable fact that with God all things are possible.

## Prayer

Lord, let me trust in You like an infant trusts in its mother. No doubts. No fears.

Jesus, have mercy on us and on the whole world.

# *January 17*

## PLEASE HIM WITH YOUR DEEP FAITH

**I am pleased by the deep faith you have.** (*Diary*, 1487)

### *Reflection*

Deep faith is hoping, trusting, and believing despite all the circumstances life throws at you. How did St. Faustina grow in faith? She said:

"I fervently beg the Lord to strengthen my faith, so that in my drab, everyday life I will not be guided by human dispositions, but by those of the spirit. Oh, how everything drags man towards the earth! But lively faith maintains the soul in the higher regions and assigns self-love its proper place; that is to say, the lowest one" (210).

During difficult times she wrote: "There are moments when one should be silent … and when the soul feels as weak as a little child. Then the soul clings to God with all its might. At such times, I live solely by faith, and when I feel strengthened by God's grace, then I am more courageous in speaking and communicating with my neighbors" (944).

### *Prayer*

May my ever-growing faith console Your Heart, dear Lord.

Jesus, have mercy on us and on the whole world.

# *January 18*
## BREAD OF THE STRONG

**My child, that you may answer My call worthily, receive Me daily in Holy Communion. It will give you strength ...** (*Diary*, 1489)

### *Reflection*

"Every morning during meditation, I prepare myself for the whole day's struggle. Holy Communion assures me that I will win the victory; and so it is. I fear the day when I do not receive Holy Communion. This Bread of the Strong gives me all the strength I need to carry on my mission and the courage to do whatever the Lord asks of me. The courage and strength that are in me are not of me, but of Him who lives in me—it is the Eucharist" (91).

### *Prayer*

Thank you, dear Lord, that on days I can't get to Mass and Communion You give me the opportunity to make a "Spiritual Communion."

Jesus, have mercy on us and on the whole world.

# *January 19*
## CHILDLIKE TRUST

I saw a tiny insect on the ground and thought: how did it get here in the middle of winter: Then I heard the following words in my soul: **You see, I am thinking of it and sustaining it, and what is it compared to you? Why was your soul fearful for a moment?** (*Diary*, 922)

## *Reflection*

Fear and worry are like the two legs of a rocking chair—always in motion, but never getting you anywhere. With fear and worry, we torment ourselves, doing Satan's job for him. Childlike prayer that trusts in God wins heavenly help and obtains victory. When St. Faustina was afraid God might not hear her prayers, Jesus asked why she was fearful. She apologized for her lack of trust and said: "Jesus wants me to always be a child and to leave all care to Him, and to submit blindly to His holy will" (922). As "mature" adults we're under that illusion that we're in control. The truth is—most things aren't. But God is. Just as He takes care of the "lilies of the field" and watches over insects in winter, so God numbers the "hairs of your head." Fear and worry don't change anything, but childlike trust does.

## *Prayer*

God, my loving Father, form my heart to have a childlike trust in You.
    Jesus, have mercy on us and on the whole world.

# *January 20*

## GOD SPEAKS WITH A DESPAIRING SOUL

O Lord, now I see all my ingratitude and Your goodness.
You were pursuing me with Your grace, while I was
frustrating Your benevolence. I see that I deserve the
depths of hell for spurning Your graces. (*Diary*, 1486)

## *Reflection*

**Do not be absorbed in your misery—you are still too weak to speak of it—but, rather, gaze on My Heart filled with goodness, and be imbued with My sentiments. Strive for meekness and humility; be merciful to others, as I am to you; and, when you feel your strength failing, if you come to the fountain of mercy to fortify your soul, you will not grow weary on your journey.** (1486)

## *Prayer*

Lord Jesus, draw all souls to gaze on Your Heart, filled with goodness. Draw us to Your fountain of mercy, so that we may not grow weary on our journey. Give us the grace to be merciful as You are to us.

Jesus, have mercy on us and on the whole world.

# *January 21*

## HOME — A PLACE OF LOVE AND PRAYER

**That evening Jesus said to me, I want you to stay home.** (*Diary*, 64)

### *Reflection*

Family schedules are jam-packed. Oftentimes, families don't even find time to have dinner together, because of school activities, sports, and other things. Once, when St. Faustina was given permission by her superior to take some time out for pleasure, Jesus told her to "stay home" instead. It's not that we can't enjoy pleasures or be involved in activities, but sometimes it's good to stay home too. The Irish priest Venerable Father Patrick Peyton once remarked, "The family that prays together stays together." As he encouraged families to pray the daily Rosary, we're reminded that prayer binds the family together. Scripture says a threefold cord is not easily broken. It's paramount for spouses to pray together with their children, because it creates a spiritual bond in their marriage and family. Pope Emeritus Benedict XVI commented: "The family is the 'little Church' because it transmits God, it transmits the love of Christ, by the power of the sacrament of matrimony." Make the "little church" of your home a place of love and prayer.

### *Prayer*

Lord, please bring us together as we are meant to be.
  Jesus, have mercy on us and on the whole world.

# *January 22*
## IDLE SOULS

> **When boredom and discouragement beat against your heart,
> run away from yourself and hide in My Heart.** (*Diary*, 1760)

## *Reflection*

Idle souls are easy prey for demons. Struggling with boredom, we are led into discouragement. Discouragement is the devil's tool for wreaking havoc, as an old legend records:

> "Once upon a time, the devil had a garage sale. Selling his tools, he marked each with a high price: hatred, envy, lust, deceit, lying, and pride. Set apart from these was a rather harmless-looking but well-worn tool marked much higher than the rest. It was marked: 'Not for Sale.'
>
> A shopper asked, 'What is that tool? Why isn't it for sale?'
>
> 'Well,' Satan whispered, "I can't afford to sell it! That's my chief tool—discouragement. I can pry open a heart with it, and once I'm there, I can do anything I want.'"

While discouragement can paralyze us, we can overcome it with confidence in God. When we practice charity, we get out of our miserable little selves and enter the immense Heart of God. Sacrificial love like this, no matter how small, evicts the enemy.

## *Prayer*

Come, Holy Spirit, and inspire me to make sacrifices for love of God and my neighbor.

Jesus, have mercy on us and on the whole world.

# *January 23*

## STARVE YOUR FEARS TO DEATH

**Do not be afraid; I am always with you.** (*Diary*, 627)

### *Reflection*

In the darkness, Christ shines the light. Plato said: "We can easily forgive a child who is afraid of the dark; the real tragedy of life is when men are afraid of the light." We're daily faced with a choice. We can feed our fears or nourish our faith. Tired of letting fear win? Stop feeding your fear. Feed your faith, and your fears will starve to death.

### *Prayer*

Lord, when fears overcome my heart and fill my mind with darkness, be the Light of my salvation.

Jesus, have mercy on us and on the whole world.

# *January 24*
## UNFATHOMABLE MERCY

Do not tire of proclaiming My mercy. In this way you will refresh this Heart of Mine, which burns with a flame of pity for sinners. Tell My priests that hardened sinners will repent on hearing their words when they speak about My unfathomable mercy, about the compassion I have for them in My Heart. To priests who proclaim and extol My mercy, I will give wondrous power; I will anoint their words and touch the hearts of those to whom they will speak. (*Diary*, 1521)

## *Reflection*

Don't ever think that anyone is beyond the scope of God's mercy. That is why Jesus wants the ministers of His Church to reach out and let even the most hardened sinners know that He loves them and went to the Cross to save them. Incredible miracles will happen if we follow Jesus' command to spread this message that comes straight from the Heart of God.

## *Prayer*

Those who do not know You, Lord, have been blinded to the truth. Lift the veil and open their eyes to see that You are the only way to ultimate freedom.

Jesus, have mercy on us and on the whole world.

# *January 25*

## THE POWERFUL WORDS
## OF THE CHAPLET OF MERCY

Say unceasingly the chaplet that I have taught you. Whoever will recite it will receive great mercy at the hour of death. Priests will recommend it to sinners as their last hope of salvation. Even if there were a sinner most hardened, if he were to recite this chaplet only once, he would receive grace from My infinite mercy. I desire that the whole world know My infinite mercy. I desire to grant unimaginable graces to those souls who trust in My mercy. (*Diary*, 687)

## *Reflection*

The Divine Mercy Chaplet is powerful because it so succinctly and beautifully expresses God's desire for the human family: that we place all of our trust in Him, and avail ourselves of His mercy which will unleash unimaginable graces. Even if it is recited only one time! Nevertheless, it is of great benefit to make the Chaplet a regular part of your daily life. Pray it unceasingly.

## *Prayer*

May the Divine Mercy Chaplet spread the message of Jesus and His mercy to all people.

Jesus, have mercy on us and on the whole world.

# *January 26*

## GOD SPEAKS WITH A SINFUL SOUL

Lord, I doubt that You will pardon my numerous sins;
my misery fills me with fright. (*Diary*, 1485)

## Reflection

My child, do you fear the God of mercy? My holiness does not prevent
Me from being merciful. Behold, for you I have established a throne of
mercy on earth—the tabernacle—and from this throne I desire to enter
your heart (1485).

## Prayer

"I invite You to my heart" (1485).

Jesus, have mercy on us and on the whole world.

# *January 27*

**The graces of My mercy are drawn by means of one vessel only, and that is — trust. The more a soul trusts, the more it will receive.** (*Diary*, 1578)

## *Reflection*

Trust is so important to Jesus, because He wants us to acknowledge that He alone is all we will ever need. He knows that we get into terrible trouble, all the way back to Adam and Eve, when we try to live contrary to His ways. Yet, when we put all of our trust in Him, anxiety takes flight, and the joy of life envelops us.

## *Prayer*

Dear Lord, increase my trust in You. Teach me to cling to You and to never let go, for You are always there for me.

Jesus, have mercy on us and on the whole world.

# *January 28*

## COUNTLESS AS THE STARS

**Look at the sky.** And when I looked at the sky I saw the stars and the moon shining. Then the child asked me, **Do you see this moon and these stars?** When I said yes, he spoke these words to me, **These stars are the souls of faithful Christians....** (*Diary*, 424)

## *Reflection*

We know that the stars aren't actually the "souls of faithful Christians," but balls of hot gases and other substances. However, Jesus isn't giving us a science lesson. He is telling us that those who have believed in Him are as countless as the stars. When you feel discouraged or begin to think that the world is penetrated with evil, look up and realize that all those who have gone before you who now make up the Church Triumphant are cheering you on.

## *Prayer*

Faithful departed who now share in the vision of God, pray for me and those I love.

Jesus, have mercy on us and on the whole world.

# *January 29*
## GOD AND THE CHURCH

... consider the life of God which is found in the Church
for the salvation and the sanctification of your soul.
Consider the use that you make of these treasures of
grace, of these efforts of My love. (*Diary*, 1758)

### *Reflection*

St. Faustina was "lifted up above earth and heaven into the inner life of God"
(734). God opens His spiritual treasury for us too, so we'll taste the sweetness
of His mercy. The inner life of God, found in the Church, is a treasure of
grace. Faustina herself was always a loyal daughter of the Church. Despite her
visions, she found her strength and comfort in the sacraments. Jesus tells us
that the "life of God," which is expressed through the sacraments, is "found
in the Church." As tempting as it is to have a personal spirituality—a me-
and-God experience—Jesus reminds us that salvation and sanctification are
found only in the communal experience of His Church and the sacraments.
We need the Church.

### *Prayer*

"O Holy Trinity, in whom is contained the inner life of God,... honor and
glory be to Your holy name forever and ever. Amen" (525).

Jesus, have mercy on us and on the whole world.

# *January 30*

## UNITED IN LIFE, UNITED IN DEATH

**As you are united with Me in life, so will you be united at the moment of death.** (*Diary*, 1552)

### *Reflection*

If we live our life in unity with the Lord, then, at the hour of death, that relationship will continue. Take some time today to analyze how your relationship with the Lord is. Is it only for Sundays? Do you spend time each day with Jesus? Do you look forward to your prayer time, or is it a duty? Ask yourself, "What will happen when I die if I am not united to Jesus now?"

### *Prayer*

Dear Jesus, help me never to be separated from You.

Jesus, have mercy on us and on the whole world.

# *January 31*

## LOVE LOVES EVERYONE

> What a paradise it is for a soul when the heart knows
> itself to be so loved by God ... (*Diary*, 1756)

### *Reflection*

God's got plenty of reasons not to love us. But God doesn't know how to hate—God is love! When we contemplate God's immense love for us, we enter a paradise of love. There in the Garden of Eden, God made us and blew His breath into us. This Breath of God is His love. And while we're fickle, as C. S. Lewis once said, "our feelings come and go, God's love for us does not." The sign of God's love was firmly planted hanging on the Cross, with His arms outstretched. The very sight of Jesus is a sermon of love for us. In the vastness of the universe, it seems we'd be insignificant to God, but St. Augustine teaches: "God loves each of us as if there were only one of us." The love of God is the world's greatest motivating force in the world, and His love doesn't discriminate, because Love loves everyone.

### *Prayer*

Breathe into me, O Breath of God, and fill me with Your love.
Jesus, have mercy on us and on the whole world.

# CHAPTER TWO

# Reflections

FOR

# *February*

# *February 1*

## ENTERING GOD'S HEART

**My daughter, look at My merciful Heart.** (*Diary*, 177)

### *Reflection*

The Lord, won't leave us wanting whenever we strive to follow the beat of His Heart.

His Heart is also a gate—the gate opening the Kingdom of Heaven. When Adam and Eve were banished from paradise, God placed the cherubim with a flaming sword at Eden's gates to protect the way that led to the Tree of Life. But if this first path were closed by the sword, a second path would be opened for us, also by the sword. Jesus' side was pierced with a spear and blood and water gushed out. Jesus wanted His Heart to be pierced—to be opened—so we'd be washed in the cleansing tide coming from His. As in the time of Noah, when God saved only those who passed through the door of the ark, so now, in the same way, only those who enter through the door of the Heart of Jesus will be saved.

### *Prayer*

My sweet Jesus, teach me how to contemplate the message of love carved in Your flesh by the soldier's lance. Enter the secret recesses of my heart and "Let every beat of my heart be a new hymn of thanksgiving to You, O God" (1794).

Jesus, have mercy on us and on the whole world.

# *February 2*

## HIS "BELOVED"

At that moment, the light of God penetrated my being,
and I felt that I was God's exclusive property ... **You
are My well-beloved daughter**. (*Diary*, 1681)

## *Reflection*

David, whose name in Hebrew means "beloved," was zealous for Lord. When
mighty Goliath mocked the God of Israel, this little shepherd marched out to
defend the Lord. Little runt that he was, David cut off Goliath's head. David
found his enemy's weak spot. Even the invincible have weak spots. Achilles
had his heel and Goliath his forehead. That weak spot represented a bigger
weakness. Proud Goliath, puffed up with self-confidence, lacked heart. But
David was God "beloved" because of the greatness of his heart. Like David,
we're God's beloved. We're His exclusive property. At Calvary Jesus' Blood
purchased our salvation at a "great price," and what God the Father said to
Jesus, He wants to say to you today: "You are My beloved ... in you, I am well
pleased."

## *Prayer*

Loving Father, I am Your beloved child.

Jesus, have mercy on us and on the whole world.

# *February 3*
## "HELP ME"

**Help Me to save souls.** (*Diary*, 1797)

### *Reflection*

There are two small words in today's quote that need our attention. The Lord said to St. Faustina: "Help Me." He says the same to you. Consider for a moment that enormity of Jesus' request to help Him save souls. He entrusts us to help Him with this, the most important task of eternity. How are we to do this? Jesus explains that one way is to recite the Chaplet of Divine Mercy for the dying. St. Faustina cries out: "Oh, if only everyone realized how great the Lord's mercy is and how much we all need that mercy, especially at that crucial hour!" (811). Today, pray the Chaplet for the dying around the world.

### *Prayer*

Dear Lord, grant those who will die this day the grace of a happy death, to die in the state of grace.

Jesus, have mercy on us and on the whole world.

# *February 4*

## I AM ALWAYS WITH YOU

I felt like a child in the hands of the best of fathers, and I heard these words: **Do not fear anything. I am always with you.** His love penetrated my whole being. I felt I was entering into such close intimacy with Him that I cannot find words to express it. (*Diary*, 629)

## *Reflection*

Over and over, Jesus tells us not to fear anything. Clearly, He knows that fear is hardwired into most of us, or He wouldn't have to repeat it so often. Granted, there are any number of things that can make us afraid, but Jesus reassures us that when we're in His presence, when we pray nothing can harm us. Now that doesn't mean we can't get injured or sick or have something bad happen to us. What it means is that when we stay close to the Lord, we need not fear the future, the devil, his temptations, or even hell itself.

## *Prayer*

Jesus, when I am afraid, be with me. When I am fearful, comfort me. When I am worried, remind me that You are my strength.

Jesus, have mercy on us and on the whole world.

# *February 5*

## GOD SPEAKS TO A SUFFERING SOUL

Poor health detains me on the way to holiness. I cannot fulfill my duties. I am as useless as an extra wheel on a wagon. I cannot mortify myself or fast to any extent, as the saints did. Furthermore, nobody believes I am sick, so that mental pain is added to those of the body, and I am often humiliated. Jesus, how can anyone become holy in such circumstances? (*Diary*, 1487)

## *Reflection*

**True, my child, all that is painful. But there is no way to heaven except the way of the cross. I followed it first. You must learn that it is the shortest and surest way** (1487).

## *Prayer*

Jesus, You followed the way of the Cross first. It is the only way to heaven. The shortest and surest way. Help me understand that. Then give me strength to follow You.

Jesus, have mercy on us and on the whole world.

# *FEBRUARY 6*

## BE COURAGEOUS IN CHRIST

**Temptation gives you a chance to show Me your fidelity.** (*Diary*, 1560)

## *Reflection*

Since Adam and Eve tasted the forbidden fruit in Eden's Garden, mankind has struggled with temptation. Whether we're tempted by venial sins or mortal sins, Satan and his minions make it their business to lay traps of temptation before us. Temptation in itself isn't a sin. But when we act deliberately and intentionally upon it, sin takes it root. St. Faustina wisely counsels us to reveal our temptations to the priest in the sacrament of Confession. When we resist temptation, we grow in virtue, glorifying God. But we can't do it alone. The Bible tells us: "Blessed is anyone who endures temptation. Such a one has stood the test and will receive the crown of life that the Lord has promised to those who love Him" (Jas 1:12). Jesus encourages us: "Do not fear struggle; courage itself often intimidates temptations, and they dare not attack us" (1760). Let us find our courage in Christ. In Him we will be victorious!

## *Prayer*

Lord, when tempted, I call upon You to strengthen me, that I might show You my fidelity.

Jesus, have mercy on us and on the whole world.

# *February 7*

## EAT THE ORANGES

Today, I received some oranges. When the sister had left, I thought to myself, "Should I eat the oranges instead of doing penance and mortifying myself during Holy Lent? After all, I am feeling a bit better." Then I heard a voice in my soul: **My daughter, you please Me more by eating the oranges out of obedience and love of Me than by fasting and mortifying yourself of your own will.** (*Diary*, 1023)

## *Reflection*

At times, we can get the idea that all God wants from us is our self-discipline; that He rejoices when we fast and mortify ourselves. While it is true that He does appreciate our acts of penance, especially during Lent, He values obedience and love more than any self-imposed penance. When we decide what penance we are going to do, we are asserting our own will. We are doing things *our* way, and that may not be what God wants at all. What if, instead of our being so hard on ourselves, God would like to spoil us a little bit? Maybe He would like to give us, as He did Faustina, some oranges out of season. If so, it would be displeasing to Him if we refused.

## *Prayer*

Jesus, help me to remember that You value obedience and love more than any penance I do out of my own self-will.

Jesus, have mercy on us and on the whole world.

# *February 8*

> **I often wait with great graces until towards
> the end of prayer.** (*Diary*, 268)

## *Reflection*

Prayer requires conversion, it is no less true that conversion requires prayer. Our daily efforts to live consistently as apostles of Jesus, according to His teaching, reveals this truth. Conversion is hard work, but hard work is not enough. Our experience of failing at the task so often tells us so.

We need grace, God's help, God's presence, and God's infinite patience with us. Ongoing conversion requires the grace that is available to us, that we become open to receive, in prayer.

## *Prayer*

Convert me, Jesus, from my lack of prayer. Your great graces come through prayer.

Jesus, have mercy on us and on the whole world.

# *February 9*

## SACRIFICE FOR CONVERSIONS

> ... it is less difficult for Me to grant a soul much rather than a little, but every conversion of a sinful soul demands sacrifice. (*Diary*, 961)

### *Reflection*

One of the greatest sacrifices we can make on behalf of the conversion of souls is fasting.

But fasting has been forgotten, overlooked, and underappreciated in recent time. We need to rediscover its power to help us conquer sin. St. Faustina fasted exhaustively. It's one of the best ways to love God and our neighbor, and it helps us say "no" to temptation by inviting the Holy Spirit into our hearts. If we are more virtuous, we will naturally be kinder to our neighbor. Fasting also (it's a little funny to say) "adds weight" to our prayer intentions, so if we are praying and fasting for others, we are loving our neighbor. If we offer up our sufferings and our sacrifices, we are loving our neighbor. If we pray and fast for the holy souls in purgatory, we are loving our neighbor.

### *Prayer*

Thank you, dear Lord, for giving me the gift of fasting. Thank you for this way for me to rid myself of bad habits.

Jesus, have mercy on us and on the whole world.

# *February 10*

## PATIENCE!

**Bear with yourself with great patience.** (*Diary*, 1760)

### *Reflection*

St. Faustina remarked: "The Lord gave me an occasion to practice patience through a particular person with whom I have to carry out a certain task. She is slower than anyone I have ever seen. One has to arm oneself with great patience to listen to her tedious talk" (1376). Are you patient? God's patience is greater. When Nineveh's destruction was at hand, God provided time for repentance. The Ninevites would have perished if God had a short fuse. St. Faustina believed "the greatest power is hidden in patience. I see that patience always leads to victory ..." (1514). Perhaps the hardest kind of patience is to be patient with oneself. "Physical weakness was," for St. Faustina, "a school of patience" (37). When human frailty limits us, we succumb to frustration. Patience in overcoming spiritual trials is harder still. It was a consolation that St. Faustina learned: "Before every major grace, my soul undergoes a test of patience ..." (1084).

### *Prayer*

Strengthen me, O God, to bear with myself in patience, so that my heart might be readied for the graces You are sending me.

Jesus, have mercy on us and on the whole world.

# *February 11*

*Feast of Our Lady of Lourdes*
## PRAY FOR THE SICK

I now see how much the sick have need of prayer ... immediately after Holy Communion I returned to my room. Then I saw the Lord, who said to me, **Know, My daughter, that the ardor of your heart is pleasing to Me.** (*Diary*, 826)

## *Reflection*

In 1992 St. John Paul II instituted the World Day of the Sick, to be marked on February 11, the Feast of Our Lady of Lourdes. It was to be, he wrote, "a special time of prayer and sharing, of offering one's suffering for the good of the Church and of reminding everyone to see in his sick brother or sister the face of Christ who, by suffering, dying and rising, achieved the salvation of mankind."

## *Prayer*

Jesus, today I pray for N.

Our Lady of Lourdes, be with those who are suffering and those who are dying.

Jesus, have mercy on us and on the whole world.

# *February 12*

## WHY GOD LOVES REDEMPTIVE SUFFERING

> **You will not be in good health.** (*Diary*, 1464)

## *Reflection*

Most people have some kind of health issue. Some suffer from serious illnesses such as cancer, but all of us get ordinary aches and pains and colds. We spend billions of dollars trying to feel better, often to little avail. The bitter reality is that, as Jesus told Faustina, we will not be in good health—at least not all of our lives. Instead of endlessly seeking a new cure, we can use our suffering on behalf of others. St. Bernadette was once asked by a very sick person why she couldn't die and be free of her pain. Bernadette told her that God wanted her to offer her suffering to save souls. Is He asking the same thing of you?

## *Prayer*

Jesus, I offer You the pains of my life on behalf of the soul most in need of Your mercy.

Jesus, have mercy on us and on the whole world.

# *February 13*

## UNBEARABLY LUKEWARM

> Souls without love and without devotion, souls full of egoism and self-love, souls full of pride and arrogance, souls full of deceit and hypocrisy, lukewarm souls who have just enough warmth to keep them alive: **My Heart cannot bear this.** (*Diary*, 1702)

## *Reflection*

The word "lukewarm" comes from an old English word meaning "tepid." No one likes a lukewarm bowl of soup or a lukewarm glass of ice tea. We want our hot to be hot and our cold to be cold. Jesus uses this example from ordinary life to remind of the need to be passionate in our love, lest, as it says in Scripture: "So because you are lukewarm, and neither hot nor cold, I will spew you out of my mouth" (Rev 3:16).

## *Prayer*

My Lord, may my love and devotion for You always be red-hot.

Jesus, have mercy on us and on the whole world.

# *February 14*

## INTIMACY WITH THE HEART OF GOD

**Give Me, give Me your heart.** (*Diary*, 1718)

## *Reflection*

The cry of the human heart is heard in the Psalms: "My soul thirsts for God, for the living God. When shall I come and behold the face of God?" (Ps 42:2). If we look at the heart of intimacy, we find trust. For intimacy to be in a relationship, there must first be trust. When we sin, oftentimes we fear approaching God. We don't trust Him. We are wary of harsh judgment. We can't fathom the depths of God's mercy and the sweet love Jesus has for us when we're wounded by sin. But St. James exhorts us: "Draw near to God, and he will draw near to you" (Jas 4:8). Have you been betrayed? Then the school of life has taught you that intimacy fades when trust is violated. But the Lord's mercy is trustworthy. It is good to draw near to Him.

## *Prayer*

My sweet Lord, take my heart. Happy Valentine's Day!
Jesus, have mercy on us and on the whole world.

# *February 15*

## THE IMPORTANCE OF PERSEVERANCE

**I use you as the instrument of their conversion.** (*Diary*, 1357)

## *Reflection*

You might be surprised at how often St. Faustina wrote about conversion. In chapter after chapter, her *Diary* speaks of Jesus' call for the conversion of sinners. But conversion is just the beginning. The real test comes with perseverance. It's a little like marriage. When you are first dating, you want to spend all your time with that person. You want to know every little detail about their likes and dislikes. You find their habits, like sneezing after every meal, to be endearing. Your heart beats faster at the thought of being together. But after many years of marriage, you may find yourself enjoying your alone time, and the likes and dislikes you found so charming are now just irritating. It takes perseverance to make a marriage last. The same is true of our relationship with the Lord. We need God's love, grace, and mercy, not just when we convert, but as we persevere in our journey of faith that we can persevere in any relationship.

## *Prayer*

Dear Jesus, help me to continually work on my relationship with You, so that I may persevere until the end of my days.

Jesus, have mercy on us and on the whole world

# *February 16*
## KEEP IT EASY

Those whom you love in a special way, I too love in a special way, and for your sake, I shower My graces upon them. I am pleased when you tell Me about them, but don't be doing so with such excessive effort. (*Diary*, 739)

## *Reflection*

St. Faustina had been speaking to the Lord about those whom she loved. After a while, Jesus told her that she didn't need to do so with "such excessive effort." Talking with God through a vibrant prayer life is an excellent path toward holiness, but remember that it is even easier than you may have first realized. After all, you are speaking with God Almighty. He is omniscient and already knows what is in your heart before a single syllable crosses your lips. So, let your prayers be a simple expression of what your soul wants to say to its Creator. Belt it out like a song to God's ears. Even if you think your voice sounds terrible, that's okay. He created it that way.

## *Prayer*

Lord, keep my prayers heartfelt and simple, for You alone know my soul in all its fullness.

Jesus, have mercy on us and on the whole world.

# *February 17*
## GIVE ME A PUSH

> **Do not put off the Sacrament of Penance, because this displeases Me.** (*Diary*, 1464)

### *Reflection*

Let's face it. Going to Confession isn't always at the top of our "to do" lists. We delay.

The Church recommends monthly Confession, but many people can't even remember the last time they went to Confession. Jesus tells us that putting off the sacrament of Penance displeases Him. He wants us to take advantage of the sacrament, not for His sake, but for our sake. We are in the presence of the Divine Physician, who can truly heal our deepest wounds.

Stubborn? You may need a push. A young Father Fulton Sheen was in church when a famous singer entered. This woman, entangled in sin, needed that push. And he gave it—literally. Sheen explains that she made a good Confession and later became a nun at Tyburn. God was greatly pleased. But when Archbishop Fulton Sheen told this story forty years after the fact, he said: "I didn't ask her to go to Confession, I pushed her in."

### *Prayer*

Lord, when I'm reluctant to confess my sins, give me a push.

Jesus, have mercy on us and on the whole world.

# *February 18*

> **I give you eternal love that your purity may be untarnished and as a sign that you will never be subject to temptations against purity.** Jesus took off His golden cincture and tied it around my waist. (*Diary*, 40)

## *Reflection*

In 1917, Our Lady of Fatima said: "More souls go to Hell because of the sins of the flesh than for any other reason." Her message today has greater force because our culture is sex-craved—plagued by every impurity imaginable. Purity is a struggle—even for saints. Reflecting on his former life, St. Augustine said: "Lust indulged became habit, and habit unresisted became necessity." Lust ruled him like a tyrant. God restores purity, but it takes courageous cooperation. Because temptations of the flesh abound today, St. Faustina teaches us to watch and pray: "A soul which is pure and beautiful must pray, or else it will lose its beauty … for every single grace comes to the soul through prayer" (146). Turn to Jesus. You'll defeat lust's power. Through frequent Confessions and fervent Holy Communions, Christ will cool the fires of passion, strengthening you in purity of heart, soul, and body.

## *Prayer*

"O my Mother, cover my soul with your virginal mantle and grant me the grace of purity of heart, soul, and body" (79).

Jesus, have mercy on us and on the whole world.

# *February 19*

## REFUGE IN HIS WOUNDS

> **From all My wounds, like from streams, mercy flows for souls, but the wound in My Heart is the fountain of unfathomable mercy. From this fountain spring all graces for souls. The flames of compassion burn Me. I desire greatly to pour them out upon souls. Speak to the whole world about My mercy.** (*Diary*, 1190)

### *Reflection*

We can't know Jesus without knowing His wounds—they tell the price of our salvation. Those wounds were made as our sins nailed him to the Cross.

An eyewitness of Jesus' crucifixion, St. John, tells us that "one of the soldiers pierced his side with a spear, and at once blood and water came out" (Jn 19:34). As His Heart was pierced, the floodgates of mercy gushed open. From the wound of His Heart, streams of grace and mercy poured forth to wash away our sins. Plagued by doubts or tempted by sin? Follow St. Faustina and "take refuge in the wounds of Jesus …" (226).

### *Prayer*

Eternal Father, I offer You the wounds of our Lord Jesus Christ to heal our souls.

Jesus, have mercy on us and on the whole world.

# *February 20*

## THE PEOPLE OF GOD WILL BE HOLY

> I place in your care two pearls very precious to My Heart: these are the souls of priests and religious. You will pray particularly for them; their power will come from your diminishment. You will join prayers, fasts, mortifications, labors and all sufferings to My prayer, fasting, mortifications, labors and sufferings and then they will have power before My Father. (*Diary*, 531)

### *Reflection*

In Dom Chautard's classic book *The Soul of the Apostolate*, we find this old saying: "If the priest is a saint the people will be fervent; if the priest is fervent, the people will be pious; if the priest is pious, the people will at least be decent. But if the priest is only decent, the people will be godless." We need priests to pursue sanctification. But we also need saintly nuns and holy monks, because consecrated religious strengthen Christ's Mystical Body through their life of prayer and sacrifice. If we diminish and humble ourselves before the Father by fasting, praying, and offering our sufferings on behalf of priests and religious, God will not be outdone in generosity. The Lord will send us many saintly priests and religious—perhaps even from our own families. And the people of God will be holy.

### *Prayer*

Lord, I offer You my prayers and sufferings, that priests and consecrated religious may shine like pearls before Your Heart.

Jesus, have mercy on us and on the whole world.

# *February 21*
## NOTHING TO FEAR

**Do not fear anything; nothing will happen
to you against My will.** (*Diary*, 541)

## *Reflection*

We're utterly convinced that if everything would "go our way," life would be
much better. Few are those who choose to set aside their plans to seek God's
will. The paradox is that mankind only finds true and everlasting happiness
when we muster the courage to do God's will, forsaking our own. Once, when
St. Faustina was praying, she heard voices from the holy souls: "We are happy
in the measure that we have fulfilled God's will" (515). We're afraid of His
will, believing the lie that God's plan isn't right for us. When Jesus told St.
Faustina to forsake fear and follow Him, He strengthened her with His power;
she exclaimed: "I rejoiced greatly that God is so good" (541). God's will leads
us to the truth, so we've nothing to fear.

## *Prayer*

"O Lord, You who penetrate my whole being and the most secret depths of
my soul, You see that I desire You alone and long only for the fulfillment of
Your holy will, paying no heed to difficulties or sufferings or humiliations or
to what others might think" (1360).

Jesus, have mercy on us and on the whole world.

# *February 22*

## LISTEN TO MY VOICE

**Meditate on the Prophet Jonah and his mission.** (*Diary*, 331)

### *Reflection*

One evening, before going to bed, St. Faustina asked Jesus upon what He'd want her to meditate the next morning. Christ replied: "Meditate on the Prophet Jonah and his mission." The next morning, she meditated on Jonah. St. Faustina writes: "I recognized myself in the person of the prophet, in the sense that often I, too, try to make excuses to the Lord, claiming that someone else would do His holy will better [than I could], and not understanding that God can do all things and that His omnipotence will be all the more manifest if the tool is poorer" (331). That afternoon in Confession, St. Faustina mentioned to the priest her fear of carrying out the special mission Jesus was giving her. Then the priest started encouraging her. He used the example of Jonah the Prophet. St. Faustina took this as clear confirmation that God was working through the priest to confirm what Jesus had told her.

### *Prayer*

My Jesus, strengthen Your priests to speak with the clarity of Your voice.

Jesus, have mercy on us and on the whole world.

# *February 23*
## GOD DELIGHTS IN SINCERITY OF HEART

The Lord said to me, **I am delighted with your love. Your sincere love is as pleasing to My Heart as the fragrance of a rosebud at morning tide, before the sun has taken the dew from it.** (*Diary*, 1546)

## *Reflection*

Out of jealousy, Saul pursued David for seven years and plotted to take his life. David cried to God. When the Lord delivered David, he sang a song of thanksgiving to the Lord: "He delivered me from my strong enemy, from those who hated me ... He delivered me, because He delighted in me" (2 Sam 22:18-20). The Lord is seeking in our hearts a true "love that issues from a pure heart and a good conscience and sincere faith" (1 Tim 1:5). When we try to reflect God's love, mercy, and righteousness, He delights in us. God loves a sincere heart that is striving to follow Him, just like David.

## *Prayer*

Heavenly Father, give me a sincere heart so that You may delight in my soul as the fragrance of a rosebud at morning.

Jesus, have mercy on us and on the whole world.

# *February 24*

## HIS MOST MERCIFUL HEART

**I do not want to punish aching mankind, but I desire to heal it, pressing it to My Merciful Heart.** (*Diary*, 1588)

## *Reflection*

We often tremble at the thought of God's anger, as well we should, given how offensive sin is to Him. Yet, without being presumptuous, we must also remember that punishing us is not what the Lord truly desires for His children. Rather, His deepest desire is to heal us, to bring us out of our sinful condition through His merciful Heart, and transform us into His image as was His original purpose in creation from the very beginning. We must yield to His efforts, like clay waiting patiently for a great sculptor to complete a breathtaking masterpiece.

## *Prayer*

I deserve Your punishment, Lord, but I seek refuge in Your Merciful Heart. I come to You, Jesus, awaiting Your miraculous healing.

Jesus, have mercy on us and on the whole world.

# *February 25*
## SPIRITUAL ARMOR

**Let three virtues adorn you in a particular way; humility, purity of intention and love.** (*Diary*, 1779)

## *Reflection*

Faustina was very devoted to humility, purity of intention, and love. She lived her life accordingly. Following her example, we can enjoy the peace that comes from never worrying about "being better" than anyone else (humility), focusing our mind on what is pure and wholesome, and wanting to do only what is right (purity of intention) and keeping love alive in our hearts. With these three virtues, our spiritual armor is always polished and ready.

## *Prayer*

O Jesus, keep my spiritual armor polished with the aid of humility, purity of intention, and love.

Jesus, have mercy on us and on the whole world.

# *February 26*

## OPEN YOUR HEART

**Tell souls not to place within their own hearts obstacles to My mercy, which so greatly wants to act within them. My mercy works in all those hearts which open their doors to it.** (*Diary*, 1577)

## *Reflection*

Life is a precious gift from God. His love for all of His children is what makes His mercy so powerful. Jesus suffered unimaginable agonies because He believed we are worth it. Is the door to your heart open to all the merciful graces He longs to pour into it? That's all that is needed. He will do the rest.

## *Prayer*

Lord, open the door to my heart. Let the ray of Your graces be with me my entire life, and especially at the hour of my death.

Jesus, have mercy on us and on the whole world.

# *February 27*

> **Everything that exists is enclosed in the bowels of My mercy, more deeply than an infant in its mother's womb. How painfully distrust of My goodness wounds Me! Sins of distrust wound Me most painfully.** (*Diary*, 1076)

## *Reflection*

We should never doubt God for even a nanosecond, for to do so is a serious offense against Him. People will, of course, not always be completely honest with us, and we may question their trustworthiness; but in God, there is no deceit whatsoever. He keeps each and every one of His promises, and all of His words are truth itself. When we distrust the Lord, we not only cheat ourselves, but we wound Him as well.

## *Prayer*

Jesus, help me to place all of my trust in You, with all my heart. In a world of uncertainty, You are my Rock and my Salvation.

Jesus, have mercy on us and on the whole world.

# *February 28*

## ALL OF THIS THAT IS MINE IS THINE

I went across the garden one afternoon and stopped on the shore of the lake; I stood there for a long time, contemplating my surroundings. Suddenly, I saw the Lord Jesus near me, and He graciously said to me, **All this I created for you, My spouse; and know that all this beauty is nothing compared to what I have prepared for you in eternity.** (*Diary*, 158)

## *Reflection*

A story from Merrie Olde England recounts how the Lord of Burleigh fell in love with a poor village girl. Because he dressed humbly and never bragged about his wealth, she'd no idea who he really was. On their wedding day, she was excited to go to his cottage. However humble it might be, she'd be happy there with her beloved. As they arrived at his mansion, he surprised her: "All of this is mine and thine." She was now the "Lady of Burleigh"—a woman of dignity and wealth. Christ leads His Mystical Bride to His mansion, and He endows the members of His royal household with a glorious title: "Saint." We contemplate all that He's created for us—the garden of eternal paradise. Jesus says to His Mystical Bride and *you*: "All of this is mine and thine."

## *Prayer*

Dear Lord, my heart is filled with thanks, great gratitude, and tremendous joy for all You have created for me in this world and the next.

Jesus, have mercy on us and on the whole world.

# *February 29 (Leap Year)*

## RECYCLED GIFTS

I want to give Myself to souls and to fill them with My love, but few there are who want to accept all the graces My love has intended for them. My grace is not lost; if the soul for whom it was intended does not accept it, another soul takes it. (*Diary*, 1017)

## *Reflection*

Our planet is becoming overrun with things we discard. But that's not God's way. God is not wasteful. God never discards grace. If we don't accept God's gifts, God offers them to someone else in the ultimate act of recycling. How many gifts of grace might you have unthinkingly discarded? What grace is God offering you right now?

## *Prayer*

Dear Lord, let me accept every good gift of grace You offer to me, especially those I am in most need of.

Jesus, have mercy on us and on the whole world.

# CHAPTER THREE

# Reflections
## FOR
## *March*

# *March 1*

## A CRUCIFIED MASTER

**Do not forget, My disciple, that you are a disciple of a crucified Master.** (*Diary*, 1513)

## *Reflection*

"When I am asleep I offer Him every beat of my heart; when I awaken I immerse myself in Him without saying a word. When I awaken I adore the Holy Trinity for a short while and thank God for having deigned to give me yet another day, that the mystery of the Incarnation of His Son may once more be repeated in me, and that once again His sorrowful Passion may unfold before my eyes. I then try to make it easier for Jesus to pass through me to other souls. I go everywhere with Jesus; His presence accompanies me everywhere" (486).

## *Prayer*

O Jesus, save me!

Jesus, have mercy on us and on the whole world.

# *March 2*

## ENTERING INTO THE PASSION

**Look, and enter into My Passion.** (*Diary*, 1663)

## *Reflection*

There are many ways you can enter "into" the Lord's Passion, such as by reading the account of His Passion in Scripture (Mk 15:21-41).

St. Faustina loved to meditate on the Lord's Passion by praying the Way of the Cross. The brutal scourging, the hours of agony as He hung on the Cross, the profuse loss of His Precious Blood and suffocation—all of these excruciating sufferings. She joined her prayers with the sorrows of Our Lady. Whenever possible she prayed lying face down on the chapel floor, with her arms outstretched assuming the position of one crucified. She believed that posture best expressed the atoning and penitential character of the prayers.

St. Faustina stated:

When I meditate upon the Passion of Jesus, I get a clear understanding of many things I could not comprehend before. I want to resemble You, O Jesus,—You crucified, tortured, and humiliated. Jesus, imprint upon my heart and soul Your own humility. I love You, Jesus, to the point of madness ... (267).

He invites you. He suffered all of this for you as if you were the only person in the world. And He would do it over again for love of you!

## *Prayer*

Transform me, Jesus, in my heart, my mind, and my soul.

Jesus, have mercy on us and on the whole world.

# *March 3*

## CONSOLING HIM

During adoration, Jesus said to me, **My daughter, know that your ardent love and the compassion you have for Me were a consolation to Me in the Garden** [of Olives]. (*Diary*, 1664)

## *Reflection*

It must have come as a great honor for such a humble person as Faustina to hear that Jesus actually found consolation through her pious actions. Yet it's true. Jesus has allowed us, like Simon of Cyrene, who helped to carry the Cross, the grace of bringing consolation to His Heart through our acts of compassion, motivated by our love of Him and of others. Are you ready to lend a hand today?

## *Prayer*

Jesus, open my eyes to new opportunities to please You and to help bring about Your mission of mercy for the entire world. Even the smallest role would be the greatest honor for me, and I pray for whatever portion You want.

Jesus, have mercy on us and on the whole world.

# *March 4*

## READING SCRIPTURE WITH THE HEART

> **Take chapter nineteen of Saint John's Gospel, and read it, not only with your lips, but with your heart....** (*Diary*, 1765)

## *Reflection*

John 19 tells the story of Jesus's Passion. Did you ever wonder why John says simply, "There they crucified him," while he goes into much more detail about everything from the scourging to the sour wine to the burial ritual? The answer is shocking to our modern ears: crucifixion was such a common punishment in Roman times that there was no need for John to describe any of the details for his audience; they would have seen crucifixions almost every day. We have to remember that at the time everyone knew that death on a cross was the most painful, most public, and most humiliating of all punishments. Once we truly "get" this fact, we can begin to read not with our lips, but with our heart.

## *Prayer*

Lord, help me to realize the magnitude of Your Passion so that I might appreciate the depths of Your love.

Jesus, have mercy on us and on the whole world.

# *March 5*

## THE SORROWFUL PASSION

… meditate frequently on the sufferings which I have undergone for your sake, and then nothing of what you suffer for Me will seem great to you. You please Me most when you meditate on My Sorrowful Passion. Join your little sufferings to my Sorrowful Passion. (*Diary*, 1512)

### *Reflection*

When we think about Jesus' Passion, we usually think about the scourging and the crucifixion. But the Agony in the Garden is part of the Passion as well. In fact, the Agony in the Garden, when Jesus was so distressed that He sweat blood, might be one of the most heartrending parts of His suffering. Basically, Jesus was having such severe panic and anxiety that His blood vessels broke. If you have ever experienced anxiety, you know how horrific it is. Now imagine that your panic was so great you began to sweat blood! In light of Jesus' Passion, our sufferings are "little." Yet, Jesus encourages us to join them, regardless of their size, to His own Sorrowful Passion. In that way, we, too, can contribute to the salvation of the world.

### *Prayer*

Jesus, help me always to remember how much You suffered for me.

Jesus, have mercy on us and on the whole world.

# *March 6*

> **Consider these words: "And being in agony, he prayed more earnestly."**
> When I started to think about them more deeply, much light streamed
> into my soul. I learned how much we need perseverance in prayer and
> that our salvation often depends on such difficult prayer. (*Diary*, 157)

## *Reflection*

Jesus taught St. Faustina to pray the Chaplet "unceasingly," especially for dying sinners. He taught her to pray and intercede for the conversion of sinners. She prayed for the women she cared for, the sick, the religious, her country, and the world. She was like a child who keeps pestering until she achieves what she wants. God loves to be pestered, so trustingly and continually did she receive the answers. St. Faustina reflected: "Jesus gave me to understand how a soul should be faithful to prayer despite torments, dryness, and temptations; because oftentimes the realization of God's great plans depends mainly on such prayer. If we do not persevere in such prayer, we frustrate what the Lord wanted to do through us or within us" (872).

## *Prayer*

Dear St. Faustina, pray for me and for my loved ones.
Jesus, have mercy on us and on the whole world.

# *March 7*

## VIEW FROM THE CROSS

> Once, Jesus said to me, **My gaze from this image
> is like My gaze from the cross.** (*Diary*, 326)

## *Reflection*

The artist James Tissot's painting "View from the Cross" shows the scene of the crucifixion from Jesus' perspective. We see Mary, the women, the soldiers, and the crowd as Jesus might have seen them as He was dying. It is a powerful and sobering image. But what did those present on that fateful day see as they looked up? Jesus tells us that when we look at the image of Divine Mercy, we see Him as He looked down from His cross. While the figures in Tissot's painting are filled with sorrow, disdain, and even boredom, Jesus looks out with utter compassion and mercy. The next time you want to know how Jesus sees you, look at the image of Divine Mercy.

## *Prayer*

Dear Lord, help me see myself as You see me.

Jesus, have mercy on us and on the whole world.

# *March 8*

## THE CROWN OF SALVATION

**Your suffering will become a source of your sanctification.** (*Diary*, 1487)

## *Reflection*

Blessed Henry Suso, a Dominican priest whose writings centered on Christ's Passion, has these encouraging words to say on suffering: "He who evaluates suffering at its true worth must accept it from God as a precious gift. Suffering guards men against grave falls; it gives a man self-knowledge, makes him firm toward himself and compassionate toward his neighbor. Suffering preserves the soul in humility, teaches patience, guards purity, and brings the crown of eternal salvation.

"It is practically impossible that suffering does not benefit a man in some way, whether he is yet in the state of sin, is just converted, making progress, or already arrived at perfection, because it scours the iron, purifies the gold, and embellishes the precious stones. Suffering takes away sin, shortens purgatory, drives away temptations, quenches carnal desires, and renews the spirit.... Suffering gives a man wisdom and experience. A man who has not suffered: what does he know?"

## *Prayer*

When I am crushed by suffering, Lord, give me the faith to trust You.

Jesus, have mercy on us and on the whole world.

# *March 9*

## WE NEED INTERIOR MORTIFICATION

**Do not neglect interior mortification.** (*Diary*, 1760)

## *Reflection*

Denying our natural inclinations isn't easy. When an old monk was busy praying, noisy children were playing nearby. Angered, he wanted to drive them away. Instead, he held his tongue and said to himself: "If I cannot endure as little as this, how shall I endure greater trials?" When irritated, it is easy to give into frustration. But we ought to mortify ourselves interiorly and see the opportunity that awaits us in our daily trials. When someone gets on your nerves, don't be blinded by frustration. Rather, see the opportunity for sanctification before you. Choke back words of anger and give the Holy Spirit time to bring forth fruits of patience, long-suffering, and charity. Interior mortifications are powerful weapons of spiritual warfare to conquer our sinfulness. St. Francis de Sales comments: "Believe me that the mortification of the senses in seeing, hearing, and speaking is worth much more than wearing chains or hair-cloth."

## *Prayer*

My sweet Jesus, prepare my soul for the right remedy.
   Jesus, have mercy on us and on the whole world.

# *March 10*

## THE SACRIFICE OF FASTING

> **I need sacrifice lovingly accomplished, because
> that alone has meaning for Me.** (*Diary*, 1316).

## *Reflection*

A sacrifice done without love, but done only out of duty accomplishes nothing. This is particularly true of fasting. Fasting done without holy intent is little more than glorified dieting. St. Basil says: "There is both a physical and a spiritual fast. In the physical fast, the body abstains from food and drink. In the spiritual fast, the faster abstains from evil intentions, words and deeds. One who truly fasts abstains from anger, rage, malice, and vengeance. One who truly fasts abstains from idle and foul talk, empty rhetoric, slander, condemnation, flattery, lying and all manner of spiteful talk, in a word, a real faster is one who withdraws from all evil.... As much as you subtract from the body, so much you will add the strength of the soul ... by fasting."

## *Prayer*

Thank you for this way for me to move closer to You today as You gently transform my heart, my mind, and my soul through the small sacrifices I make. Amen.

Jesus, have mercy on us and on the whole world.

# *March 11*

## PUTTING OTHERS FIRST

> **I turn to you, you—chosen souls ...** (*Diary*, 367)

## *Reflection*

Talk about unsung heroes! The holy men and women hidden in their convents love us so much that they pray for us constantly. Although we will probably never even hear about them, much less ever meet them this side of heaven, they are the unsung heroes of the world. Be grateful for such selfless intercession. Satan attacks them precisely because he knows how effective they are in delivering God's message of mercy, snatching them away from the clutches of the evil one. As the monk, historian, and theologian Pseudo Rufinus once said, "The human race lives thanks to a few; were it not for them, the world would perish...."

## *Prayer*

Lord, let me join those special brothers and sisters in Christ as they glorify You day in and day out. Thank You for them!

Jesus, have mercy on us and on the whole world.

# *March 12*

## HOW DO I KNOW IF I AM TRULY CONVERTING?

I saw a large ciborium filled with sacred hosts. A hand placed the ciborium in front of me, and I took it in my hands. There were a thousand living hosts inside. Then I heard a voice, **These are hosts which have been received by the souls for whom you have obtained the grace of true conversion during this Lent.** (*Diary*, 640)

### *Reflection*

Our Lord mentions the words "true conversion." How do we know if we are truly converting? We go to Mass, we say our Rosaries, we fast on Fridays. Isn't that enough?

A Benedictine priest gives a clear description of what conversion truly looks like:

"I was a regular confessor to a woman who took great pride in telling me that she was reading St. Teresa of Avila, St. John of the Cross, and the works of the mystics. She felt she made great strides in her prayer. But in Confession, she could think of nothing to confess. But how could that be, if she was truly growing closer to the Lord in authentic prayer? Perhaps it was quite true that she could think of no particular acts of sin—at least of any serious nature—but how can one draw close to the God of Infinite Love and not see more deeply one's own failure to love through a greater spirit of generosity, patience, hospitality or service?"

### *Prayer*

Jesus, give me the graces I need to truly convert!

Jesus, have mercy on us and on the whole world.

# *March 13*

## QUINTILLION UPON QUINTILLION

> Let the weak, sinful souls have no fear to approach Me, for even if it had more sins than there are grains of sand in the world, all would be drowned in the unmeasurable depths of My mercy.... (*Diary*, 1059)

## *Reflection*

Scientists calculate that there are at least seven quintillion, five hundred quadrillion grains of sand in the world. Just in case you've forgotten, a quadrillion is 1,000,000,000,000,000 and a quintillion is 1,000,000,000,000,000,000. Such a number is beyond our comprehension, yet Jesus tells us that even if we had sinned that many times, we can still be forgiven. If you want to have a visual image of what that means, the next time you are at the shore, pick up a handful of sand. You couldn't count the grains if you tried! And yet God's mercy on sinners is greater even than the sand.

## *Prayer*

Lord, help me believe that no matter how grave my sin, You will always forgive me.

Jesus, have mercy on us and on the whole world.

# *March 14*

## DO NOT FEAR

**Do not fear, My child; but remain faithful
only to My grace....** (*Diary*, 1166)

## *Reflection*

One of the things that Jesus tells Faustina over and over is "Do not fear."
That's because fear comes much more naturally to us than trust. We see all
the dangers out there and our instinctive reaction is to be afraid. Now there's
nothing wrong with being afraid. Most of our fears exist only in our mind.
We worry about what will happen tomorrow ... or next week ... or next year.
Jesus tells us that those kinds of fears are useless. All that is needed is to be
faithful to the grace that God gives us for the present moment.

## *Prayer*

Dear Jesus, when fear enters my heart, help me to turn to You for Your peace.
    Jesus, have mercy on us and on the whole world.

# *March 15*

## DEFEATING TEMPTATION

**Do not bargain with any temptation; lock yourself immediately in My Heart and, at the first opportunity, reveal the temptation to the confessor.** (*Diary*, 1760)

## *Reflection*

St. John Vianney said, "With the Name of Jesus we shall overthrow the demons." St. Antony of the Desert put this into practice. The devil beat him and left him half dead. "Well," said St. Antony, "here I am, ready to fight again. You will not be able to separate me from Jesus Christ." The demons tried to terrify St. Antony, but he trusted God. We ought to put total confidence in God. Christ will strengthen us with sanctifying grace whenever we come to Him in Confession and reveal our temptations, weaknesses, and sins. Our Lord told St. Faustina: "I Myself am waiting there for you" (1602). Leaving the confessional, we do works of penance. As we pray, fast, and give alms with humble hearts, Satan cannot separate us from our loving Lord Jesus in this world or the next.

## *Prayer*

Merciful God, graciously hear my prayer. Free my heart from the temptations of evil thoughts, that I may worthily become a fit temple for Your Holy Spirit.

Jesus, have mercy on us and on the whole world.

# *March 16*

## UNITE YOURSELF WITH HIM

I demand of you a perfect and whole-burnt offering; an offering
of the will. No other sacrifice can compare with this one. I
Myself am directing your life and arranging things in such a
way that you will be for Me a continual sacrifice and will always
do My will. And for the accomplishment of this offering, you
will unite yourself with Me on the Cross. (*Diary*, 923)

## *Reflection*

A nun on duty at a motherhouse was doing a final check before retiring.
Things had to be in perfect order because they had a visiting bishop. She
heard a noise in the chapel. Nothing in the choir stalls and kneelers. But in
the aisle she saw the bishop making the Way of the Cross, going from station
to station "on his knees." She didn't disturb him. The next day she shared
this at recreation with the nuns—not realizing that he would become St.
John Paul II.

This man of simple piety, suffering with the people of his time, knowing
hardship and personal pain, had long united and summed up everything in
that quiet practice of going from station to station in many a church and
chapel.

## *Prayer*

Jesus, take my will and give me Yours, united with You on the Cross.

Jesus, have mercy on us and on the whole world.

# *March 17*

## TOUGH LOVE

> **It is because you are not of this world that the world hates you. First it persecuted Me. Persecution is a sign that you are following in My footsteps faithfully.** (*Diary*, 1487)

## *Reflection*

Jesus taught St. Faustina to love her persecutors, even when she didn't feel like it. Practicing mercy means putting love into action—willing the good of our neighbor in all things. When mistreated, be at peace and do good to those who hate you. C. S. Lewis nails it: "To love at all is to be vulnerable.... If you want to make sure of keeping it intact, you must give your heart to no one ... lock it up safe in the casket or coffin of your selfishness. But in that casket—safe, dark, motionless, airless—it will change. It will not be broken; it will become unbreakable, impenetrable, irredeemable." To be like Christ, we need the "tough love" of the Cross, a love that is vulnerable but indestructible.

## *Prayer*

Lord, take away my feelings and give me Your feelings.

Jesus, have mercy on us and on the whole world.

# *March 18*

## BATTLING TEMPTATIONS

Jesus again gave me a few directives: **First, do not fight against a temptation by yourself, but disclose it to the confessor at once, and then the temptation will lose all its force.** Second, during these ordeals do not lose your peace; live in My presence; ask My Mother and the Saints for help. Third, have the certitude that I am looking at you and supporting you. Fourth, do not fear either struggles of the soul or any temptations, because I am supporting you; if only you are willing to fight, know that the victory is always on your side. Fifth, know that by fighting bravely you give Me great glory and amass merits for yourself. (*Diary*, 1560)

## *Reflection*

Jesus taught St. Faustina to not fight temptation alone. Just as high frequencies of ultraviolet light can kill bacteria and viruses, so our temptations lose their force under the Light of Christ when we reveal them in Confession. As the Sacrament of Mercy knocks the wind out of our temptations, Christ strengthens us. He brings us peace in the midst of temptation, and whenever we turn to Jesus, Mary, or the saints to help us, heaven rushes to our aid. Through Christ, we're victorious in overcoming our temptations.

## *Prayer*

When temptations rage against me and a wave of doubts beats against my soul, come to my aid, O most gracious Virgin Mary with all the saints.

Jesus, have mercy on us, and on the whole world.

# *March 19*

## POWER IN THE BLOOD

> **My child, unite yourself closely to Me during the Sacrifice and offer My Blood and My Wounds to My Father in expiation for the sins of that city. Repeat this without interruption throughout the entire Holy Mass. Do this for seven days.** (*Diary*, 39)

## *Reflection*

Behold Christ's wounds on the Cross: the thorns pressed into His brow; the nails painfully piercing His flesh, and the crimson Blood watering Calvary. Jesus' Blood atones for sin. Because the Lord is patient, He gives us time to repent. Like a loving father chastises his children when they need it, God chastises us to set us right. When God was going to chastise a city because of its many sins, St. Faustina interceded for seven days. She offered Christ's Blood and Wounds through the Holy Mass. St. Faustina said Jesus "made a big sign of the cross over our country" (39). When we enter Jesus' Wounds, we find there's power in His Blood.

## *Prayer*

Lord, I offer Your Blood and Your Wounds in reparation for my sins and for those of my city.

Jesus, have mercy on us and on the whole world.

# March 20

## POWER OF CHRIST'S PASSION

**It is in My Passion that you must seek light and strength.** (*Diary*, 654)

## Reflection

On her spiritual journey, Jesus called St. Faustina to meditate upon the sufferings of His Sacred Passion. She remarked: "When I meditate upon the Passion of Jesus, I get a clear understanding of many things I could not comprehend before" (267). The Lord imparted spiritual light as she immersed herself in His Passion. She once described how, during Mass, she beheld Jesus nailed to the Cross. "A soft moan issued from his Heart.... He said, 'I thirst. I thirst for the salvation of souls.'" He asked Faustina to help Him save souls by joining her sufferings to His Passion and offering them to the Father for sinners. Christ was teaching her how to unite her little daily trials to the suffering He bore on Calvary—a lesson in redemptive suffering. Our prayer draws us into His Sacred Heart—a Heart which beats for us.

## Prayer

"O my Jesus, my only hope, thank You for the book which You have opened before my soul's eyes. That book is Your Passion which You underwent for love of me. It is from this book that I have learned how to love God and souls" (304).

Jesus, have mercy on us and on the whole world.

# *March 21*

## WOUNDS OF LOVE

**Remember My Passion, and if you do not believe My words, at least believe My wounds.** (*Diary*, 379)

## *Reflection*

Before the crucifix, meditate upon Christ's precious wounds. That's what Dismas, the good thief, did. As he hung upon his own cross, paying the penalty for his crimes, he cast his gaze upon the man next to him. He saw an innocent man being slain for the guilty. Dismas had the courage to ask: "Jesus, remember me when you come into your kingdom" (Lk 23:42). Gazing into Jesus' wounds, he found faith in the power of the Precious Blood. Once he claimed Jesus as Lord and Savior, Christ poured forth His saving graces, because God's grace always enters through our wounds. Like the Good Samaritan who poured oil into the wounds of the man left for dead along the roadside, Jesus pours forth His grace into our wounds and heals us. Turn to Jesus and put your faith in Him, He is your Savior. Doubting still? Behold the Wounds of His Love!

## *Prayer*

Eternal Father, I offer you the Wounds of Our Lord, Jesus Christ, to heal the wounds of our souls.

Jesus, have mercy on us and on the whole world.

# *March 22*

## A DISTINCT AND BEAUTIFUL SOUL

> **By meditating on My Passion, your soul
> acquires a distinct beauty.** (*Diary*, 1657)

## *Reflection*

There are many wonders in this world. There's much to please the eye and the ear, from the snow-covered Alps to the sound of birds chirping in the morning breeze. But nothing's so beautiful to God as the human soul. When God created the universe, He had a master plan. Saving the best for last, God revealed His genius by making man in His own image and likeness. We're beautiful because we're fashioned after God, who is the source of all beauty. The depth of beauty is unlocked when the soul becomes more and more united to God. In each moment of our lives, Jesus invites us to meditate on His Passion to purify and beautify our souls. St. Augustine remarked: "Since love grows within you, so beauty grows. For love is the beauty of the soul."

## *Prayer*

Sweet Lord, when the beauty of my soul is marred by sin, cleanse me and make my soul reflect the beauty of Your love.

Jesus, have mercy on us and on the whole world.

# *March 23*

## THE GREAT THIRST

Good Friday. At three o'clock, I saw the Lord Jesus, crucified, who looked at me and said, **I thirst.** (*Diary*, 648)

### *Reflection*

Jesus was not merely thirsting for water as He was dying upon the Cross; much more to the point, as He was in the very act of sacrificing His life, He was thirsting for the salvation of souls. He wanted Faustina to help Him. She did. She longed to do anything she could to bring people to God's throne of grace. Does the Crucified One, who looks at you, move you to action, too?

### *Prayer*

Burn a thirst for souls in my heart, Lord, that I may be a beacon of hope for them.

Jesus, have mercy on us and on the whole world.

# *March 24*

## INTERCESSORY POWER OF THE CHAPLET

Jesus listened to these outpourings of my heart with gravity and interest, as if He had known nothing about them, and this seemed to make it easier for me to talk. And the Lord said to me, **My daughter, those words of your heart are pleasing to Me, and by saying the chaplet you are bringing humankind closer to Me.** (*Diary*, 929)

### *Reflection*

St. Faustina poured out her heart to Jesus. So, much like today, she suffered, realizing how sinners offend God—fearing how souls rush headlong toward hell's abyss. She was troubled at how Jesus' friends are oppressed and persecuted for following Him. Remembering those who profess love of God, she lamented their lack of fervor. St. Faustina said pains gnawed at her heart and bones. How precious her love for Jesus—her contemplation on the sufferings of His Heart. She told Him, "I desire that all mankind turn with trust to Your mercy. Then, seeing the glory of Your name, my heart will be comforted" (929). He exhorted her to pray with confidence and trust in Him, placing great trust in the intercessory power of the Chaplet.

### *Prayer*

Lord, I pour out my heart to You, in atonement for the sins of the whole world.
Jesus, have mercy on us and on the whole world.

# *March 25*

Is it possible that there is yet mercy for me? (*Diary*, 1486)

## *Reflection*

**There is my child. You have a special claim on My mercy. Let it act in your poor soul; let the rays of grace enter your soul; they bring with them light, warmth, and life** (1486).

## *Prayer*

Lord Jesus, shine Your rays of light, warmth, and life into my life. Let me never despair of Your mercy.

Jesus, have mercy on us and on the whole world.

# *March 26*

## BE ALWAYS MERCIFUL

The Lord said to me, **It should be of no concern to you how anyone else acts; you are to be My living reflection, through love and mercy.** I answered, "Lord, but they often take advantage of my goodness." **That makes no difference ... That is no concern of yours. As for you, be always merciful toward other people, and especially toward sinners.** (*Diary*, 1446)

## *Reflection*

Just like the rest of us, Faustina would sometimes get frustrated when other people, seeing how kind, loving and merciful she was, would take advantage of her for those traits, selfishly using her generosity beyond what was reasonable. She brought her complaint to Jesus, but the answer He gave was to ignore their rude behavior. Her focus needed to be on following Jesus, and always doing things His way. If we truly want to follow Him, that applies to us, too.

## *Prayer*

Lord, keep my eyes fixed on You, never on the shortcomings or offenses of others.

Jesus, have mercy on us and on the whole world.

# *March 27*

## EVERYTHING IS UNDER CONTROL

When I asked the Lord to be so good as to cast a glance upon a certain soul [probably Father Sopocko] who was struggling alone against many difficulties, the Lord gave me to know, in an instant, that all people are as dust under His feet. **So do not worry; you see that they cannot do a thing of themselves. And if I allow them to seem to triumph, I do this for the sake of My impenetrable decrees.** I experienced great peace in seeing how all things are determined by the Lord. (*Diary*, 1610)

## *Reflection*

We all have a tendency to be so self-absorbed that we seem to believe the world revolves around us. It doesn't. God is at the center of all creation; it all belongs to Him, including us, the creatures He made in His own image. That keeps everything in perspective. Even when it comes to our greatest accomplishments, all of the glory belongs to God, without whom we could do nothing. When you see a beautiful painting, the praise goes to the artist—not to the paintbrushes or the canvas! And so it is with the greatest Artist, whose creation is the masterpiece that surpasses and sustains all others.

## *Prayer*

O Lord and King of the Universe, let me humbly serve You in gratitude.
 Jesus, have mercy on us and on the whole world.

# *March 28*

## IT'S A MARATHON, NOT A SPRINT

**I do not reward for good results but for the patience and hardship undergone for My sake.** (*Diary*, 86)

## *Reflection*

Sometimes, it really isn't whether you win or lose; it is how you play the game. God knows that our efforts will not always end up with the results that we want, at least not immediately, but that's not what is important to Him. Rather, do we patiently persevere in doing what is right? That is what He will reward.

## *Prayer*

Strengthen me, O Lord. When obstacles come, give me the courage to face them bravely, and to never give up.

Jesus, have mercy on us and on the whole world.

# *March 29*

## THE SEA OF MERCY

I have opened My Heart as a living fountain of mercy. Let all souls draw life from it. Let them approach this sea of mercy with great trust. Sinners will attain justification, and the just will be confirmed in good. Whoever places his trust in My mercy will be filled with My divine peace at the hour of death. (*Diary*, 1520)

### *Reflection*

It's not very often that we receive anything for free—but here is something precious, of infinite value. The Lord is giving away a fountain of mercy through which we can be filled with peace at the hour of death. In an amazing outpouring of His grace, Jesus offers every human being what we need even more than the air we breathe.

### *Prayer*

God, let me draw from the fountain of Your mercy. I place all my trust in Your divine goodness.

Jesus, have mercy on us and on the whole world.

# *March 30*

## HE IS MERCY

**My Heart rejoices in the title of Mercy.** (*Diary*, 300)

## *Reflection*

Emmanuel. Prince of Peace. God-Hero. Father-Forever. Lord. Son of God. Son of man. These are a few of the titles of Jesus. But of all the titles we have bestowed on Him, one of them causes His Heart to rejoice. It isn't a title we use, but perhaps it is one we should use more often: *Mercy*.

## *Prayer*

Mercy, have mercy on me, a sinner.

Jesus, have mercy on us and on the whole world.

# *March 31*

## LOVE IS STRONGER THAN DEATH

**If My death has not convinced you of My love, what will?** (*Diary*, 580)

## *Reflection*

Everyone loves a good love story, and the best ones end with weddings—"They got married and lived happily ever after." The Bible begins and ends with marriage. In Genesis, Adam and Eve are married and begin the human family. The love poetry of the Song of Songs points to Jesus' love for His Bride. Jesus, the Bridegroom of our souls, comes to rescue His holy Bride. He's tender, merciful, kind, humble, meek, patient and forgiving. On the Cross, He paid the ransom for our lack of love. Christ's love is stronger than death. If this doesn't convince you, what will?

## *Prayer*

Sweet Jesus, I believe and am convinced of Your love for me. Now strengthen me to live in that love.

Jesus, have mercy on us and on the whole world.

# CHAPTER FOUR

# Reflections

FOR

## *April*

# *April 1*

## THE PRESENCE OF PEACE

During the Mass of Resurrection, I saw the Lord in beauty and splendor, and He said to me, **My daughter, peace be with you ...** My heart was fortified for struggle and sufferings. (*Diary*, 1067)

## *Reflection*

St. Faustina has peace in her soul. Where does such peace come from? Does it come from the world? From riches? Can it be gained by dialogue, by treaties, or by war? No! Peace comes from Jesus Christ. Worldly peace is temporary, but God's peace is eternal. St. Faustina's heart was "fortified for struggle and sufferings" when Jesus greeted her: "Peace be with you." What is Christ's peace? In Hebrew, the word for peace, *shalom*, describes a life of freedom, security, and contentment. We get a snapshot of what this is like in Isaiah, chapter 66. There we see a portrait of peace in the child nursing at his mother's breast. That is peace—freedom—contentment. A mother and child's bond of peace hints at the everlasting bond of peace between God and people, because peace is not an "absence," like an absence of war. Rather, peace is a "presence"—the Divine Presence of Jesus, risen from the dead.

## *Prayer*

Risen Lord, strengthen me with Your presence of peace.
Jesus, have mercy on us and on the whole world.

# *April 2*

## MAKING A DIFFERENCE

**Today, bring to Me all Mankind ...** (*Diary*, 1210)

## *Reflection*

We must realize that we are all in this together. As Pope Emeritus Benedict XVI states in his encyclical *Spe Salvi*: "No man is an island. No one lives alone. No one sins alone. No one is saved alone. The lives of others continually spill over into mine ... and my life spills over into that of others: for better and for worse." We bring each other to heaven. Each one of us benefits from the prayers of others, and for our part we should make intercession for whoever needs the Lord's help. How beautiful it is that Jesus has designed things this way, allowing us the privilege of becoming vessels of His grace for the living and deceased.

## *Prayer*

Lord, may my prayers always include (add names).

Jesus, have mercy on us and on the whole world.

# *April 3*
## THE FEAST OF MERCY

Your assignment and duty here on earth is to beg for mercy for the whole world. No soul will be justified until it turns with confidence to My mercy, and this is why the first Sunday after Easter is to be the Feast of Mercy. On that day, priests are to be administrators of My mercy. Tell the confessor that the Image is to be on view in the church and not within the enclosure in that convent. By means of this Image I shall be granting many graces to souls; so, let every soul have access to it. (*Diary*, 570)

## *Reflection*

When Jesus appeared to Faustina, He told her to have an image painted according to the vision that she saw before her. This image is now known around the world. Countless testimonies of healings and conversions have been obtained through this miraculous image. Especially important in the image is Jesus' Sacred Heart. The two rays of blood and water defeat Satan's only two weapons: sin and death. Sin is wiped away by the cleansing waters of Baptism and the healing words of Confession. These rays represent what Christ asks us to do on the Feast of Divine Mercy Sunday: Go to Confession and receive Holy Communion.

## *Prayer*

Merciful Lord, keep alive in me all year long the adoration of Your divine mercy. Open my heart to others to share this wonderful message of hope and healing.

Jesus, have mercy on us and on the whole world.

# *April 4*

## WHAT IS YOUR MOTIVE?

... the Lord gave me an understanding of God's incomprehensible love for people. He lifts us up to His very Godhead. His only motives are love and fathomless mercy ... (*Diary*, 1172)

## *Reflection*

We always have a motive for the things we do. Sometimes we act out of good and uplifting motives—like when we donate to a good cause because we believe in the mission of the cause. But other times we act out of less honorable motives—like cutting someone off in traffic because we are running late. God's only motives are love and mercy. Think how amazing that is. God never does anything except for love or mercy. How would your life be different if everything you did was based on God's motives? How would the world be changed if everyone did that?

## *Prayer*

Jesus, give me the courage to examine the motives for my behavior.

Jesus, have mercy on us and on the whole world.

# *April 5*

## FOR THE CONSOLATION OF THE WORLD

**The Feast of My Mercy has issued forth from My very depths
for the consolation of the whole world.** (*Diary*, 1517)

### *Reflection*

The world needs God's mercy today. From every continent, the depth of human misery cries for Mercy. God in His goodness bends down to us sinners. He heals our weaknesses. Jesus, reigning from the Cross embraces us with His arms, open wide with Love and Mercy. God has given us the Feast of Divine Mercy to console us and comfort us with His grace—to give sweet hope for sinners.

### *Prayer*

"O inconceivable and unfathomable Mercy of God, who can worthily adore You and sing Your praises? O greatest attribute of God Almighty, You are the sweet hope of sinners" (951).

Jesus, have mercy on us and on the whole world.

# *April 6*

## ACCEPTING GOD'S PARDON

> **I want to grant a complete pardon to the souls that will go to Confession and receive Holy Communion on the Feast of My mercy.** (*Diary*, 1109)

## *Reflection*

In 1830, a postal clerk, George Wilson, stole a federal payroll off a train, endangering the life of a guard. Found guilty, Wilson was sentenced to death by hanging. The public believed capital punishment was extreme. It was Wilson's first offense. A plea for presidential pardon was raised, which President Andrew Jackson mercifully granted. Wilson refused it. The nation was shocked. The bizarre case was brought before the U.S Supreme Court. Chief Justice John Marshall handed down the decision: "A pardon is a parchment whose only value must be determined by the receiver of the pardon. It has no value apart from that which the receiver gives to it. George Wilson refused to accept the pardon.... We cannot conceive why he would do so, but he has. Therefore, George Wilson must die." In the spiritual life, many insist, "I'm a good person." Yet, before God, we're sinners. To accept God's pardon is to first admit we're guilty of sin. God's pardon is a gift of grace. He offers it to us, but it can be experienced only if we accept it.

## *Prayer*

Lord, thank you for winning pardon for my salvation. As I daily accept Your grace, let me show pardon towards my neighbor.

Jesus, have mercy on us and on the whole world.

# *April 7*

## JESUS, SHOW ME YOUR MERCY

At three o'clock, implore My mercy, especially for sinners; and, if only for a brief moment, immerse yourself in My Passion, particularly in My abandonment at the moment of agony. This is the hour of great mercy for the whole world. I will allow you to enter into My mortal sorrow. In this hour, I will refuse nothing to the soul that makes a request of Me in virtue of My Passion.... (*Diary*, 1320)

### *Reflection*

When we enter into the mystery of Christ's Passion we'll find mercy. Our human nature—naturally repulsed by His Passion—fears of suffering, not wanting to touch us. We tiptoe around the Cross from a safe distance. We are afraid to embrace the Cross. In Jesus' agony, we're tempted to abandon Him, fleeing like most did. But Our Lady didn't run. She stood. She didn't faint. Why? Because she was totally united to God's will. There was no tomb. She trusted.

Joseph of Arimethea came forward. She and her holy companions invite us to kneel there at the foot of the Cross and immerse ourselves in His Passion. They teach us to kneel before Our Savior and pray with confidence, "Jesus, show me your mercy."

### *Prayer*

Lord, I trust in Your mercy—save me!

Jesus, have mercy on us and on the whole world.

# *April 8*

## GOD SPEAKS WITH A SINFUL SOUL

Lord, I hear your voice calling me to turn back from the path of sin, but I have neither the strength nor the courage to do so. (*Diary*, 1485)

### *Reflection*

**I am your strength, I will help you in the struggle** (1485).

### *Prayer*

"Jesus, source of life, sanctify me. O my strength, fortify me. My Commander, fight for me. Only light of my soul, enlighten me. My Master, guide me" (1490).

Jesus, have mercy on us and on the whole world.

# *April 9*

## A WITNESS TO MERCY

**You are a witness of My mercy. You shall stand before My throne forever as a living witness to My mercy.** (*Diary*, 417)

## *Reflection*

As Jesus called Faustina, He also calls us to be witnesses to His mercy. That commission requires both prayer and presence. He wants us to pray for relatives, family, friends and people on the margins, asking for His mercy. And He wants us to bring His mercy to everyone we encounter, letting them feel His love in the ways we relate to them.

## *Prayer*

Lord Jesus, please give me the wisdom and grace to be an effective witness to Your mercy.

Jesus, have mercy on us and on the whole world.

# *April 10*

## SHARING GRACE

> **The graces I grant you are not for you alone, but for a great number of other souls as well ...** (*Diary*, 723)

## *Reflection*

John Donne said, "No man is an island entire of itself; every man is a piece of the continent, a part of the main." Jesus revealed this truth to Faustina, and He reveals it to us as well. The graces He gives us are not for us to hide away for our personal pleasure. We are to use the graces we are given for the benefit of other souls. That's the purpose of this book. Just think, Jesus speaks to *you*. He loves you. He desires your love. But along with that, He wants you to let the entire world know of His love. If you don't share His love, who will?

## *Prayer*

My dear Jesus, I graciously receive the graces You wish to give me. Never allow me to hoard Your grace, but to give freely what I have been given.

Jesus, have mercy on us and on the whole world.

# *April 11*

## GOOD INTENTIONS

**I am pleased with what you are doing.** (*Diary*, 1499)

### *Reflection*

It's comforting to know that if we have good intentions, even if it doesn't turn out the best, it's okay in Jesus' eyes. St. Faustina makes that clear. She writes: "If one does not know what is better, one must reflect, consider and seek advice, because one must not act with an uncertain conscience. When uncertain, say to yourself: 'Whatever I do will be good. I have the intention of doing good.' The Lord God accepts what we consider good, and the Lord God also accepts and considers it as good. One should not worry if, after some time, one sees that these things are not good. God looks at the intention with which we begin and will reward us accordingly. This is a principle which we ought to follow" (800).

### *Prayer*

Thank You, Lord for caring about *why* I do something.

   Jesus, have mercy on us and on the whole world.

# *April 12*

## THE MEANING OF NINE

The Lord told me to say this chaplet for nine days before the Feast of Mercy. It is to begin on Good Friday. **By this novena, I will grant every possible grace to souls.** (*Diary*, 796)

## *Reflection*

Have you ever wondered why the Chaplet of Mercy novena—like all novenas—is said for nine days? It's not because the number nine is magical, but there are some interesting things about nine. Multiply a number by nine and then add the digits of the answer. They will add up to nine. Try it: 9x9 is 81; 8+1 is 9. 9x3 is 27; 2+7 is 9. Jesus died at the ninth hour, or 3 p.m. Mary and the Apostles waited in the Upper Room for nine days. And, of course, we spend nine months in the womb awaiting birth! In Scripture, nine represents completion or finality. Little wonder then that the Lord tells us to say His Chaplet for nine days so that we might bring the fulfillment of His grace to souls.

## *Prayer*

Lord, bring Your work of mercy to completion in my soul.

Jesus, have mercy on us and on the whole world.

## *April 13*

I saw the Lord Jesus clothed in a white garment. One hand [was] raised in the gesture of blessing, the other was touching the garment at the breast. From beneath the garment, slightly drawn aside at the breast, there were emanating two large rays, one red, the other pale. In silence I kept my gaze fixed on the Lord; my soul was struck with awe, but also with great joy. After a while, Jesus said to me, **Paint an image according to the pattern you see, with the signature: Jesus, I trust in You.** (*Diary*, 47)

### *Reflection*

Our trust in Jesus grows as we see Him working through our lives. Living by faith, our life is a training ground in trust. Scripture says, "Whenever you face trials of any kind, consider it nothing but joy, because you know that the testing of your faith produces endurance …" (Jas 1:2-4). In our weakness, He gives us strength. In our littleness, we find our true greatness is in God. St. Faustina teaches us to trust in God's mercy completely and to pray from the inner recesses of our being: "Jesus, I trust in You."

### *Prayer*

"I trust in Your mercy because You are the God of mercy …" (1730).

Jesus, have mercy on us and on the whole world.

# *April 14*

## PROCLAIM HIS MERCY

And who knows anything about this feast? No one! Even those who should be proclaiming My mercy and teaching people about it often do not know about it themselves. That is why I want the image to be solemnly blessed on the first Sunday after Easter, and I want it to be venerated publicly so that every soul may know about it. (*Diary*, 341)

## *Reflection*

Secular society has no place for mercy. They have only justice. By keeping justice without mercy in it, they are relentless and unforgiving. We have an obligation to proclaim God's mercy in this merciless society.

## *Prayer*

Lord, grant me the grace to always be merciful.

Jesus, have mercy on us and on the whole world.

# *April 15*

## WHAT DOES IT MEAN TO VENERATE?

I promise that the soul that will venerate this image will not perish. I also promise victory over [its] enemies already here on earth, especially at the hour of death. I Myself will defend it as My own glory. (*Diary*, 48)

## *Reflection*

The Divine Mercy image is a vessel of grace, from which gushes a fountain of mercy. Jesus says that He will grant many graces to souls and asks that every soul be able to venerate it. We ought to give the Divine Mercy image a place of honor in our parishes and homes, adorning it with flowers and candles—outward signs of veneration. But true veneration of the image of Divine Mercy begins in the heart—the human heart pierced by the love of Jesus. Worshipping the mercy of God, "victory is always on your side" (1560) because we put our trust in Him. God protects as His own possession His own children—the beloved of God who venerate the image of His Mercy.

## *Prayer*

"Most Merciful Jesus, whose Heart is Love Itself, receive into the abode of Your Most Compassionate Heart the souls of those who particularly extol and venerate the greatness of Your mercy" (1225).

Jesus, have mercy on us and on the whole world.

# *April 16*

## LIKE SUN THROUGH CRYSTAL

When my soul was flooded with God's happiness, I heard these words in my soul: **My mercy has passed into souls through the divine-human heart of Jesus as a ray from the sun passes through crystal.** I felt in my heart and understood that every approach to God is brought about by Jesus, in Him and through Him. (*Diary*, 528)

## *Reflection*

Ever look at the sunlight as it shines through a crystal? The invisible rays are revealed to be made up of every color of creation. Flashes of pure white light illuminate everything around the crystal. At that moment, it is as if you are granted a tiny glimpse at the colors of heaven. In the same way, Jesus reveals the Father to us in all His glory. Just as all the brilliance of the sunlight is shown only when diffused through a crystal, so the love and mercy of God are made real and tangible through the Heart of Jesus.

## *Prayer*

Dear Jesus, help me to see the Father by and in and through You.

Jesus, have mercy on us and on the whole world.

# *April 17*

## GOOD ENOUGH TO BE TRUE

> **The flames of mercy are burning Me—clamoring to be spent; I want to keep pouring them out upon souls; souls just don't want to believe in My goodness.** (*Diary*, 177)

## *Reflection*

The passion that God has, in His tremendous desire to pour out mercy upon all of humanity, is nothing short of remarkable. We see here that He is "burning" and "clamoring" to do so. The only problem? People don't want to believe in His goodness. Perhaps they fear that the message of Divine Mercy sounds "too good to be true." Well, that may be the case with an offer from a fellow human being ... but coming from the Lord God Almighty, it is absolutely 150 percent true. Our only duty is to believe it and fully embrace it.

## *Prayer*

Jesus, may the world understand Your burning eagerness for Your children to accept Your amazing offer of complete and total forgiveness.

Jesus, have mercy on us and on the whole world.

# *April 18*

## THE COURAGE OF TRUE MERCY

> I am giving you three ways of exercising mercy toward your neighbor:
> the first—by deed, the second—by word, the third—by prayer.
> In these three degrees is contained the fullness of mercy, and it is
> an unquestionable proof of love for Me.... You must not shrink
> from this or try to excuse or absolve yourself from it. (*Diary*, 742)

### *Reflection*

False mercy is common today. It tickles the ear; it trivializes sin. But without repentance, mercy is false. Because society today relativizes truth and attacks Christian morality, people enmeshed in various situations embrace a false mercy that soothes their consciences. But the Gospel calls us to radical conversion in Christ. Showing false mercy, we cajole people to embrace sin's false allurements—not the true mercy of God, which their souls desperately need. To love our neighbor, we must show true mercy, not displaced compassion, by proclaiming the Gospel truth. Putting love of God and neighbor into action demands that we show true mercy through deeds, through words, and by prayer. We must not shrink from this or try to excuse ourselves from this duty toward others.

### *Prayer*

Lord, let me love my neighbor by bringing them truth wrapped in mercy—in deeds, in words, and by prayer.

Jesus, have mercy on us and on the whole world.

# *April 19*

## JUST LET GO

**If souls would put themselves completely in My care,
I Myself would undertake the task of sanctifying them, and
I would lavish even greater graces on them.** (*Diary*, 1682)

## *Reflection*

We cling so tightly to our sense of control! We think we have the future in
our grasp, or at least in our planner. But Jesus' way is so much better. It's the
only way, of course. We just have to let go and open ourselves to His grace,
which is far more powerful than any effort we could dream up on our own.
To abandon ourselves completely to God's will and not be afraid. Everything
that is best for us, everything that leads us to eternal life, will be given to us.
Can you imagine the extraordinary peace that comes with being completely
in His care?

## *Prayer*

Compassionate Heart of Jesus, take over my life.

Jesus, have mercy on us and on the whole world.

# *April 20*

## PLEADING FOR MERCY

Pure love gives the soul strength at the very moment of dying.
When I was dying on the cross, I was not thinking about Myself,
but about poor sinners, and I prayed for them to My Father. I
want your last moments to be completely similar to Mine on the
cross. There is but one price at which souls are bought, and that
is suffering united to My suffering on the cross. (*Diary*, 324)

### *Reflection*

When Napoleon sentenced a man to death, the man's mother pleaded for her son's life. Napoleon insisted that the crime's gravity demanded her son's life in justice. Sobbing, she cried, "Sir, I don't seek justice, but mercy." He said, "He's undeserving of mercy." She argued, "Sir, if he deserved it, it would not be mercy." With that, Napoleon's heart opened, "I will have mercy." You want God's mercy? Then show mercy. Whenever we can be merciful to someone, we ought to show that person the same mercy we desire from God at life's last moment. A Christian woman, lying on her deathbed was asked, "Are you going to receive your reward?" With tears filling her eyes, she faintly whispered with pure love, "No. I am going to plead for mercy."

### *Prayer*

Crucified Lord, permit my last moments to be like Yours on the Cross, pouring forth love and mercy to my last breath.

Jesus, have mercy on us and on the whole world.

# *April 21*

## HIS HOLY WILL

> **Now I know that it is not for the graces or gifts that you love me, but because My will is dearer to you than life.** (*Diary*, 707)

## *Reflection*

When a first-grader brings home an A, Mom and Dad cheer and applaud. But a doctoral student finishing his dissertation isn't rewarded with ice cream from his professor. He sacrificed and worked hard as he or she cracked the books. Translate this into the spiritual life. When God rewards us for doing good, this reinforces what's truly good in us. These rewards are His gifts of grace—spiritual consolations. Consolations make us feel good about doing good—nothing's wrong with that. But to help us mature spiritually, God withdraws consolations to help us grow. This tests us but also strengthens us. When God does this to us, He purifies our intentions, so that we follow His will and do the right thing simply because it is the right thing. St. Faustina teaches us to please God, seeking that which had become dearer to her than life—His Holy Will.

## *Prayer*

Lord, help me to do Your will, not simply for graces and gifts, but because You are dearer to me than life.

Jesus, have mercy on us and on the whole world.

# *April 22*

## GOD CONDEMNS NO ONE

**Do not fear, My little child, you are not alone. Fight bravely, because My arm is supporting you; fight for the salvation of souls, exhorting them to trust in My mercy, as that is your task in this life and in the life to come.** After these words, I received a deeper understanding of divine mercy. Only that soul who wants it will be damned, for God condemns no one. (*Diary*, 1452)

## *Reflection*

St. Faustina received from Jesus the sure knowledge that no soul will be eternally lost unless they "want it," meaning they have deliberately rejected God's offer of mercy. Her mission was to tell the world about the great mercy that our Father wants to extend to all of us. We need to make it our mission, too.

## *Prayer*

Father, You condemn no one. We condemn ourselves. May I always remember that truth.

Jesus, have mercy on us and on the whole world.

# *April 23*

## GOD SPEAKS WITH A PERFECT SOUL

Lord, first let me pour out my heart at Your feet in a fragrant anointing of gratitude for the many blessings which You lavish upon me; even if I wanted to, I could not count them. I only recall that there has never been a moment in my life in which I have not experienced Your protection and goodness ... You have covered me with the cloak of Your mercy ... You always had pity on me, giving me a new life of grace ... You have entrusted me to the loving care of Your Church ... there is one more secret in my life, deepest and dearest to my heart: it is You Yourself when you come to my heart under the appearance of bread. Herein lies the whole secret of sanctity.... (*Diary*, 1489)

## *Reflection*

**Your words please Me, and your thanksgiving opens up new treasures of graces. But, My child, we should talk in more detail about the things that lie in your heart. Let us talk confidentially and frankly, as two hearts that love one another do** (1489).

## *Prayer*

O Lord, although eternity will hardly suffice for me to give due praise to Your unfathomable mercy and Your compassion for me, I will never cease to praise and thank you here and in eternity!

Jesus, have mercy on us and on the whole world.

# *April 24*

## FOR THE HOLY FATHER

> **Make a novena for the Holy Father's intention. It should consist of thirty-three acts; that is repetition that many times of the short prayer—which I have taught you—to the Divine Mercy.** (*Diary*, 341)

## *Reflection*

Jesus cares deeply about His Church and those who lead the faithful. That is why He instructed Faustina and us to pray this novena (nine successive days of a particular prayer). He points to the power of novenas. The Divine Mercy novena prayer is, as its name says, all about divine mercy. The Lord clearly wants those who lead the Church to teach this vital lesson to the entire Body of Christ. Along with Faustina, pray, "Today, Jesus, I offer you all my sufferings, mortifications, and prayers for the intentions of the Holy Father" (340).

## *Prayer*

Dear Lord, strengthen the Holy Father in his mission as Vicar of Christ to those of the Universal Church throughout the four corners of the earth.

Jesus, have mercy on us and on the whole world.

# *April 25*

## BOUNTIFUL GRACE

> Tell [all people] ... that I am Love and Mercy itself. When a soul approaches Me with trust, I fill it with such an abundance of graces that it cannot contain them within itself, but radiates them to other souls. (*Diary*, 1074)

## *Reflection*

We've all heard the expression, "my cup overfloweth." That is precisely what happens when we trust in the Lord. He blesses us with so many graces that our souls cannot contain them all, and they flow out to the benefit of other souls as well. No blessing is meant to be hoarded, but to be shared with others; therefore, we should desire to have a heart that always seeks to radiate the graces that we have received to all souls.

## *Prayer*

Build up my trust in You, O Lord, so that I may overflow with Your bountiful graces for the benefit of many.

Jesus, have mercy on us and on the whole world.

# *April 26*

## GRACE FOR THE HUMBLE

**Be absolutely as frank as possible with your confessor.** (*Diary*, 1499)

### *Reflection*

A priest shared his thoughts on this entry from the *Diary*: Walking toward St. Peter's Basilica, you cross the Tiber River. As you walk over the Sant'Angelo Bridge, you see this inscription: *Hinc humilibus venia* (Here, there's forgiveness for the humble). *Hinc retribuito superbis* (Here, there's punishment for the proud). As you enter the confessional, keep these words in mind. Want to make a good confession? Be humble and honest. Keep confession simple. When we confess sin, exhaustive detail isn't necessary. We shouldn't be vague or hide our sins. We ought to just say plainly what we did and leave it at that. Want to be close to God? Want to enjoy peace of heart? St. Faustina advises that we be frank with our confessor, because "God opposes the proud, but gives grace to the humble" (Jas 4:6).

Wise advice.

### *Prayer*

Come, Holy Spirit, and enlighten me to see my sins and the grace to speak frankly.

Jesus, have mercy on us and on the whole world.

# *April 27*

## THE MERIT OF ALL THINGS LIES
## IN THEIR DIFFICULTY

**Do not be guided by feeling, because it is not always under your control; but all merit lies in the will.** (*Diary*, 1760)

## *Reflection*

When someone hurts us, our innermost feelings come to the surface. If we're not careful, we'll be guided by our hurt feelings and do something foolish—something we'll later regret. When emotions dominate us, we need to let God's love strengthen our wills. Jesus told Faustina: "It is love that has meaning and power and merit" (822). Indeed, all merit resides in the will, because love's an act of the will. Faustina learned how God "allows certain difficulties precisely for our merit so that our fidelity might be clearly manifest." She explains that "through this, I have been given strength for suffering and self-denial" (1409). Alexandre Dumas, the famed author of *The Three Musketeers*, put it this way: "The merit of all things lies in their difficulty."

## *Prayer*

"O Lord, deify my actions so that they will merit eternity; although my weakness is great, I trust in the power of Your grace, which will sustain me" (1371).

Jesus, have mercy on us and on the whole world.

# *April 28*

## ONE OF GOD'S BROKEN VESSELS

I saw the suffering Jesus, who spoke these words to me: **My daughter, do not pay so much attention to the vessel of grace as to the grace itself which I give you, because you are not always pleased with the vessel, and then the graces, too, become deficient ... Let all the attention of your soul be concentrated on responding to My grace as faithfully as possible.** (*Diary*, 1599)

## *Reflection*

Flip through the pages of the Bible and you'll see God uses imperfect people as vessels of His grace. Moses had speech impediment; Samson was a womanizer; David committed adultery and murder; Rahab was a prostitute; Zacchaeus was a money-hungry tax collector; Martha complained and worried; and Peter denied Jesus three times. Jesus oftentimes sends the best graces through people who are broken vessels. Like Faustina, we can pay too little attention to the message of grace that God's sending and focus too much on the person who brought the message — one of God's broken vessels.

## *Prayer*

"O most compassionate Jesus, I have not always known how to profit from these priceless gifts, because I have paid too little attention to the gift itself and too much to the vessel in which You were giving me Your gifts" (1759).

Jesus, have mercy on us and on the whole world.

# *April 29*

## HAPPINESS IN GOD

> I do not know how to live without God, but I also
> feel that God, absolutely self-sufficient though He is,
> cannot be happy without me.... (*Diary*, 1120)

## *Reflection*

God's children should live focused on what matters to God, "love, love, and once again, love" (997). St. Faustina commented that even though God "... is happy in Himself and has absolutely no need of any creature, still, His goodness compels Him to give Himself to the creature ..." (244). Just as we're happiest when we do good for the needy, God rejoices to do good to us. Want to receive God's love? Avoid sin like the plague, because sin separates us from God. It's impossible to be happy apart from God. C. S. Lewis commented: "All that we call human history—money, poverty, ambition, war, prostitution, classes, empires, slavery—[is] the long terrible story of man trying to find something other than God which will make him happy." But the human heart is made for love because we're made for God. Happiness is in God alone.

## *Prayer*

O God, wrap me in Your arms of love and let me seek happiness in nothing else but You!

Jesus, have mercy on us and on the whole world.

# *April 30*

## THE LOVE OF GOD FOR SOULS

**O child, especially beloved by Me, apple of My eye ...** *(Diary, 1489)*

### *Reflection*

God's wants us to rest in His Heart because He loves us so much. But people don't understand. Just as St. John reclined upon His Heart at the Last Supper, so Jesus wants us to make His Heart our refuge. You're precious to Him—His beloved child. St. Padre Pio echoes that when he says, "Our Lord loves you and loves you tenderly...." Be utterly convinced of the love of God for you. "When I was leaving the chapel, in an instant, God's omnipotence enveloped me. I understood how greatly God loves us. Oh, if people could at least partly comprehend and understand this!" (574).

### *Prayer*

Heavenly Father, I am the apple of Your eye. You love me more than anybody else and more than anybody can. Thank you.

Jesus, have mercy on us and on the whole world.

CHAPTER FIVE

# Reflections

FOR

# *May*

# *May 1*

## THE HUMILITY OF MARY

When I was left alone with the Blessed Virgin, she instructed me concerning the interior life. She said, *The soul's true greatness is in loving God and in humbling oneself in His presence, completely forgetting oneself and believing oneself to be nothing, because the Lord is great, but He is well-pleased only with the humble, He always opposes the proud.* (Diary, 1711)

## *Reflection*

If we're working "to be humble," we're striving to be "something" — to be noticed. If we're "something," we've not been seeking the "lowest place" like Mary. If we're seeking a humble heart, the Virgin Mother will be our guide. In his pilgrimage to Mary's home at Loreto, "the sanctuary of humility," Pope Emeritus Benedict XVI said: "In following Christ and imitating Mary, we must have the courage of humility ..." (Homily, September 2, 2007). Our Lady formed St. Faustina in this too, teaching her that the "soul's true greatness is in loving God and in humbling oneself in His presence" (1711).

## *Prayer*

O God, mold me in the humility of Mary.

Jesus, have mercy on us and on the whole world.

# *May 2*

## A CONSOLING THOUGHT

**A single act of pure love pleases Me more than
a thousand imperfect prayers.** (*Diary*, 1489)

## *Reflection*

Do random acts of kindness and see how pure love makes you feel close to
others. Now you get an inkling of what God feels.

## *Prayer*

"O inexhaustible treasure of purity of intention which makes all our actions
perfect and so pleasing to God!" (66).

Jesus, have mercy on us and on the whole world.

# May 3

*The Feast of the Holy Trinity*

## ADORE THE HOLY TRINITY

During Holy Mass, I heard the rustling of garments and saw the most holy Mother of God in a most beautiful radiance. Her white garment was girdled with a blue sash. She said to me, *You give Me great joy when you adore The Holy Trinity for the graces and privileges which were accorded Me.* (*Diary*, 564)

## Reflection

St. Faustina tells us the saints in heaven forever contemplate the Holy Trinity: "Today I was in heaven, in spirit, and I saw its inconceivable beauties and the happiness that awaits us after death. I saw how all creatures give ceaseless praise and glory to God. I saw how great is happiness in God, which spreads to all creatures making them happy; and then all the glory and praise which springs from this happiness returns to its source; and they enter into the depths of God, contemplating the inner life of God, the Father, the Son, and the Holy Spirit, whom they will never comprehend nor fathom.... Now I understand St. Paul who said: 'Eye has not seen, not has ear heard, nor has it entered into the heart of man what God has prepared for those who love Him'" (777).

## Prayer

"Be adored, O Most Holy Trinity, now and for all time. Be adored in all Your works and all Your creatures. May the greatness of Your mercy be admired and glorified, O God" (5).

Jesus, have mercy on us and on the whole world.

# *May 4*

## SAFE BY DAY OR NIGHT

**In a soul that lives on My love alone, I reign in heaven.
I watch over it day and night.** (*Diary*, 1489)

## *Reflection*

Jesus wants us to respond to His love by giving ourselves entirely to Him. In response to our surrender, He promises to guide and protect us. He wants us to give what we can't keep to gain what we can't lose.

## *Prayer*

Jesus, as You reign in heaven, reign in my heart day and night.
Jesus, have mercy on us and on the whole world.

# May 5

## TWO DEAR FRIENDS

**What are you doing here so early?** I answered, "I am thinking of You, of Your mercy and Your goodness toward us. And You, Jesus what are You doing here?" **I have come out to meet you, to lavish new graces on you.** (*Diary*, 1705)

## Reflection

In May, 1938, Faustina went out to the hospital gardens after Mass. There were no patients around, so she could contemplate the blessings of God. Her heart burned so strong with love for God that she felt it would burst. Many saints had this experience. (St. Philip Neri experienced this same intense love so that his heart was enlarged). Then Jesus stood before Faustina, and this beautiful exchange between two loving hearts took place. Faustina lived in such intimacy with Him for such a long time that she treated Jesus like her dearest friend. Two dear friends lavishing each other with love and grace. That's what friends are for.

## Prayer

My Lord, I want this friendship with You.

Jesus, have mercy on us and on the whole world.

# *May 6*

## TEMPTATIONS AREN'T SINS

> **All temptations united together ought not disturb your interior peace, not even momentarily.** (*Diary*, 1488)

### *Reflection*

Don't mistake a temptation for a sin. As long as you resist the temptation, it can never be a sin. For that reason, Jesus says not to let temptations upset your peace. Now sin, on the other hand, is another story. Any sin, large or small, ought to cause enormous unrest in your soul.

### *Prayer*

When I am tempted to sin, help me resist. And when I have resisted, help me never to think of it again.

Jesus, have mercy on us and on the whole world.

# *May 7*

## KEEP ON ASPIRING

**I am pleased with your efforts, O soul aspiring for perfection.** (*Diary*, 1488)

## *Reflection*

Good news! We don't actually have to be perfect for God to love us. He is pleased with our efforts as we strive for perfection. To be great in God's eyes it is necessary to do His will at every waking moment. If you have a natural inclination to smile, use it often. Are you good at figures? Become the best you can be! Do you have a singing voice? Strive for the most exquisite notes! Be focused on what gifts God gave you and perfect them!

## *Prayer*

Jesus, I want to use all my efforts to be perfect for You!
Jesus, have mercy on us and on the whole world.

# *May 8*

## TOTAL UNDERSTANDING

**I understand all your troubles and miseries.** (*Diary*, 1487)

## *Reflection*

Who can understand us? Our turbulent changes of emotion. Our contradictory and at times confusing likes and dislikes. If we seek out Jesus, His divine mercy gives us the greatest desire of the human heart, to be fully understood and more importantly, to be fully accepted.

## *Prayer*

Lord, thank You for Your total understanding and accepting of every part of me.

Jesus, have mercy on us and on the whole world.

# *May 9*

I recognize your holiness and fear you. (*Diary*, 1485)

## *Reflection*

Be not afraid of your Savior; O sinful soul. I make the first move to come to you, for I know that by yourself you are unable to lift yourself to me. Child, do not run away from your Father; be willing to talk openly with your God of mercy who wants to speak words of pardon and lavish his graces on you. How dear your soul is to Me! I have inscribed your name upon My hand; you are engraved as a deep wound in My Heart (1485).

## *Prayer*

My name is inscribed upon Your hand, dear Lord. There's no place I'd rather be ... now and forever.

Jesus, have mercy on us and on the whole world.

# May 10

**Pray with all your heart in union with Mary ...** (*Diary*, 32)

## Reflection

Sailor's call Polaris the Stella Maris, "star of the sea." This is their "guiding star" or "steering star" because it has been used for celestial navigation at sea since antiquity. Mary is the "Star of the Sea," as she guides us safely to her Son. In the twelfth century, St. Bernard of Claivaux wrote:

> "If the winds of temptation arise; if you are driven upon the rocks of tribulation, look to the star. Call on Mary. If you are tossed upon the waves of pride, of ambition, of envy, of rivalry, look to the star, call on Mary. Should anger, or avarice, or fleshly desire violently assail the frail vessel of your souls, look at the star, call upon Mary."

## Prayer

Help me, dear Mother, to do what Jesus tells me to do.
Jesus, have mercy on us and on the whole world.

# *May 11*

## BLESS EVERYONE

**Is your love for neighbor guided by My love. Do you pray for your enemies? Do you wish well to those who have, in one way or another, caused you sorrow or offended you?** (*Diary*, 1768)

### *Reflection*

It's easy to pray for those who love us, but what about those who have mistreated us?

Praying for God's blessing on someone who has hurt us doesn't feel natural. We'd rather strike back than wish them well. Yet Jesus wants us to love our enemies with the same kind of love He has for us. That means that even when we are hurt or angry, we recognize that we are all children of the same loving Father, and we extend the same forgiveness and grace to others that we would have given to us. Remember, this doesn't have to be a big thing. Jesus says to wish them well. For instance, the next time someone cuts you off in traffic or says a sharp word, silently pray that the rest of their day goes more smoothly.

### *Prayer*

Dear Jesus, help me to love all those around me, especially those who have hurt me, with the same love You have for me.

Jesus, have mercy on us and on the whole world.

# May 12

## GOD SPEAKS TO A SOUL STRIVING AFTER PERFECTION

Lord, the reason for my sadness is that, in spite of my sincere resolutions, I fall again into the same faults. I make resolutions in the morning, but in the evenings I see how much I have departed from them. (*Diary*, 1488)

### Reflection

You see, My child, what you are of yourself. The cause of your falls is that you rely too much upon yourself and too little on Me. But let this not sadden you so much. You are dealing with the God of mercy, which your misery cannot exhaust. Remember, I did not allot only a certain number of pardons (1488).

### Prayer

"I trust in You, Jesus, for You are unchangeable. My moods change, but You are always the same, full of mercy" (1489).

Jesus, have mercy on us and on the whole world.

# *May 13*

## BECOMING HUMBLE

> **More favor is granted to a humble soul than the soul itself asks for....** (*Diary*, 1361)

## *Reflection*

Great gifts are given to the humble soul, but what does being humble mean to the Lord? It means to be kinder, more compassionate, and more merciful. So how does one learn to be kinder, more compassionate, and more merciful? The first thing is to remember we are all God's children. That includes yourself. You are a child of God, and sometimes God's children are nice; other times not so much. When you do something that you wish you did not do, be kind to yourself. Try to remember that to be humble before the Lord means we can make mistakes as long as we acknowledge them and work not to repeat them. Let's say we are brusque with a friend. We can go to our friend and say we are sorry. The opposite is true as well. If someone apologizes to us for being rude with us, learn to accept the apology graciously. This is the beginning of the path to humility.

## *Prayer*

Dear Lord, help me to understand that being humble means remembering I am a beloved child of God.

Jesus, have mercy on us and on the whole world.

# May 14

**Yes, when you are obedient I take away your weakness and replace it with My strength.** (*Diary*, 381)

## Reflection

St. Faustina professed the vow of obedience. Jesus deeply touched her heart because of her trust in Him. When He spoke, she listened: "By obedience you give great glory to Me and gain merit for yourself" (28). As she obeyed, He strengthened her. To obey is to listen to God with the "ear of our hearts," as St. Benedict taught. Christian faithful live in obedience to their state in life, following the commandments. Children obey their parents, and employees obey their bosses. When we don't obey God in our lives, trouble and chaos follow. The ancient saying, "Obedience is good, but only when it's done for God's sake," rings true today and reminds us to seek God's guidance in everything. We discern God's will and seek wise counsel. When we hear God, obedience says "yes" to His will, desires, and dreams for our lives. Ultimately, to obey is say to "yes" to God's love.

## Prayer

"O my Love, my eternal Master, how good it is to obey; because when obedience infuses the soul, it brings with it power and strength to act" (1686).

Jesus, have mercy on us and on the whole world.

# *May 15*

**My daughter, your compassion for Me refreshes Me.** (*Diary*, 1657)

## *Reflection*

During Mass, Jesus permitted St. Faustina, in a remarkable way, to experience the pain his soul experienced during His Sacred Passion. She described it like a "painful echo in his Sacred Heart" (1657). "My soul, too, was inundated by a sea of bitterness," she wrote, as she mysteriously entered into Christ's suffering. Her compassion for Jesus intensified because she was increasingly willing to suffer with Him. The friends of the Cross are few. But St. Faustina had courage. She reached out to her Savior: "My whole soul was drawn close to Jesus" (1657). St. Faustina teaches us: "Suffering is a great grace; through suffering the soul becomes like the Savior; in suffering love becomes crystallized; the greater the suffering, the purer the love" (57).

## *Prayer*

Lord, deepen my desire to suffer for You.

Jesus, have mercy on us and on the whole world.

# May 16

Tell sinners that no one shall escape My Hand; if they run away from My Merciful Heart, they will fall into My Just Hands. Tell sinners that I am always waiting for them, that I listen intently to the beating of their heart.... when will it beat for Me? (*Diary*, 1728)

## Reflection

St. Bernard of Clairvaux speaks of mercy and judgment as God's two feet. We ought not to neglect either foot. "But keep the law and the commandments, and be merciful and just, so that it may be well with you" (Tob 14:9). Our Lord told St. Faustina that "before I come as a just Judge, I first open wide the door of My mercy. He who refuses to pass through the door of My mercy must pass through the door of My justice ..." (1146). In the book of Revelation, St. John the Divine was shown in heaven an open door. This must be the door of Mercy that Jesus spoke of to St. Faustina. Those who turn away from that open door of God's Mercy open for themselves the door of His Justice.

## Prayer

My sweet Jesus, make me turn to You and run toward the open door of Your Mercy.

Jesus, have mercy on us and on the whole world.

# *May 17*

## A LIFE OF RECOLLECTION

Strive for a life of recollection so that you can hear My voice, which is so soft that only recollected souls can hear it.... (*Diary*, 1779)

## *Reflection*

God calls his children to a mysterious encounter with Himself. He invites us, but we must reciprocate. Keeping a spirit of recollection first requires a spirit of self-control over the tongue. St. Faustina remarked that the "tongue is a small member, but it does big things" (118). She said that "in order to hear the voice of God, one has to have silence in one's soul and to keep silence; not a gloomy silence, but an interior silence; that is to say, recollection in God" (118). Without that silence of mind and heart, a prayerful spirit cannot be formed, "for the Spirit of God to act in the soul, peace and recollection are needed" (145).

## *Prayer*

Lord, may I be like a bee enclosed in the hive, busily making the sweet honey of prayer.

Jesus, have mercy on us and on the whole world.

# *May 18*

## MORTAL SIN — DEATH TO THE SOUL!

**Know without doubt, and once and for all, that only mortal sin drives Me out of a soul, and nothing else.** (*Diary*, 1181)

## *Reflection*

St. Faustina described how she saw a priest in danger of committing mortal sin. Horrified by the thought, she begged God to send her "all the torments of hell ... if only this priest would be set free and snatched from the occasion of committing a sin" (41). St. Faustina was uniquely inspired to unite these sufferings to the Cross of Christ in a most mystical way. When Jesus granted her request, she said: "I felt a crown of thorns on my head. The thorns penetrated my head with great force right into my brain. This lasted for three hours; the servant of God was set free from this sin, and his soul was strengthened by a special grace of God" (41). When we're comfortable with sin, we ought to recall that "the wages of sin is death" (Rom 6:23). Mortal sin is death to the soul! If we've succumbed to mortal sin, we have recourse to the sacrament of Confession—as Jesus says, "where the greatest miracles take place"—at a parish near you.

## *Prayer*

Son of David, Son of the living God, have mercy on me, a sinner.

Jesus, have mercy on us and on the whole world.

# *May 19*

## LOVE NEVER DECEIVES

One of the Mothers [probably Mother Jane], when she learned about my close relationship with the Lord Jesus, told me that I must be deluding myself. She told me that the Lord Jesus associates in this way only with the saints and not with sinful souls "like you, Sister!" After that, it was as if I mistrusted Jesus. In one of my morning talks with Him I said, "Jesus, are You not an illusion?" Jesus answered me, **My love deceives no one.** (*Diary*, 29)

## *Reflection*

When we start listening to negative, critical voices, we must realize that this is a test. Your trust and faith in God are on the line when others try to convince you that you are somehow "unworthy" of God's love and attention. Nothing could be further from the truth. The Lord's love for each of us is real indeed. Pay no attention to anyone claiming otherwise.

## *Prayer*

Test my heart, O Lord. Never let me for one single moment doubt Your love for me.

Jesus, have mercy on us and on the whole world.

# *May 20*
## CHOSEN SOULS

The Lord has given me to know how much He desires the perfection of chosen souls. **Chosen souls are, in My hand, lights which I cast into the darkness of the world and with which I illumine it. As stars illumine the night, so chosen souls illumine the earth.** (*Diary*, 1601)

## *Reflection*

These "chosen souls" are those consecrated religious who have dedicated their lives to God in a special way for the benefit of all humanity. These holy men and women bring God's light into our world, casting out the darkness of evil and sin. It is God's will to sanctify them to perfection, so that others may see their shining example and learn from them, to seek their own perfection as they themselves draw closer to the Lord every day.

## *Prayer*

Lord, grant that the light of all those in religious orders brighten the hearts of those living in the gloom of darkness and despair.

Jesus, have mercy on us and on the whole world.

# *May 21*

## GOD'S DELIGHT

> Today after Holy Communion, the Lord told me, **My delight is to unite myself with you. It is when you submit yourself to My will that you give Me the greatest glory and draw upon yourself a sea of blessings. I would not take such special delight in you if you were not living by my will.** (*Diary*, 954)

## *Reflection*

Uniting ourselves with God is literally what life is all about. It delights God because what is more delightful than being in love? God literally created us out of love, to love us and for us to love Him back. It is so profoundly beautiful, not only for us, but for Him, when that love is fulfilled and expressed, in meaningful ways. For our part, it's living by His holy will. That's how we demonstrate our love for our Father. It brings a sea of blessings into our lives and fills His heart with unspeakable joy. And in His mighty hands we are never alone.

## *Prayer*

Father, from the moment I awaken to when I fall asleep at night, may I always seek Your holy will in my every thought and deed. True happiness and peace lies in doing Your will.

Jesus, have mercy on us and on the whole world.

# May 22

> I desire that priests proclaim this great mercy of Mine towards souls of sinners. Let the sinner not be afraid to approach Me. (*Diary*, 50)

## Reflection

Jesus takes great pleasure in freely dispensing His mercy to all who come to Him. It is an endless supply of gifts, and He will bestow them with tremendous joy for the glory that it brings to the Father. He asks His priests to tell everyone about His unfathomable mercy. He asks St. Faustina to speak to priests about this. "Tell My priests that hardened sinners will repent on hearing their words when they speak about My unfathomable mercy, about the compassion I have for them in My Heart. To priests who proclaim and extol My mercy, I will give wondrous power; I will anoint their words and touch the hearts of those to whom they will speak" (1521). "O priests, you bright candles enlightening human souls, let your brightness never be dimmed" (75).

## Prayer

Lord, may all the people of God, but most especially Your priests, proclaim in the Church and to the world the message of divine mercy that Jesus brings to us.

Have mercy on us and on the whole world.

# *May 23*

**Be merciful to others, as I am to you.** (*Diary*, 1486)

## *Reflection*

St. Faustina spoke a lot about God to the "wards" (those she took care of) who helped her in the kitchen and garden. She encouraged them to make small sacrifices, to take small steps to change their lives. But she also offered up her own mortifications and penances that she had taken on for their needs. With her pleas, she obtained God's mercy for them.

## *Prayer*

Dear Jesus, make my actions speak louder than my words.

Jesus, have mercy on us and on the whole world.

# *May 24*

## DELIGHT OF MY HEART

My daughter, delight of My heart, it is with pleasure that I look into your soul. I bestow many graces only because of you. I also withhold My punishments only because of you. You restrain Me, and I cannot vindicate the claims of My justice. You bind My hands with your love. (*Diary*, 1193)

## *Reflection*

Jesus called St. Faustina the "delight" of His Heart. Because of her prayers, many punishments for others were withheld. Her love restrained His justice and supplanted it with His mercy. Although she was a saint, we can also become God's "delight." Imagine what good you might be able to do in the world if you commit yourself body and soul to His work!

## *Prayer*

Jesus, I want to be Your delight. I want to serve You on behalf of others. Give me the grace to do that.

Jesus, have mercy on us and on the whole world.

# *May 25*

## PRAISE HIS GOODNESS

> **... every soul will praise My goodness.** (*Diary*, 1059)

## *Reflection*

It's not only every soul that praises God's goodness. All of creation sings of
His glory. As the geophysicist Enrico Medi prayed, in the spirit of St. Francis
of Assisi: "O Galaxies of the immense heavens, give praise to my Lord, for he
is omnipotent and good. O atoms, O protons, O electrons, O bird-songs, O
blowing of the leaves and of the air, in the hands of man as prayer, sing out
the hymn which returns to God!" Amen!

## *Prayer*

Lord, loosen my tongue to sing Your praises.

Jesus, have mercy on us and on the whole world.

# *May 26*

## ACCEPT YOURSELF AND OTHERS

A heart, which thus far is envious, now begins to be filled with hate. And they are already at the edge of the precipice. They are jealous of my gifts in other souls, but they themselves are unable and unwilling to accept them. (*Diary*, 1717)

## *Reflection*

We are all gifted by God. We have different stations in life. Ask God to help you find your calling. Don't force your way into what others have. You will lose peace and go on the wrong path. Pray to be what God is calling you to be. Be satisfied with your role. All roles are equal. No one has your role. Only you can fulfill it. Be the best you can be without comparing yourself to others. Rejoice in others' gifts. You will always be happy fulfilling the role God gave you because it is a perfect fit!

## *Prayer*

Dear Lord, thank You for creating me. When I am doing what I love, what You called me to do, that's what makes me the happiest.

Jesus, have mercy on us and on the whole world.

# *May 27*

## MISSION NOT IMPOSSIBLE

> ... give Me souls. Know that it is your mission to win souls for Me by prayer and sacrifice, and by encouraging them to trust in My mercy. (*Diary*, 1690)

## *Reflection*

If you ever feel like you don't have much purpose in your life, take a moment to truly contemplate what Jesus is saying to us. He wants us to encourage our brothers and sisters to literally put their lives in His hands and to trust in His mercy without reservation. That means telling others about God's mercy and performing acts of mercy toward others in our own life experiences. When we "practice what we preach," others take notice, and they too will be drawn toward the ocean of God's mercy.

## *Prayer*

Strengthen me, O Jesus, in my mission to proclaim Your mercy to the world. Let me consistently show others that forgiveness and compassion are always the right way.

Jesus, have mercy on us and on the whole world.

# *May 28*

## A GOOD RECEIVER

Act like a beggar who does not back away when he gets more alms [than he asked for], but offers thanks the more fervently. You, too, should not back away and say that you are not worthy of receiving greater graces when I give them to you. I know you are unworthy, but rejoice all the more and take as many treasures from my heart as you can carry, for then you will please Me more. And I will tell you one more thing—take these graces not only for yourself, but also for others. (*Diary*, 294)

## *Reflection*

Have you ever met an ungracious receiver? This kind of ungracious receiver goes on and on, saying things like "You really shouldn't have. I don't deserve this." At some point, you might almost feel like taking back the gift. The same thing can happen with the gifts God wants to give us. When we keep saying how unworthy we are, we aren't being humble. We are actually looking for more affirmation of our worth. We don't honor God with false humility. So rejoice when God gives you a treasure, knowing that God truly wants you to have the gift. (And be willing to accept "as many treasures" as God offers! If not for yourself, then for those around you.)

## *Prayer*

Lord, help me to learn how to become a good receiver of Your gifts.

Jesus, have mercy on us and on the whole world.

# May 29

> After some time, Jesus said to me, **All this is for the salvation of souls. Consider well, My daughter, what you are doing for their salvation.** I answered, "Jesus, when I look at Your suffering, I see that I am doing next to nothing for the salvation of souls." And the Lord said to me, **Know, My daughter, that your silent day-to-day martyrdom in complete submission to My will ushers many souls into heaven. And when it seems to you that your suffering exceeds your strength, contemplate My wounds, and you will rise above human scorn and judgment. Meditation on My Passion will help you rise above all things.** (*Diary*, 1184)

## Reflection

Jesus reminded Faustina of the incredible suffering He endured for us, and that He allows us the privilege of using our own daily martyrdom, when joined with His Passion, as a means of saving souls. St. Faustina said: "Today I felt the Passion of Jesus in my own whole body, and the Lord gave me knowledge of the conversion of certain souls" (1627). Her pain is great, but all for the sake of immortal souls. We should meditate on His wounds often. It brings Jesus great joy. It is never in vain when you allow God to use you for the salvation of souls.

## Prayer

O immense Passion, O profound Wounds, O Most Precious Blood, help me rise above all things.

Jesus, have mercy on us and on the whole world.

# *May 30*

## CURIOUS ROADS

**Do not examine with curiosity the roads
down which I lead you.** (*Diary*, 1760)

## *Reflection*

As we travel through life, we take many roads. We are naturally curious about
what is coming around the corner. We want to prepare. We cross over rough
terrain and have many winding paths to navigate. We run into potholes and
have flat tires along the way. Even though faith is "one foot on the ground,
one foot in the air, and a queasy feeling in the stomach," as Mother Angelica,
foundress of EWTN, remarked, God wants us to put our hand in His with total
trust. The soul consumed with curiosity seeks knowledge to gain control over
the future—to manipulate and dominate. The contemplative soul trusts God
each step of the way, walks "through the valley of the shadow of death," and
says, "I will fear no evil, for you are with me" (Psalm 23).

## *Prayer*

Lord, teach me to have confidence in Your guidance. Grant me the grace to
curb my curiosity, so that I will not worry about my future. Mold my heart to
desire Your holy will.

Jesus, have mercy on us and on the whole world.

# *May 31*

## HEART TO HEART

**I am taking your heart....** (*Diary*, 42)

### *Reflection*

Venerable Fulton J. Sheen shares this about the heart: "The human heart is not shaped like a valentine heart, perfect and regular in contour; it is slightly regular in shape, as if a small piece of it were missing out of its side. The missing part may very well symbolize a piece that a spear tore out of the universal heart of humanity on the Cross, but it probably symbolizes something more. It may very well mean that when God created each human heart, He kept a small sample of it in heaven, and sent the rest of it into the world, where it would each day learn the lesson that it could never be really happy, that it could never be really wholly in love, that it could never be really wholehearted until it rested with the Risen Christ, in an eternal Easter."

### *Prayer*

"O my Jesus, take my heart. I thank you for Your Heart — it's all I need" (240). Jesus, have mercy on us and on the whole world.

CHAPTER SIX

# Reflections

FOR

*June*

# June 1

## THE BEST OF FATHERS

If only they could understand that I am the best of fathers to them and that it is for them that the Blood and Water flowed from My Heart as from a fount overflowing with mercy. (*Diary*, 367)

## Reflection

There are biological fathers, absentee fathers, stepfathers, and even deadbeat dads.

No matter what kind of earthly father you might have had, God is there for you as the "best of fathers." When even the best earthly fathers sometimes fail their children, Our Heavenly Father loves us with a perfect love. His love never fails. He desires our greatest good at all times—a true father, a loving father to all. St. Faustina describes this. When God's presence enveloped her one day in the chapel as she was thanking Him for His graces, she writes: "I felt like a child in the hands of the best of fathers, and I heard these words: Do not fear anything. I am always with you" (629). Like St. Faustina, contemplate Our Father's immense love for us. The blood and water flowing from Jesus' side wash over us. We are being healed of all the wounds of our hearts and enveloped in the merciful love of the Father.

## Prayer

My loving Father, enfold me in Your loving and merciful arms.

Jesus, have mercy on us and on the whole world.

# *June 2*

## JESUS MAKES THE FIRST MOVE

**I wait for you.** (*Diary*, 1489)

### *Reflection*

It can be difficult to share with a loved one things that we are ashamed about.
But when we have the courage to share our shame with them we can feel our
whole body and soul relax. As with the prodigal son, the Father waits and
reaches out to His son with words of pardon and lavish graces. He makes the
first move. So it is with us and our Savior.

### *Prayer*

Thank you, Lord, for reaching out to me when I have been fearful to reach
out to You.

Jesus, have mercy on us and on the whole world.

# *June 3*

## MEDICINE OF MERCY

> **My daughter, you have not offered Me that which is really yours.** (*Diary*, 1318)

### *Reflection*

When St. Faustina "nestled close to the Most Sacred Heart of Jesus," she relied entirely on His Mercy. Reflecting on her sinfulness, she exclaimed, "Happy is the soul that calls upon the mercy of the Lord" (598). I believe, O Jesus, that You would not reject me, but would absolve me through the hand of Your representative (1318).

God's representative is the priest patiently waiting for you in the confessional. He's there to forgive your sins and apply the balm of mercy. Don't leave earth without it.

### *Prayer*

Jesus, I offer You my sins.

Jesus, have mercy on us and on the whole world.

# June 4

> **Speak, My beloved child, for I am always listening
> ... What do you desire to say?** (*Diary*, 1489)

## Reflection

We must remember that the Lord loves all parts of us and that includes those parts of us that we find difficult to accept. Loving someone means we are willing to risk sharing thoughts that make us frightened and vulnerable.

## Prayer

Jesus, when I am tempted to hide behind flowery words, remind me that You value simple, plain speech.

Jesus, have mercy on us and on the whole world.

# June 5

**My Spirit shall be the rule of your life.** (*Diary*, 438)

## Reflection

In the words of St. Faustina: "Faithfulness to the inspirations of the Holy Spirit—that is the shortest route [*to holiness*]" (291). And she said that a key to being aware of those inspirations (from the Latin for "breathe into") is to stop and be quiet. Or, to quote the psalmist: "Be still, and know that I am God" (Ps 46:10).

## Prayer

Come, Holy Spirit!
  Jesus, have mercy on us and on the whole world.

# *June 6*

## NEVER-ENDING PARDONS

> **You are dealing with the God of mercy, which your misery cannot exhaust. Remember, I did not allot only a certain number of pardons.** (*Diary*, 1488)

### *Reflection*

A wounded man is lying in misery along the roadside. Everyone passes him by. But a kind man stops, kneels down, and pours oil into his wounds to heal, cleanse, and purify. This act of tenderhearted love applies the balm of God's mercy. As this Good Samaritan binds the poor man's wounds, so Christ binds us in the healing bonds of Divine Charity. Like the man wounded along life's road, we're prone to stumble and fall, because we fail to rely on the Lord. Yet in every fall, Christ comes as our Good Samaritan. While worldly men pass us by, Jesus finds us. Having fallen so many times, we're tempted to hide under a blanket of shame. But we should have no fear, because God doesn't allot us only a certain number of pardons. When you were born, God didn't say, "Okay, this one only gets a dozen pardons and after that, it's direct to hell." No! There's no poverty of forgiveness in the Heart of God, because Jesus is rich in mercy.

### *Prayer*

"You carry me in the bosom of Your mercy and forgive me every time that I ask Your forgiveness with a contrite heart" (1332).

Jesus, have mercy on us and on the whole world.

# *June 7*

## A TENDER HEART

During the June devotions, the Lord said to me, **My daughter, My favor rests in your heart. When on Holy Thursday I left Myself in the Blessed Sacrament, you were very much on My mind.** (*Diary*, 1774)

### *Reflection*

In the Litany of the Sacred Heart, we pray: "Heart of Jesus, formed by the Holy Spirit in the womb of the Virgin Mary, have mercy on us." The forming of Christ's human Heart in Mary's womb fulfills Ezekiel's prophecy: "I will take the stony heart out of their flesh and give them a heart of flesh ... and they shall be my people, and I will be their God" (Ezek 11:19-20). We find favor with God when we obey Him. Enjoying God's approval is a treasure that nothing on earth can rival. Because St. Faustina delighted in obeying God and seeking His wisdom, Jesus told her that He found great favor in her heart.

### *Prayer*

Loving Lord, may You find favor in my heart as You did with St. Faustina.
   Jesus, have mercy on us and on the whole world.

# *June 8*

## FOLLOWING CHRIST INTO BATTLE

---

**I will not delude you with prospects of peace and consolations; on the contrary, prepare for great battles.** (*Diary*, 1760)

---

## *Reflection*

As a "good soldier of Christ" (2 Tim 2:3), we fight in Christ's army. We battle the devil, who "prowls around like a roaring lion, seeking someone to devour" (1 Pet 5:8). Satan attacks, but he is like a dog tied to a tree. God limits his reach. Jesus is our sole defense. St. Faustina remarks: "I begin my day with battle and end it with battle. As soon as I conquer one obstacle, ten more appear to take its place.... When the burden of the battle becomes too much for me, I throw myself like a child into the arms of the heavenly Father and trust I will not perish" (606). Let us foster a holy fear of awe for Jesus in the Most Blessed Sacrament, because, as St. John Paul II taught: "Every Mass is stronger than all the evil in the Universe."

## *Prayer*

Blessed are You, O Lord, my rock, who train my hands for battle. In the spiritual attacks of this day, I ask You to cover me with Your protecting wings and keep me safe from all harm.

Jesus, have mercy on us and on the whole world.

# June 9

**I claim veneration for My mercy from every creature ...** (*Diary*, 1572)

## Reflection

The universe is simply inconceivable to our human intellect. Just one fact: Scientists think there could be as many as three sextillion stars in the universe. That's 3 followed by 23 zeros. Now given that our sun is a single star, the idea of three sextillion suns is unfathomable. But what is even more unfathomable is that God loves us so much that He allows us to call upon the whole universe and His creation to glorify His mercy. Try to wrap your mind around that fact!

St. Faustina cried out: "I call upon the whole universe to glorify Your mercy. Oh, how great is Your goodness, O God!" (1749).

## Prayer

"O my most compassionate Creator, I want to give You worship on behalf of all creatures and all inanimate creation" (1749).

Jesus, have mercy on us and on the whole world.

# June 10

## DWELLING PLACE OF THE TRINITY

I heard these words: **You are Our dwelling place.** (*Diary*, 451)

### Reflection

St. Faustina understood that the Divine Spirit—the Holy Spirit—works within each of us to make us holy. To fill our life and our soul with His fruits and gifts. To make us saints. Setting an example for all of us, in the midst of busy work periods she would often pause for a moment and pray: "Most Holy Trinity, I adore you!" Jesus tells us we are the "dwelling place" of the Trinity. We are the temples of the Holy Spirit. The indwelling Spirit gives spiritual gifts (God-given abilities) to serve the Lord effectively. The indwelling Holy Spirit empowers us to live for Christ, to do His will for His glory. Thus, how we behave, think, and speak, and what we let into the temple through our eyes and ears, becomes critically important. Every thought, word, and deed are in His view. In Ephesians 4:30, St. Paul tells them to "get rid of all bitterness, rage and anger, brawling and slander, along with every form of malice. Be kind and compassionate to one another, forgiving each other, just as Jesus Christ forgave you." You are His dwelling place.

### Prayer

"O Holy Trinity, honor and glory be to Your name forever and ever. Amen" (525).

Jesus, have mercy on us and on the whole world.

# *June 11*

## RESTING IN THE LORD

**Lay your head on My shoulder, rest and regain your strength.** (*Diary*, 498)

### *Reflection*

Is there anything better than your bed after a good day's work? That feeling of letting go of the worries of the day and sinking into the pillow is one of life's great pleasures. Jesus understands that working for the Kingdom is as hard as any other labor, so He encourages us to take our rest in His Heart. But what does that mean? One way is to turn off all electronics, go to a quiet, peaceful place, and just allow yourself to "be" in the presence of the Lord. Meditate on His blessings, but don't worry if you fall asleep. Even great saints like St. Thérèse of Lisieux sometimes fell asleep during meditative prayer.

### *Prayer*

Jesus, show me how to rest close to Your Heart.

Jesus, have mercy on us and on the whole world.

# June 12

## KINGDOM ON EARTH

> My delight is to act in a human soul and to fill it with My mercy and to justify it. My kingdom on earth is My life in the human soul ... [and] I Myself am the spiritual guide of souls. (*Diary*, 1784)

### Reflection

When the Apostles asked Jesus about the Kingdom of heaven, He gave somewhat obscure answers like saying that the Kingdom was like a mustard seed. When St. Faustina asked about the Kingdom of God on earth, Jesus gave a more straightforward answer: the Kingdom here is Jesus' life in our souls. What an awesome thought! We, in all our frailty and sin, are the embodiment of Jesus' Kingdom on earth. If we truly believe this, how can we show that Kingdom to everyone we meet? One way to do so is to treat each person you encounter as if he or she were Jesus in the flesh.

### Prayer

My Lord, let my life be representative of Your kingdom here on earth.

Jesus, have mercy on us and on the whole world.

# *June 13*

Jesus, transform me into another host! I want to be a living host for You. You are a great and all-powerful Lord; You can grant me this favor." And the Lord answered me, **You are a living host, pleasing to the Heavenly Father. But reflect: What is a host? A sacrifice.** (*Diary*, 1826)

## *Reflection*

When St. Faustina asked to become a living host, she didn't mean a Communion host! She meant a place where Jesus could dwell. Jesus reassured her that she was already was a living host, but reminded her that being a host means becoming a living sacrifice. Sacrifice doesn't mean becoming a missionary martyr. Every day, we are offered the opportunity to sacrifice for our Lord. Let someone who has only a few items go before you in the checkout line. Refrain from insisting that you are right ... even if you are. Turn over the TV clicker and let others choose a show. The opportunities for sacrifice are everywhere if we only look for them.

## *Prayer*

God, open my eyes to the places where I can sacrifice on Your behalf.
Jesus, have mercy on us and on the whole world.

# June 14

> Approach each of the sisters with the same love
> with which you approach Me; and whatever you
> do for them, you do it for Me. (*Diary*, 285)

## Reflection

Jesus' request applies to us as well. Even though St. Faustina lived in a convent, she said: "Oh, how sweet it is to live in a convent among sisters, but I must not forget that these angels are in human bodies" (1126). If we approach Jesus in Communion or at church with love and reverence and then snap and snarl at those around us, we might as well have snapped and snarled at Jesus, for He says to all of us, "Truly, I say to you, to the extent that you did it to one of these brothers of mine, even the least of them, you did it to me" (Matt 25:40). Or, to paraphrase the Golden Rule: Do unto others as you would do unto Jesus.

## Prayer

Jesus, let me see You in all I meet today.
Jesus, have mercy on us and on the whole world.

# June 15

> **Be at peace, My child. See, you are not alone.**
> **My Heart watches over you.** (*Diary*, 799)

## Reflection

As humans, we respond both intellectually and emotionally to repetition. It's one reason children like the same stories read over and over. This promise Jesus made to St. Faustina—and by extension to us—makes a wonderful prayer to be repeated over and over to soothe our souls: *I am at peace. I am never alone. Jesus watches over me.*

## Prayer

Lord God, thanks for reminding me over and over that "I am not alone."
　　Jesus, have mercy on us and on the whole world.

# *June 16*

LOVE FOR LOVE

> **You know what love demands: one thing
> only, reciprocity....** (*Diary*, 1770)

## *Reflection*

In the sublime moment of Holy Communion, St. Faustina encountered God's loving presence: "At that moment, I was drawn into the bosom of the Most Holy Trinity, and I was immersed in the love of the Father, the Son and the Holy Spirit" (1670). Filled with Christ's presence in Holy Communion, we're called to reciprocate His love in our lives. Jesus' love isn't wimpy love. Christ's courageous love demands we move out of our comfort zone, because the love of God is daring. His love changes us—saves us! Accepting God's love means we grasp the other end of the rope that binds us to Him—in bonds of everlasting love. If true love is measured by the "thermometer of suffering" (343), as St. Faustina says, then the love of Jesus on Calvary is proof positive of God's love for sinners.

## *Prayer*

My sweet Jesus, fill me with Your Presence, so that I may return love for love. Jesus, have mercy on us and on the whole world.

# *June 17*

## INTIMACY WITH GOD

I heard these words in my soul: **You are my spouse forever; your chastity should be greater than that of the angels, for I call no angel to such intimacy as I do you. The smallest act of My spouse is of infinite value.** (*Diary*, 534)

## *Reflection*

God had great plans for St. Faustina—a mission for her to fulfill. Jesus invited her to taste of the delights of His presence in spiritual intimacy. Calling her to a chastity "greater than that of the angels," Christ invited her into deeper communion with Himself. She responded, and the Lord helped her accomplish the work of His Kingdom. As with St. Faustina, God's got something special planned for you. No matter how insignificant the world may think you are, God has other ideas. Because God's got a mission in mind for everyone, God's calling us to live a virtuous life. What virtues may Jesus call you to put into action today—prudence, justice, fortitude, temperance? That's just the beginning of the list. Put greater trust in God and respond to the call He's given you, and enter into the intimate working of God.

## *Prayer*

"O Love Eternal, now I understand in what close intimacy my heart was with You! For what else can satisfy me in heaven or on earth except You, O my God, in Whom my soul is drowned" (469).

Jesus, have mercy on us and on the whole world.

# June 18

When the priest exposed the Blessed Sacrament, and the choir began to sing, the rays from image pierced the Sacred Host and spread out all over the world. Then I heard these words: **"These rays of mercy will pass through you, just as they have passed through this Host, and they will go out through all the world."** (*Diary*, 441)

## *Reflection*

Jesus wants us to use our whole being, body, and soul when we pray. The next time you receive Communion, as you kneel in thanks, imagine that Jesus' mercy is radiating out from you to touch everyone in the Church. Feel His love flowing like ripples on a pond until everyone is bathed in the glory of God. Then, when you leave Church, try to extend that sense of love and mercy to everyone you meet.

## *Prayer*

Dear Lord, let me be an instrument of Your mercy to a broken world.

Jesus, have mercy on us and on the whole world.

# June 19

## FORGIVENESS AND CONTRITION

**Know that as often as you come to Me, humbling yourself and asking My forgiveness, I pour out a superabundance of graces on your soul ...** (*Diary*, 1293)

## *Reflection*

Sometimes we think that to forgive someone means to overlook what that person has done, even if the person doesn't express any sorrow or regret. Because we are supposed to forgive, we think that we have to ignore what the person has done, or even pretend that it didn't hurt us. We act as if forgiveness is the same as amnesia. Before the person even acknowledges what they have done, we say, "Oh, that's okay. I forgive you. Not a problem." That's not how God's forgiveness works. God's forgiveness starts with us. We must first acknowledge what we have done. We must ask forgiveness with a contrite heart. Today, ask God for forgiveness for all that you have done that has offended Him, those things you remember and those that you have forgotten or are too blind to see.

## *Prayer*

Dear Jesus, forgive my trespasses; wipe away my sins.
Jesus, have mercy on us and on the whole world.

# *June 20*

## LIVING FAITH

In place of the monstrance, I saw the glorious face of the Lord, and He said to me, **"What you see in reality, these souls see through faith. Oh, how pleasing to Me is their great faith!"** (*Diary*, 1420)

## *Reflection*

St. Louis IX, king of France, didn't live in stained-glass isolation. He was real—quick-tempered and gluttonous. But his love for the Eucharist transformed this king into a saint. While St. Louis was working in his study, a servant burst in, exclaiming: "Your Majesty, a beautiful miracle is taking place in the palace chapel. The Infant Jesus is appearing in the Host upon the altar!" St. Louis didn't lift his head but calmly replied: "I couldn't believe more firmly in Christ's presence in the Eucharist if I were to see a miracle! Miracles aren't needed for those who already believe!"

We need living faith.

## *Prayer*

Give us, Lord, a living faith like Your saints.

Jesus, have mercy on us and on the whole world.

# June 21

## THE HOST IS YOUR POWER

**In the Host is your power; It will defend you.** (*Diary*, 616)

### Reflection

We find courage in the Eucharistic witness of forty-nine Christians martyrs who died in A.D. 304 in Abitene, North Africa. Their crime was to violate the emperor Diocletian's order forbidding Christians, under pain of death, from gathering on Sunday for the Eucharist. When the proconsul Anulinus asked why they'd disobeyed, a man named Emeritus replied, "*Sine Dominico non possumus*," "we cannot live without Sunday." They believed that Sunday Mass was worth dying for. The power of the Host defended their faith and gave them courage in Christ. As St. Faustina said, "This Bread of the Strong gives me all the strength I need to carry on my mission and the courage to do whatever the Lord asks of me. The courage and strength that are in me are not of me, but of Him who lives in me—it is the Eucharist" (91). Like the saints, may we find power in the Eucharist!

### Prayer

"O Blessed Host, take up Your dwelling within my soul, O Thou my heart's purest love!" (159).

Jesus, have mercy on us and on the whole world.

# *June 22*

## PROOF OF MY LOVE

> If you knew what great merit and reward is earned by one act of pure love for Me, you would die of joy. I am saying this that you may constantly unite yourself with Me through love, for this is the goal of the life of your soul. (*Diary*, 576)

## *Reflection*

We're told, "Love your neighbor as yourself." It's hard. We can't pick and choose. Dorothy Day's words cut to the heart: "You only love God as much as you love the person you love the least." St. Faustina wisely taught: "Love must be reciprocal. If Jesus tasted the fullness of bitterness for me, then I, His bride, will accept all bitterness as proof of my love for Him" (389). To imitate the love of God, we have to imitate the love of Jesus, because the Love loves everyone without exception.

## *Prayer*

Lord, let me perform just one act of pure love for You today.

Jesus, have mercy on us and on the whole world.

# *June 23*

## SALVATION OF SOULS

**I desire their salvation.** (*Diary*, 186)

## *Reflection*

Holy Mother Church exists to save souls—to make saints. Every good work the Church does, from feeding the hungry to liberating souls from demonic possession, are only means to one end: the salvation of souls. St. Catherine of Siena explained that everything of God "is ordained for the salvation of man, because "God does nothing without this goal in mind." Every grace God sends is directing us heavenward. But these graces aren't just for us. We're not to be stingy with them. We're to help our neighbors too—so that everyone may know salvation in Jesus Christ. St. Faustina reminds us: "We do not know the number of souls that is ours to save through our prayers and sacrifices; therefore, let us always pray for sinners" (1783). Let's proclaim God's mercy and make this our daily pledge: to save souls.

## *Prayer*

"O most compassionate Jesus, grant me the grace to forget myself that I may live totally for souls, helping You in the work of salvation, according to the most holy will of Your Father" (1265).

Jesus, have mercy on us and on the whole world.

# June 24

## FOR A NEW GENERATION

> ... prayer joined to the act of mercy ... will defend the souls of children against the spirit of evil. (*Diary*, 1156)

## Reflection

Our faith needs to be presented to each new generation, and we must never take for granted that our children will automatically continue with attending Mass, frequenting the sacraments, just because we are their parents and expect them to do so. Parents have a special obligation to talk to their children about God and to show them the ways of love and mercy in not only our words, but more importantly in our actions and behavior, especially in acts of mercy. To form kind and merciful hearts in their children, parents need to plant the seed of God and prayer in those young hearts, or else children depart into godlessness. Children are like sponges—they absorb all that they see and hear. So, make sure it is the message of the Gospel.

## Prayer

Lord, may my acts of mercy, small though they may be, help defend the children I know against the spirit of evil of this age.

Jesus, have mercy on us and on the whole world.

# June 25

Jesus made known to me how very pleasing to Him were prayers of atonement. He said to me, **The prayer of a humble and loving soul disarms the anger of My Father and draws down an ocean of blessings.** (*Diary*, 320)

## Reflection

These are such powerful words—"disarming the anger of the Father." What we are being told, in no uncertain terms, is that God's righteous anger toward sin can be appeased by the prayers of humble and loving souls. We should take this as a challenge. Do we pray daily, not only for ourselves but for others, begging the Father in all humility to not extend the punishment we have all earned in one way or another? Remember, the Father would much rather cover us in an ocean of blessings than to spend one second chastising us.

## Prayer

Dear God, forgive me my sins and help me to always approach You with a humble and contrite heart.

Jesus, have mercy on us and on the whole world.

# June 26

## KYRIE ELEISON (LORD, HAVE MERCY)

> Know that My Heart is mercy itself. From this sea of mercy, graces flow out upon the whole world ... I desire that your heart be an abiding place of My mercy. I desire that this mercy flow out upon the whole world through your heart. (*Diary*, 1777)

### Reflection

The story of the prodigal son paints a picture of God's mercy. The son leaves home, wastes his inheritance on immoral living, and ends up living in a pigsty. There, at rock bottom, he remembers his father, repents, and returns home. The father, who is waiting to embrace his son, declares a feast. Mercy flowed out from his heart to his son. That's God's mercy. The miracle is that God's mercy is waiting for us each time we turn back to Him with humble and contrite hearts. Jesus said: "No soul that has approached Me has ever gone away unconsoled. All misery gets buried in the depths of My mercy, and every saving and sanctifying grace flows from this fountain" (1777). As prodigal children before the Father's throne, our only cry is *Kyrie eleison* ... Lord, have mercy.

### Prayer

As my soul is plunged in the ocean of Your mercy, let my heart sing *Kyrie eleison*, Lord have mercy.

Jesus, have mercy on us and on the whole world.

# June 27

## A PURE AND HUMBLE HEART

Today, penetrate into the spirit of My poverty and arrange everything
in such a way that the most destitute will have no reason to
envy you. I find pleasure, not in large buildings and magnificent
structures, but in a pure and humble heart. (*Diary*, 532)

### *Reflection*

When we seek to please God, a pure and humble heart is priceless to Him.
The value of each human being is their soul, not their bank account. Material
things will pass away, but the soul lives forever. God shares His eternal kingdom with all of us equally, regardless of our circumstances or status in this life.

### *Prayer*

Empty me, Lord, of all pretense and instill in me Your priceless gift of a pure
and humble heart.

Jesus, have mercy on us and on the whole world.

# June 28

For me there is no mercy. (*Diary*, 1486)

## Reflection

**My child, listen to the voice of your merciful Father....**

Jesus calls to the soul a third time, but the soul remains deaf and blind, hardened and despairing. Then the mercy of God begins to exert itself, and without any cooperation from the soul, God grants it final grace. If this, too, is spurned, God will leave the soul in this self-chosen disposition for eternity. This grace emerges from the merciful Heart of Jesus and gives the soul a special light by means of which the soul begins to understand God's effort; but conversion depends on its own will. The soul knows that this, for her, is final grace and, should it show even a flicker of goodwill, the mercy of God will accomplish the rest.

"My omnipotent mercy is active here. Happy the soul that takes advantage of this grace" (1486).

## Prayer

Lord Jesus, when my soul despairs, give me all the graces I need.

Jesus, have mercy on us and on the whole world.

# *June 29*

**What joy fills My Heart when you return to Me.
Because you are weak, I take you in My arms and carry
you to the home of My Father.** (*Diary*, 1486)

## *Reflection*

Sometimes we can become so caught up recognizing our own sinful nature that we almost think God created us just to punish us. Nothing could be further from the truth. God created us, not to watch us fail and then send us to hell, but to bring us home to eternity with Him. What's more, He knows that we are weak and subject to sin, but He loves us anyway. When we turn to Him in faith, He does not condemn us, but He lifts us in His loving arms and takes us home to the Father.

## *Prayer*

Jesus, I give myself to You. I trust that You will be with me all the way to my final heavenly home.

Jesus, have mercy on us and on the whole world.

# *June 30*

## CRADLED IN LOVE

God filled my soul with the interior light of a deeper knowledge
of Him as Supreme Goodness and Supreme Beauty. I came
to know how very much God loves me. (*Diary*, 16)

## *Reflection*

God has given each of us the wonderful gift of His love. We can't even begin
to fathom "what is the breadth and length and height and depth and to know
the love of Christ that surpasses knowledge ..." (Eph 3:18-19). When you
peer through a telescope and gaze at the heavens, you have a glimpse of the
immense greatness of God's creation. We ask, *Does the Creator of the universe
really know me? Does He truly count the hairs on my head and write my name in
His Heart?* Yet our faith teaches us that His love is beyond all knowledge or
understanding. How indescribable is the Supreme Goodness and Beauty of
God! He cradles us in the loving arms of His mercy. He fills us with awe and
amazement as we say with St. Augustine: "You are good and all-powerful,
caring for each one of us as though the only one in your care."

## *Prayer*

Lord, thank you for loving me so much.

Jesus, have mercy on us and on the whole world.

# CHAPTER SEVEN

# Reflections

FOR

## *July*

# July 1

## FORTIFICATION FOR THE JOURNEY

**I have remained on earth to comfort your aching heart and to fortify your soul, so that you will not falter on the way.** (*Diary*, 1487)

### Reflection

Through the Eucharist and Eucharistic Adoration, Jesus remains with us on earth to comfort and fortify our souls, lest we falter along the way. It was the Eucharist that gave St. Faustina the strength and courage to carry out her mission. A gift he continues to offer us to carry out our mission today!

The extension of the Eucharist is Adoration. St. Faustina was an adorer at a young age. She writes: "When I was seven years old, before the Lord in the monstrance, the love of God was imparted to me for the first time and filled my little heart" (1404). As she grew in wisdom and age and grace the love deepened. She said: "I spend every free moment at the feet of the hidden God. He is my Master; I ask Him about everything; I speak to Him about everything. Here I obtain strength and light; here I learn everything; here I am given light on how to act toward my neighbor" (704).

Faustina called herself Sister Faustina of the Blessed Sacrament. Adoration was central to her life as a religious. It was her life.

Make it part of your life and your children's life.

### Prayer

Jesus, I adore You.

Jesus, have mercy on us and on the whole world.

# *July 2*

## ABIDING PRESENCE

**Always fight with the deep conviction that I am with you.** (*Diary*, 1760)

## *Reflection*

Throughout Scripture, we see how God is close to His people. In Genesis, God walks with Adam and Eve amidst the trees of the Garden of Eden. As Isaiah taught, Jesus is "Emmanuel" — "God with us" (Is 7:14). St. Faustina's life reveals how God wants intimacy with us still today. Sometimes God permits our faith to be tried to strengthen us and prove the genuineness of our faith. Jesus reminded Faustina that suffering is a sign that He is with us. As her faith is purified and strengthened, she says with deep conviction: "With You, Jesus, I go through life, amid storms and rainbows, with a cry of joy, singing the song of Your mercy. I will not stop singing my song of love until the choir of Angels picks it up. There is no power that can stop me in my flight toward God" (761).

## *Prayer*

O incomprehensible God, permit me to feel Your abiding presence in my life, and assist me to love You above all things that exist on earth or in heaven.

Jesus, have mercy on us and on the whole world.

# *July 3*

## SATURATED WITH HIS LOVE AND FORGIVENESS

> **Be imbued with My sentiments.** (*Diary*, 1486)

### *Reflection*

A despairing soul told Jesus he deserved the depths of hell for spurning His graces.

Jesus told him to become imbued or completely saturated with His sentiments of love and forgiveness. To forgive yourself and others is often so difficult and yet there is nothing that brings us closer to others and to Our Lord. Jesus adds if we come to the "fountain of mercy" (Confession) it will fortify our souls, and we will not grow weary on the journey.

### *Prayer*

Lord, let me know that despite my awkward ways of forgiving myself and others that You love me and I can do whatever You ask.

Jesus, have mercy on us and on the whole world.

# *July 4*
## PRAYERS FOR OUR NATION

On one occasion I heard these words in my soul. **Make a novena for your country. This novena will consist of the recitation of the Litany of the Saints.** (*Diary*, 59)

## *Reflection*

The Bible tells us that if God's people humble themselves in prayer, forsaking wickedness, then God "will forgive their sin and heal their land" (2 Chr 7:14). Wherever we're from, we need to pray for our homeland, that its people be faithful to God. Jesus wanted St. Faustina to pray for her country and make a novena—nine days of prayer for her native land. Asking the intercession of the saints, St. Faustina pleaded for God to send grace to her country. Like her, we pray for our nation, so wounded by sin. But we don't pray alone. We pray in the company of the saints!

## *Prayer*

As we face uncertain times in our nation, we ask You, Lord, to dwell among us. Send Your Spirit to touch the hearts of these people and give us wisdom to know what is right, and the courage to do it.

Jesus, have mercy on us and on the whole world.

# July 5

## PATIENCE LEADS TO VICTORY

**My daughter, have patience** (*Diary*, 858). I have learned that
the greatest power is hidden in patience. I see that patience
always leads to victory, although not immediately; but that
victory will become manifest after many years. (*Diary*, 1514)

## *Reflection*

We live in an impatient world. Take stoplights, for example. While it might
feel like you sit forever at a red light, the longest red light is 120 seconds.
Anything longer than that and people start running the light. Jesus reminds
us to have patience, not because patience is all that great in and of itself, but
because, as St. Faustina explains, patience contains great power and always
leads to victory. Think about it—when you are patient you are guaranteeing
victory! Since we always have opportunities to be patient, we also always have
opportunities for victory.

## *Prayer*

Jesus, help me to be patient in all things, especially those that are the most
frustrating.

Jesus, have mercy on us and on the whole world.

# July 6

**Be grateful for the smallest of My graces, because your gratitude compels Me to grant you new graces....** (*Diary*, 1701)

## Reflection

Every day contains many small graces. It might not seem that way sometimes, but it's true.

No day passes without its moment of blessings. A parking spot in a high-rise neighborhood, finding your car keys, a friend is there just when you need them. However, we can overlook these simple joys. We have to train ourselves to pay attention and look for the grace or blessing. One way to do that is to set a time every day—perhaps 3 p.m., the hour of Our Lord's death—and consciously express gratitude for the "smallest" of graces. Jesus can't be outdone in generosity. We have the grace of eternal life! Our sincere grateful thanks compels Him to grant grace upon grace.

## Prayer

Lord, thank you for the smallest of graces. They are the best kind!

Jesus, have mercy on us and on the whole world.

# July 7

## ETERNAL LIFE BEGINS THROUGH HOLY COMMUNION

> **But I want to tell you that eternal life must begin already here on earth through Holy Communion. Each Holy Communion makes you more capable of communing with God throughout eternity.** (*Diary*, 1811)

### Reflection

Jesus shares His desire to unite Himself with us not just in eternal life but right now through the Eucharist! The more we prepare ourselves to receive Him in the state of grace hidden in the Host, the more prepared we will be to stand before Him at the hour of our death. How do we prepare to meet Him? St. Faustina understood well who she was receiving.

"Today, I prepare for the Coming of the King. What am I, and who are You, O Lord, King of eternal glory? O my heart, are you aware of who is coming to you today? Yes, He is the King of kings, the Lord of lords. Before Him, all power and dominion tremble. He is coming to my heart today" (1810). If we understood who we were receiving, could we ever not want to receive Him?

### Prayer

"I ask You for one thing only: remain forever the King of my heart; that is enough for me" (1811).

Jesus, have mercy on us and on the whole world.

# *July 8*

## HE IS GENEROUS WITH HIS MERCY

I am Thrice holy, and detest the smallest sin. I cannot love a soul which is stained with sin; but when it repents, there is no limit to My generosity toward it. My mercy embraces and justifies it. With My mercy, I pursue sinners along all their paths, and My Heart rejoices when they return to me. I forget the bitterness with which they fed My Heart and rejoice at their return. (*Diary*, 1728)

### *Reflection*

One of the greatest gifts Jesus reveals is His merciful generosity. Consider for a moment that God detests all sins ... not just the big ones like murder, but the little ones like being short-tempered as well. Since we are all guilty of at least a few small sins, no matter how horrible you have been, the wonderful news is that when we repent and are contrite, He forgives you. This is like having a "get out of jail" pass forever. As you go through your day, pay attention how you make a person feel with your words? How do they feel with your deeds?

If you find yourself falling into even the tiniest of sins, stop, ask for forgiveness, and move on, knowing that you are a dearly beloved child of God, who forgets and rejoices at your return.

### *Prayer*

Forgive me, Lord, for I know I sin in word and deed. Help me to always ask forgiveness for anything that has offended You.

Jesus, have mercy on us and on the whole world.

# July 9
## PURITY OF INTENTION

When I was apologizing to the Lord Jesus for a certain action of mine which, a little later, turned out to be imperfect, Jesus put me at ease with these words: **My daughter, I reward you for the purity of your intention which you had at the time when you acted ... I want you to always have such great purity of intention in the very least things you undertake.** (*Diary*, 1566)

## *Reflection*

Have you ever had an act be misunderstood? Perhaps you tried to help someone, but they interpreted your action as being meddling or interference. Because they misinterpreted your intention, they misjudged you. One of the wonderful things about our relationship with the Lord is that He always knows the whole of our intentions. He knows if we act out of purity or if we act out of selfishness. As we go through our life, we need not fear making mistakes or being misjudged as long as we focus on keeping our intentions pure and holy.

## *Prayer*

Dear Jesus, as I go through my day, may my every action be guided by purity of intention.

Jesus, have mercy on us and on the whole world.

# July 10

I suddenly saw Jesus at my side, Jesus racked with pain, stripped of His clothing, all covered with wounds, who spoke these words to me: **How long shall I put up with you and how long will you keep putting me off?** (*Diary*, 9)

## *Reflection*

St. Augustine wrote, "Late have I loved you, beauty so old and so new: late have I loved you."

Many of us can appreciate that sentiment. So many things clamor for our attention—our families, our work, our health, our desires. We can be tempted to put off spiritual matters until these other, seemingly more urgent demands are taken care of. Yet, what could possibly be more important than the state of our soul? While we focus on earthly cares, Jesus waits for us to stop putting Him off. We need to realize that our time here is limited.

## *Prayer*

"You touched me, and I am set on fire to attain the peace which is yours." —St. Augustine

Jesus, have mercy on us and on the whole world.

# *July 11*

The moment I knelt down to cross out my own will, as the Lord had bid me to do, I heard this voice in my soul: **From today on, do not fear God's judgment, for you will not be judged.** (*Diary*, 374)

## *Reflection*

Faustina made an "Act of Oblation," a total abandonment to the will of God which for her was love and mercy itself.

She prayed: "Bid me to stay in this convent, I will stay; bid me to undertake the work, I will undertake it; leave me in uncertainty about the work until I die, be blessed; give me death when, humanly speaking, my life seems particularly necessary, be blessed. Should You take me in my youth, be blessed; should You let me live to a ripe old age, be blessed. Should You give me health and strength, be blessed; should you confine me to a bed of pain for my whole life, be blessed. Should You give only failures and disappointments in life, be blessed ...

"From this moment on, I live in the deepest peace, because the Lord Himself is carrying me in the hollow of His hand" (1264). Abandon yourself to God's holy will and you will have no fears on the day of your judgment. Only peace.

## *Prayer*

O Jesus, may I like Faustina, have the grace of doing God's will always and everywhere. And on the day of my judgment only Your peace.

Jesus, have mercy on us and on the whole world.

# July 12

## THE STORMS OF LIFE

Today I was awakened by a great storm. The wind was raging, and it was raining in torrents, thunderbolts striking again and again. I began to pray that the storm would do no harm, when I heard the words: **Say the chaplet I have taught you, and the storm will cease.** I began immediately to say the chaplet and hadn't even finished it when the storm suddenly ceased, and I heard the words: **Through the chaplet you will obtain everything, if what you ask for is compatible with My will.** (*Diary*, 1731)

### Reflection

We often feel like the storms of life are too much for us to handle. And it can indeed be frightening. Jesus says, "Say the chaplet...." Special graces are given for various needs. (See Appendix C.) This powerful Chaplet, which implores us to always seek out God's mercy, alleviates our fears, for it reinforces in us our conviction that God is in firm control of everything, bringing good from all things—even the forces of natures—as long as they are in union with His most perfect and holy will.

### Prayer

Lord, quell the storms in my life as You urge me to pray the Chaplet.

Jesus, have mercy on us and on the whole world.

# *July 13*

## REST ON MY HEART

In the evening, the Lord said to me, **my child, rest on My Heart; I see that you have worked hard in My vineyard. And my soul was flooded with divine joy.** (*Diary*, 945)

## *Reflection*

"Those who abide in me and I in them bear much fruit, because apart from me you can do nothing" (Jn 15:5). Each child of God's Kingdom is privileged to work in the Lord's vineyard. After a good day's work, Jesus told St. Faustina, "I see that you have worked hard in my vineyard." Just as Jesus flooded her soul with joy, so He desires to fill us with His presence, saying, "My child, rest on My Heart."

## *Prayer*

Lord, help me labor in Your vineyard and let me rest on Your Heart.

Jesus, have mercy on us and on the whole world.

# July 14
## GRACE AND GRATITUDE

Know, my child, that for your sake I grant blessings to this whole vicinity. But you ought to thank Me on their behalf, as they do not thank Me for the kindnesses I extend to them. For the sake of your gratitude, I will continue to bless them. (*Diary*, 719)

## Reflection

We are often told that we should be grateful for all we have. But why is gratitude so important? On a psychological level, it can help improve our mood and create a more positive outlook. But Jesus tells us that on a spiritual level, gratitude is the source of new grace. Think of how amazing that is! When we are grateful for something, even something as simple as a perfectly-brewed cup of coffee, we may obtain grace to combat one of our faults—like impatience. We may never see the link between our gratitude and the grace we are given, but Jesus assures us that it is always there.

## Prayer

Dear Lord, help me to be grateful for all that comes into my life, including new graces that You give me every day.

Jesus, have mercy on us and on the whole world.

# *July 15*

## THE LORD WORKS IN MYSTERIOUS WAYS

When I arrived at Warsaw, I went into the small chapel for a moment to thank the Lord for a safe journey, and I asked the Lord to give me the assistance and the grace necessary for everything that was in store for me here. I submitted myself in all things to His holy will. I heard these words: **Fear nothing; all difficulties will serve for the fulfillment of My will.** (*Diary*, 634)

## *Reflection*

God uses life's difficulties to accomplish good. It's a mystery how God uses life's difficulties to accomplish good. Maria von Trapp of the Trapp Family Singers wrote: "It will be very interesting one day to follow the pattern of our life as it is spread out like a beautiful tapestry. As long as we live here, we see only the reverse side of the weaving, and very often the pattern, with its threads running wildly, doesn't seem to make sense. Someday, however, we shall understand. In looking back over the years, we can discover how a red thread goes through the pattern of our life: The Will of God." Trust in God's Providence when troubles arise. Like a child unafraid in his father's arms, Jesus tells us to fear nothing. God uses all difficulties to accomplish His will. Truly, the Lord works in mysterious ways.

## *Prayer*

"O Divine Will, be my love!" (725).

Jesus, have mercy on us and on the whole world.

# July 16
## DEATHLY SORROW

> Pray for souls that they be not afraid to approach the Tribunal
> of My mercy. Do not grow weary of praying for sinners. You
> know what a burden their souls are to My Heart. Relieve
> My deathly sorrow; dispense my mercy. (*Diary*, 975)

## *Reflection*

A man was standing in line, waiting his turn to go to Confession. He was noticeably nervous about confessing his sins. The fellow standing behind him, who'd already offered a little prayer for him, leaned over and whispered: "Satan's the only one who should be anxious about confession. Be at peace." There's nowhere we're more loved than in the Tribunal of Mercy. There we're wrapped in the Father's mercy. Jesus comes to us, knocking on the door of our hearts, with a hand that was pierced for our sins. He'll heal our souls if we come humbly like the publican, who fell to his knees, beat his breast, and with eyes downcast, pleaded "God, be merciful to me, a sinner!" No one approaches the confessional in "good shape," because, as St. John Chrysostom said: "Even if we reach the summit of virtue, we are saved only by God's mercy." Pray for reluctant souls, because in the Tribunal of Mercy, God works His greatest miracles.

## *Prayer*

Give me courage, Lord, to confess my sins with trust in Your infinite Mercy.
Jesus, have mercy on us and on the whole world.

# *July 17*
## SIMPLICITY OF HEART

Speak to Me about everything in a completely simple and human way; by this you will give Me great joy. I understand you because I am God-Man. This simple language of your heart is more pleasing to Me than the hymns composed in My honor. (*Diary*, 797)

## *Reflection*

Just as we have to declutter our kitchen countertop and clean out our desks from time to time, so we need to clear the clutter in our hearts. Faustina often said that God values simplicity. To teach her to approach Him simply and humbly, Our Lord frequently communed with her as a little child. Jesus told St. Faustina: "Because you are a child, you shall remain close to My Heart. Your simplicity is more pleasing to Me than your mortifications" (1617). We're liberated when we simplify our lives materially. In our spiritual lives, this freedom is all the more real for those who've got simplicity of heart.

## *Prayer*

"With the trust and simplicity of a small child, I give myself to You today, O Lord Jesus, my Master" (228).

Jesus, have mercy on us and on the whole world.

# *July 18*

## DO NOT BE DISTURBED

Satan gained nothing by tempting you, because you did not enter into conversation with him. Continue to act in this way. You gave Me great glory today by fighting so faithfully. Let it be confirmed and engraved on your heart that I am always with you, even if you don't feel My presence at the time of battle. (*Diary*, 1499)

## *Reflection*

When you must walk through life's darkest moments, you've got to have faith that you won't fall off a cliff along the way. Making our way through life, the devil's like the barking dog around the corner. He tries to induce fear in our hearts and minds. If we feed that fear, it can grow into a monster that torments us mercilessly. But St. Padre Pio advises us: "Have courage and do not fear the assaults of the devil. Remember this forever; it is a healthy sign if the devil shouts and roars around your conscience since this shows that he is not inside your will." Satan wanted to disturb Faustina's peace and give her exaggerated thoughts. She relied totally on the Lord to carry her through. Jesus reassures Faustina and you: "Yes, I will be with you always ... fear nothing" (295).

## *Prayer*

"O Savior, how great is your goodness!" (1802).

Jesus, have mercy on us and on the whole world.

# *July 19*

## GOD'S LOVE FOR SINNERS

**Look into My Heart and see there the love and mercy which I have for humankind, and especially for sinners.** (*Diary*, 1663)

## *Reflection*

In "The Merchant of Venice," Shakespeare wrote these famous lines: "The quality of mercy is not strained; It droppeth as the gentle rain from heaven." It is true. God's mercy rains down from heaven upon us sinners. Mercy is something we receive when we seek the Heart of God. We can't bargain for mercy, because we've nothing to offer except the misery of our sins. And yet, that is precisely what God wants. No one else wants our sins—they stink to high heaven. Yet God does. It's the only thing that's really ours to give. Being a perfect gentleman, Jesus doesn't rush into our lives. He waits for our invitation. But if we will show Him a "flicker of good will, the mercy of God will accomplish the rest" (1486). St. Faustina adds: "If Jesus sees this little bit of good will in the soul, He hurries to give Himself to the soul, and nothing can stop Him, neither shortcomings or falls—absolutely nothing" (291).

## *Prayer*

Merciful Lord, rain down your mercies upon me.

Jesus, have mercy on us and on the whole world.

# July 20

As I was praying before the Most Blessed Sacrament, my physical sufferings ceased suddenly, and I heard this voice in my soul: **You see, I can give you everything in one moment. I am not constrained by any law.** (*Diary*, 1153)

## Reflection

Who can be anything but amazed when we contemplate the incomparable power of God? If He wants something to happen, it happens. When He wants. How He wants. And for whatever purpose He deems fitting. All things are in His hands, and nothing is beyond His reach. Now, grasp the reality that this all-powerful God is our loving Father! That should obliterate all fears, all doubt, all anxiety. For as He told Faustina, there is no law (of nature or otherwise) that could ever constrain Him.

## Prayer

Lord, You are the Ruler of the Universe. I humbly bow before You.

Jesus, have mercy on us and on the whole world.

# July 21
## THE BATTLEFIELD OF LIFE

> I want you to become like a knight experienced in battle, who can give orders to others amid the exploding shells. In the same way, My child, you should know how to master yourself amid the greatest difficulties, and let nothing drive you away from Me, not even your falls. (*Diary*, 1823)

## *Reflection*

Our life can indeed feel like a battlefield sometimes. Problems explode like bombs and obstacles confront us like barbed wire. Just as Christ prepared St. Faustina to do spiritual battle, so He calls us to fight bravely against evil. We courageously follow the saints into the spiritual battle to stand up for what is right and true. Though we may stumble, Christ will raise us up to be victorious with Him. Because he is our Captain, we trust in victory.

## *Prayer*

"O truth, O life-and-death struggle, when I rose to do battle, an inexperienced knight, I felt I had a knight's blood, though still a child, and therefore, O Christ, I needed Your help and protection" (1654).

Jesus, have mercy on us and on the whole world.

# *July 22*

## A RESTING PLACE FOR JESUS

At the first altar, a flame issued from the Host and pierced my heart, and I heard a voice, **Here is My repose.** Ardor burst into flame in my heart. I felt that I am transformed completely into Him. (*Diary*, 1140)

## *Reflection*

Just as He did for Faustina, Jesus wants to make your heart His resting place. He promised that if we love Him and keep His word, He with the Father and the Holy Spirit would come and make a home in us. And the Lord's presence in us transforms us, making us more like Him.

## *Prayer*

Come, Lord Jesus, take up Your rest in my heart.

Jesus, have mercy on us and on the whole world.

# *July 23*

## THE WIDE OPEN DOOR

[Let] the greatest sinners place their trust in My mercy. They have the right before others to trust in the abyss of My mercy.... Souls that make an appeal to My mercy delight Me. To such souls I grant even more graces than they ask. I cannot punish even the greatest sinner if he makes an appeal to My compassion, but on the contrary, I justify him in My unfathomable and inscrutable mercy.... (*Diary*, 1146)

## *Reflection*

Really, how much easier could God make it for us? He is letting us know that, regardless of how badly we have gone astray, rather than slam the door in our face as we may well deserve, He instead graciously opens it wide open and lavishes His inconceivable mercy upon us. If that doesn't make us literally want to leap for joy, nothing will.

## *Prayer*

Lord, You open wide the door for me, and I will be ever grateful for what You have done for me.

Jesus, have mercy on us and on the whole world.

# *July 24*

## SEEING THROUGH FAITH ALONE

I was transported in spirit to the chapel where I saw the Lord Jesus exposed in the monstrance. where I saw Lord Jesus, exposed in the monstrance. In place of the monstrance, I saw the glorious face of the Lord, and He said to me. **You see, although there appears to be no trace of life in Me, in reality it is present in its fullness in each and every Host. But for Me to be able to act upon a soul, the soul must have faith. O how pleasing to Me is living faith!** (*Diary*, 1420)

### *Reflection*

Some of the saints like St. Faustina have been given the great grace of seeing the face of the Lord in reality. Most of us, however, see only through the eyes of faith. Jesus himself tells us not to envy those who see Him in the flesh, but rather tells Thomas "Because you have seen me, you have believed; blessed are those who have not seen and yet have believed" (Jn 20:29). Think for a moment of the implication of these words. Those of us who believe without seeing please the Lord with our faith! Which would you rather—see the Lord or please the Lord?

### *Prayer*

Lord Jesus, help me to see You more clearly through the eyes of faith so that I might please You all the more.

Jesus, have mercy on us and on the whole world.

# July 25

> **When a soul extols My goodness, Satan trembles before it and flees to the very bottom of hell.** (*Diary*, 378)

## Reflection

Spiritual warfare is very real, but those who love God have powerful weapons on their side. One of the simplest, yet most effective, is the invocation of the name of *Jesus*. The enemy is frightened when a soul that is devoted to the Lord proclaims God's goodness. Why? Because it is the light of God's righteous holiness that overcomes and crushes the darkness of evil, and Satan and all his minions can't withstand it.

## Prayer

Lord, keep me ever mindful that Your Holy Name contains great power and will always prevail over every scheme of the evil one. May the name of *Jesus* forever be upon my lips.

Jesus, have mercy on us and on the whole world.

# July 26
## AN ACT OF REPARATION

**Make reparation to My justice.** (*Diary*, 873)

## Reflection

In 1 Thessalonians 5:17, St. Paul tells us to "pray without ceasing." When we read that, our reaction can be, "Who has time to spend all the time in Church?" But that's not what Paul meant. He meant that we are to live our days in an awareness of the presence of God. In response to Jesus' request to her to help convert souls, St. Faustina said: "Throughout the whole day I lived in an act of reparation" (1816). What might an act of reparation look like? St. Faustina's favorite saint, St. Thérèse of Lisieux, said the best reparations she could ever make for sin was attending Holy Mass and worthily receiving Holy Communion. We can fast. Or refrain from saying anything negative. Or stay on task and not procrastinate. It doesn't mean being on your knees from morning to night. What it does mean is making a conscious choice to do something for God every day.

## Prayer

Jesus, may I take You with me in all I do today.
Jesus, have mercy on us and on the whole world.

# July 27

## MISERY TO MERCY

> I heard these words within me: **His heart is, for Me, a heaven on earth.** (*Diary*, 574)

### Reflection

Jesus told St. Faustina: "I am love and Mercy Itself. There is no misery that could be a match for My mercy, neither will misery exhaust it, because as it is being granted—it increases. The soul that trusts in My mercy is most fortunate, because I Myself take care of it" (1273).

We tend to wallow in our misery like pigs wallow in mud. But when we offer the Lord our misery, He meets it with mercy. To show us His love, God's goodness transforms us "from misery to mercy" said St. Augustine. God's omnipotence enveloped St. Faustina and took her into His heart. She would later write: "The love of God is the flower—Mercy is the fruit" (948).

### Prayer

O good and gentle Jesus, form my heart in Your heart.

Jesus, have mercy on us and on the whole world.

# July 28
## SERVING JESUS IN THOSE AROUND US

Suddenly I heard the bell in the next room and I went in and rendered a service to a seriously sick person ... **My daughter, you gave Me greater pleasure by rendering Me that service than if you had prayed for a long time.** I answered, "But it was not to you, Jesus, but to that patient that I rendered this service." And the Lord answered me, **Yes, My daughter, but whatever you do for your neighbor, you do for Me.** (*Diary*, 1029)

## *Reflection*

It's easy to fall into the trap of thinking that hours of prayer are more pleasing to Jesus than acts of service. While it's true that service can never take the place of prayer, we mustn't forget that acts of service can be acts of prayer. When we get up in the night to care for a sick child or when we listen patiently to an older person tell a story over and over, we please Jesus just as much or even more than if we had been on our knees in Church. By offering our service to Jesus, we can transform our actions in prayers and that gives Our Lord great joy!

## *Prayer*

Dear Lord, help me to remember that even the smallest act of service done out of love for You can become a prayer.

Jesus, have mercy on us and on the whole world.

# July 29

## HEART MURMURS

**Shun murmurs like a plague.** (*Diary*, 1760)

### Reflection

Murmuring reveals a lack of faith. We can see this in the story of the Israelites. Repeatedly, God intervened for them in their journey out of Egypt, leading them out of slavery, the angel of death passing-over their homes, the parting of the Red Sea, and making the waters of Marah sweet to drink. These miraculous works of God should have transformed them. Yet the Israelites, who had mastered the art of murmuring, showed their faithlessness with the worship of the golden calf. When they murmured against Moses and Aaron, Moses said to Israel: "Your murmurings are not against us but against the Lord" (Ex 16:8). Murmuring steals the joy out of our hearts and leaves with the spiritual disease of an ungrateful spirit. The remedy is a spirit of joy and thanksgiving, as St. Paul wrote: "Rejoice always, pray constantly, give thanks in all circumstances; for this is the will of God in Christ Jesus for you" (1Thess 5:16-18).

### Prayer

Lord, let me shun murmurs like a plague and always serve You in a spirit of joy and thanksgiving.

Jesus, have mercy on us and on the whole world.

# *July 30*

## THE NEED FOR OBEDIENCE

**You are to be obedient.** (*Diary*, 895)

### *Reflection*

"I have come to do My Father's will. I will obey my parents, I obeyed My tormentors, and now I obey the priests" (535).

In His Sacred Passion, our Savior made Himself entirely subject to His tormentors. He gave them free reign and permitted them to spit in His face, flog Him mercilessly, and nail Him to the Cross. By obeying His tormenters, Jesus teaches us to have patient endurance under trial. Through the priests of His Church, Jesus is again obedient. Despite their imperfections, He permits them to be His hands and His voice. What humility Jesus shows through His priests, as He allows them to bind and loose sins through the authority of His name, and as Our Lord is subject to them in Holy Mass under the fragile form of bread and wine. Jesus taught St. Faustina that the spirit of obedience isn't merely external, but involves also "the reason, the will and judgment" (535). We all must imitate Jesus' perfect obedience in some measure, according to our state in life. Obedience isn't just for monks and nuns. When human pride makes us think we know best, we recall the humble obedience of Jesus.

### *Prayer*

"O will of God, you are the nourishment and delight of my soul" (952).

Jesus, have mercy on us and on the whole world.

# *July 31*

## UNCHANGING LOVE

> **Before I made the world, I loved you with the love your heart is experiencing today, and throughout the centuries, My love will never change.** (*Diary*, 1754)

### *Reflection*

It's hard for our finite minds to grasp, but God's love is without limit. His love never fails. His love is unchanging. God tells us, "I have loved you with an everlasting love" (Jer 31:3). In a day and age when we're constantly looking for what's "new-and-improved," God's love for us does not change — it's already perfect. God's love doesn't falter. Nor can it change. His love is ever-steady and always true. In this ever-changing world, we've got to understand the sole thing that does not change is the one thing that matters most — God's love for us.

### *Prayer*

God, even when I forget Your love, You don't forget to love me.

Jesus, have mercy on us and on the whole world.

# CHAPTER EIGHT

# Reflections

FOR

# *August*

# *August 1*

## RETREATING *INTO* LIFE

> At the beginning of the retreat, Jesus told me, **During this retreat, I Myself will direct your soul. I want to confirm you in peace and love.** (*Diary*, 229)

### *Reflection*

Going on a formal retreat is a luxury that many of us can't afford, especially when we must go to work, take care of families, and meet other obligations. But what we really can't afford is failing to spend time in the presence of the Lord. Even if we have to take our "retreats" in small bits, like an afternoon here or a day of vacation there, set some time aside to be with Jesus. He wants to give you grace, guidance, and refreshment that you need for the growth of your soul.

### *Prayer*

Lord, help me find the time to be with You. Don't let me get so caught up in the daily grind that I neglect spending time in Your presence.

Jesus, have mercy on us and on the whole world.

# *August 2*
## SWOONING WITH LOVE

See, I have left My heavenly throne to become united with you. What you see is just a tiny part and already your soul swoons with love. How amazed will your heart be when you see Me in all My glory. (*Diary*, 1810)

## *Reflection*

In Michael Brown's book *The Other Side*, people who have claimed to have had near-death experience almost all report that they were overcome—swooning as it were—with the presence of love they felt. They struggle to find words to express just how overwhelming the experience of encountering the Lord was, even for an instant. One woman shared: "I was unbelievably happy. Nothing on earth can compare to how I felt. If all the happiness I ever had in my life were contained, it would be a mere drop in a vast ocean as to how happy I felt while in this place." Another man said: When I died it was like the weight of the world was off my shoulders. The joy. The release. The connection. The freedom. The major lesson I took from it was: "Praise Jesus. Worship Jesus." While most of us will never have that experience here on earth, we can open ourselves to the glory of God each time we are at Mass, which is closest we can be to heaven.

## *Prayer*

My God, help my earthly eyes see Your heavenly glory when I attend Mass. Jesus, have mercy on us and on the whole world.

# *August 3*
## PRAYING FOR OUR PRIESTS

Today, I saw the Lord in great beauty, and He said to me, **My loving host, pray for priests, especially during this time of harvest.** (*Diary*, 980)

### *Reflection*

It is only through the service of our priests that we can have access to the life-giving sacraments, especially the Holy Eucharist and Confession. But our priests need our prayers, especially in these times when so many scandals have emerged. We mustn't judge the majority of priests by the actions of some who have fallen. Instead, Jesus tells us to pray for all priests, asking that they have the strength and courage to be faithful to their commitments and their holy vocation.

### *Prayer*

Dear Lord, watch over and protect Your shepherds. Let them know that their sacrifice brings blessings beyond measure to the Body of Christ.

Jesus, have mercy on us and on the whole world.

# *August 4*

**Do not become discouraged by ingratitude.** (*Diary*, 1760)

## *Reflection*

In our lives, we meet people who're ungrateful for the good we've done for them. Some people seem to think we were put on earth to serve them, clean up their messes, and fix all their problems. Met with such ingratitude, it's easy to become discouraged and to give up the acts of charity toward our neighbor. When offended by the pompous attitude of selfish people, we should stop and consider instead how much worse is our ingratitude toward our all-good God. When we approach Christ with an attitude of gratitude, He won't be outdone in generosity:

> "You have shown your mercy, O God, and this, time and time again. You carry me in the bosom of your mercy and forgive me every time that I ask your forgiveness with a contrite heart." (*Diary*, 1332)

## *Prayer*

Lord, when my neighbor shows ingratitude for the good I've done, assist me to see the moments in which I've been ungrateful of Your Mercy. Then form my heart to be truly grateful, as I count the blessings which come from Your almighty hands.

Jesus, have mercy on us and on the whole world.

# *August 5*

## ADORATION WITH MARY

> **During this adoration try to unite yourself in prayer with My Mother.** (*Diary*, 32)

## *Reflection*

St. Faustina had a very intimate and tender relationship with Our Lady. In order to fulfill God's will, St. Faustina stayed very close to Our Lady. She said: "The more I imitate the Mother of God, the more deeply I get to know God" (843). And like Our Lady she adored Jesus. St. Faustina loved to pray the Rosary, Marian novenas, and consecration prayers to the Mother of God. She gave all her concerns to Mary. Faustina understood that without the Blessed Mother there would be no Eucharistic Jesus. In order to love Jesus in the Eucharist, we must love His holy Mother, the first tabernacle.

## *Prayer*

"Mary, Immaculate Virgin, take me under Your special protection and guard the purity of my soul, heart and body. You are the model and star of my life" (874).

Jesus, have mercy on us and on the whole world.

# August 6

## HE HAS HIS WAYS

One of the sisters was appointed to look after the sick, but she was so negligent that one had to practice real mortification. One day, I made up my mind to tell the Superior about it, but then I heard a voice in my soul: **Bear it patiently; someone else will tell her....** I have found that sometimes the Lord does not want us to say something on our own; He has His ways and knows when to speak out. (*Diary*, 1587)

## Reflection

When others are doing things that we know are wrong, our impulse is, of course, to speak up and do something about it. Yet Sister Faustina would often "arm herself with patience." We should first listen for God's voice and seek direction. If you are still tempted to correct another, slow yourself down and ask yourself if it is your business to get involved. It may be, but do so only after serious reflection, as God may, in fact, have other plans.

## Prayer

Lord, let me always seek Your holy will first before taking any actions. In my silence let me recall my own weaknesses and never dwell on the shortcomings of others.

Jesus, have mercy on us and on the whole world.

# *August 7*

## MORTIFY YOUR WILL

**Know that when you mortify your own self-will,
then Mine reigns within you.** (*Diary*, 365).

## *Reflection*

St. Faustina was asked to pray for a certain soul. She decided to make a novena to the Merciful Lord but added another mortification without permission from her spiritual director. She asked pardon and he changed the mortification. Jesus granted Faustina the grace she asked for on behalf of the soul for whom she interceded and begged mercy, not because of the mortification she chose but because of her obedience to His representative.

## *Prayer*

"O my Jesus, be patient with me. I will be more careful in the future. I will rely, not upon myself, but upon Your grace and Your very great goodness to miserable me" (366).

Jesus, have mercy on us and on the whole world.

# *August 8*

## DON'T GET LOST IN YOUR MISERY

**Do not be absorbed in your misery.** (*Diary*, 1486)

## *Reflection*

Sister Justine, who lived with Faustina, noted: "She often told me that when a soul fears getting close to the Lord after a fall, then it wounds the Sacred Heart of Jesus so horribly, for the lack of trust hurt Him more than the most terrible sins. She would often tell me when I had distanced myself from God for a longer period of time, 'it is a human thing to fall due to our weakness, but a thing of the devil to remain in sin and give in to distrust.' Her eyes read what was going on in the depths of my soul. She would say to me, "Sister, how could you allow such a horrible vacuum in your soul?"

## *Prayer*

Forgive me, Lord, for my lack of trust. Give me the perfect trust of a child.
Jesus, have mercy on us and on the whole world.

# *August 9*

## GOD'S BOTTOMLESS MERCY

**Look into the abyss of My mercy and give praise
and glory to this mercy of Mine.** (*Diary*, 206)

## *Reflection*

There really is an abyss here on earth. It's part of the ocean and is usually called the abyssal zone. It ranges from 9,800 to 19,700 feet below the surface, and no one has ever explored its depths. Since the word "abyss" means "bottomless," it's a good name for the area. Abyss is also a good word for God's mercy, since it, too, is bottomless. Remember that the next time you are fearful that your sins might be too great to be forgiven. No one has yet reached the bottom of God's mercy, and you aren't going to be the first.

## *Prayer*

Lord, help me to remember that Your endless mercy always awaits me for the asking.

Jesus, have mercy on us and on the whole world.

# *August 10*

## HOPE AND THE END TIMES

Speak to the world about My mercy; let all mankind recognize My unfathomable mercy. It is a sign for the end times; after it will come the day of justice. While there is still time, let them have recourse to the fount of My mercy; let them profit from the Blood and Water which gushed forth for them. (*Diary*, 848)

## *Reflection*

The end times are times of warning to awaken mankind to turn with trust to receive the Lord's mercy "who desires all men to be saved and to come to the knowledge of the truth" (1 Tim 2:4). But it depends on our cooperation with His mercy. We need to start afresh every day. We should not become focused on trying to figure out how much time we have left, but rather, as St. Paul says, "to work out your own salvation with fear and trembling" (Phil 2:12), understanding that Jesus has given us all we need. Then, like St. Faustina, we can know the peace that comes from the hope of salvation.

## *Prayer*

Lord Jesus, come now as the King of Mercy.

Jesus, have mercy on us and on the whole world.

# *August 11*
## SANCTIFY YOURSELF

> **I bless your efforts and will give you opportunities
> to sanctify yourself.** (*Diary*, 1361)

## *Reflection*

Do you want to be a saint? Really want to be a saint? All too often, we hold back a little because we think that becoming a saint means that we will have to join religious life or give up much of what we enjoy. However, each of us is called to be a saint right where we are. In our everyday lives as spouses, parents, siblings, children, workers, friends, we are given every opportunity for sanctification. Remember this the next time you ask your kids to clean their rooms or your spouse to cook. These are your opportunities to become a saint!

## *Prayer*

Dear Lord, help me see how I can become a saint by living my very best life just where I am.

Jesus, have mercy on us and on the whole world.

# *August 12*

## UNCHANGING MESSAGE OF GOD

What are you afraid of? If you are with Me, who will dare touch you? Nevertheless, I am very pleased that you confide your fears to Me ... (*Diary*, 797)

## *Reflection*

Jesus tells us and St. Faustina not to fear because He is with us, the same message that St. Paul conveys in his letter to the Romans: "If God is for us, who can be against us?" (Rom 8:31).

Jesus also knows that we are going to be afraid at times. It's just human nature. When fear comes—and it will—He wants us to confide our fears to Him, not with flowery language but with a simple, heartfelt, "Jesus, I'm afraid." Even more than that, Jesus wants us to talk to Him about everything—our sorrows, joys, fears, triumphs, defeats—as we would our best friend.

## *Prayer*

My Lord, help me remember that nothing can separate me from You.

Jesus, have mercy on us and on the whole world.

# *August 13*

## CONSTANT COMPANION

**Why are you afraid to do My will? Will I not help you as I have done thus far?...** The next morning, I saw my Guardian Angel, who accompanied me throughout the journey ... (*Diary*, 489–490)

### *Reflection*

St. Faustina loved and imitated her Guardian Angel. Blessed Clelia Merloni, founder of the Apostles of the Sacred Heart, reminds us: "We should imitate our Guardian Angel: in church, his profound worship before the Tabernacle; in prayer, his recollection and his piety; in our affairs, his union with God; in our temptations, his glorious battles against the devil; in the practice of charity, his patience in bearing the mistakes and defects of his neighbor, his gentleness, his generosity, his assistance; in short, his conformity to God's good pleasure in all things, the uprightness of his intentions and his pure innocent life."

### *Prayer*

Dearest Guardian Angel, thank you for accompanying me all the days of my life. At the hour of my death carry me home to the Heavenly Father.

Jesus, have mercy on us and on the whole world.

# *August 14*

## OUR TRUE HOME

My daughter, your struggle will last until death. Your last breath will mark its end. You shall conquer by meekness. (*Diary*, 1597)

## *Reflection*

Marketing and social media lead us to believe that there is some mythical arrival point where we will no longer have to struggle here on earth. We will have all the money, experiences, love, and happiness we could ever desire. If we can just get there, we can have a good life. We will never be perfectly happy here because this world is not our home. Our true home is in heaven, and it is only in heaven that all our struggles will end. So how do we overcome the struggles of the present time? Jesus tells us it through meekness. Meekness doesn't mean rolling over and letting everyone walk on us. It means doing things like holding your tongue when you want to lash out, taking the smallest piece of dessert, allowing someone to cut in line. Meekness is an active submission of our own desires for the love of God.

## *Prayer*

My Lord, I do not want to dwell on my struggles, but on Your promises of mercy.

Jesus, have mercy on us and on the whole world.

# *August 15*

## HOW TO GIVE THANKS

I desire to unite Myself with human souls; my great delight is to unite Myself with souls. Know ... that when I come to a human heart in Holy Communion, My hands are full of all kinds of graces which I want to give to the soul. But souls do not even pay any attention to Me; they leave Me to Myself and busy themselves with other things. Oh, how sad I am that souls do not recognize Love! They treat Me as a dead object. (*Diary*, 1385)

## *Reflection*

How often do we receive Communion as if we were on autopilot? We take the Precious Body and Blood and then go back to our pew and watch as others receive. Instead of spending the next few minutes with Jesus, we read the bulletin! Sometimes we may even dash out the door before the Final Blessing. Jesus wants our attention. He wants to give our souls all kinds of graces. We need to make a proper Thanksgiving for receiving Jesus. St. Paul VI, in his Apostolic Exhortation *Marialis Cultus*, stated that an excellent way to express thanksgiving after Mass could be the recitation of the Most Holy Rosary. Don't treat Him like a dead object. Graces are waiting for you.

## *Prayer*

Dear Lord, You come to me Body, Blood, Soul, and Divinity. Thank You for this great gift of Yourself in the Eucharist.

Jesus, have mercy on us and on the whole world.

# *August 16*

## THROUGH YOUR PRAYERS ALONE

> **For the sake of your sincere and generous love, I grant them many graces although they are not asking Me for them.** (*Diary*, 383)

## *Reflection*

Do you ever wonder if your prayers do any good? Once, when she was on retreat, St. Faustina saw Jesus looking at three sisters with great severity. Finally, she gathered her courage and asked the Lord to look upon these three with kindness, saying that she would accept the severe gaze that had been directed at them. In turn, Jesus replied that He would look with mercy on the sisters because of St. Faustina's request. Think about that for a minute. It was only through St. Faustina's prayer that the other sisters were given mercy. Who do you know who might need God's mercy? Commend that soul to Jesus right now.

## *Prayer*

Lord, "You, who are Mercy Itself ... I beg you by the power of Your mercy, to look then with kindness" on N. and N. and N. and ... who most needs Your mercy.

Jesus, have mercy on us and on the whole world.

# *August 17*

## A MOMENT LASTS A LIFETIME

**Should you be unable to step into the chapel, immerse yourself in prayer there where you happen to be, if only for a very brief instant.** (*Diary*, 1572)

## *Reflection*

While praying for an extended period of time in Church, especially before or after Mass, is ideal, we aren't always able to do that. The demands of our families and our work may make praying in Church more of a luxury than a regular occurrence. The wonderful news is that we don't have to be in a special place to pray and we don't have to have hours and hours set aside. We can pray whenever and wherever we are. Even if our prayer lasts only "for a very brief instant," God is with us, listening to and loving us.

## *Prayer*

Dear Lord, in the busyness of my life, hear my prayer.
Jesus, have mercy on us and on the whole world.

# *August 18*

## FOUNTAIN OF MERCY FOR SOULS

> Every soul, and especially the soul of every religious, should reflect My mercy. My Heart overflows with compassion and mercy for all. The heart of My beloved must resemble Mine; from her heart must spring the fountain of My mercy for souls; otherwise I will not acknowledge her as Mine. (*Diary*, 1148)

## *Reflection*

Consider Jesus's mercy. It is freely given out of His endless love. It is all-encompassing. It is extended to all people. Now think about what Jesus is telling us in these few short words. He says that just as His Heart overflows with compassion, so, too, must our souls. If that doesn't happen, He will not acknowledge us as being His! If nothing else gives you pause, this should. When we fail to be merciful, when we fail to be compassionate, when we fail to be loving, Jesus will not acknowledge us. As frightening as that thought is, the opposite can bring comfort. Each time we extend mercy and compassion, Jesus is there, drawing us ever closer to Himself.

## *Prayer*

Dear Jesus, help me to always act in ways that will allow You to acknowledge me as being Yours.

Jesus, have mercy on us and on the whole world.

# *August 19*

## IMPORTANCE OF SILENCE

The Lord gave me to know how displeased he is with a talkative soul. **I find no rest in such a soul. The constant din tires Me, and in the midst of it the soul cannot discern My voice.** (*Diary*, 1008)

### *Reflection*

We are surrounded by noise. It's rare that any of us experience complete silence, even in Church. Sometimes the inside chatter can be louder than the outside noise! Jesus tells us that all that talk (inside and out) tires Him, but more than that, it keeps us from being able to hear God's voice in our soul. St. Faustina tells us: "A silent soul is strong; no adversities will harm it if it perseveres in silence. The silent soul is capable of attaining the closest union with God. It lives almost always under the inspiration of the Holy Spirit. God works in a silent soul without hindrance" (477).

Perhaps, as it says in 1 Kings 19:12, you will experience it as "a gentle blowing." When you seek silence, you may be amazed at what you actually hear.

### *Prayer*

Lord, St. Faustina said: "Patience, prayer and silence—these are what give strength to the soul" (944). Grant me these graces.

Jesus, have mercy on us and on the whole world.

# August 20

## A PURPOSE BEHIND YOUR PROBLEMS

As I was conversing with the hidden God, He gave me to see and understand that I should not be reflecting so much and building up fear of the difficulties which I might encounter. **Know that I am with you; I bring about the difficulties, and I overcome them....** (*Diary*, 788)

### Reflection

Living life takes courage. In the face of life's difficulties and challenges, you shouldn't fear. Do the thing that's right or hard, regardless of the cost. God's with you at every step. When Padre Pio was having troubles, he said, "I do not know what will happen to me; I only know one thing for certain, that the Lord will never fall short of his promises." When you're put to the test, all eyes are on you. An old saying puts it this way: People are like tea bags—you don't know what's in them until you put them in hot water. It's true. Life's difficulties build character. When afraid, take courage in Christ, and remember His consoling words: "Know that I am with you" (788). When difficulties arise, know that God's got a purpose behind your problems.

### Prayer

"My soul is struggling through a terrible thicket of all kinds of difficulties. If You Yourself did not support me, Lord, there would be no thought of my moving forward" (1606).

Jesus, have mercy on us and on the whole world.

# *August 21*

## NEVER LOSE YOUR PEACE

During Holy Mass, I saw Jesus stretched out on the Cross, and He said to me, ... **have great love for those who cause you suffering. Do good to those who hate you.** I answered, "O my Master, You see very well that I feel no love for them, and that troubles me." Jesus answered, **It is not always within your power to control your feelings. You will recognize that you have love if, after having experienced annoyance and contradiction, you do not lose your peace ...** (*Diary*, 1628)

### *Reflection*

Don't feel bad if you have a hard time loving those who hate you—St. Faustina had the exact same problem. It's part of being human, and Jesus knows that. Yet, His simple advice to Faustina was to "not lose your peace" but to pray for her enemies despite their bitterness and her own feelings and wish them well. Excellent advice for all of us.

### *Prayer*

Dear Lord, give me the strength to bear my crosses in peace and patience and to offer up my sufferings in union with You and Your Mother.

Jesus, have mercy on us and on the whole world.

# *August 22*

## ONE THING GOD CAN'T STAND

> All the graces that I pour out upon them flow off them
> as off the face of a rock. I cannot stand them, because
> they are neither good or bad. (*Diary*, 1702)

## *Reflection*

If you've ever seen runoff in the spring, you know that the water tumbles
uncontrollably over the rocks in its way. It's next to impossible to stop the
water, which grows increasingly destructive as it speeds along. Jesus says that
when we are neither good nor bad, but a sort of mediocre middle, all the graces
that should be ours flow over us and onto others, just like water over rocks.

## *Prayer*

My Lord, I hold out my heart to capture all the graces You want to give me.
Jesus, have mercy on us and on the whole world.

## *August 23*

> **You are to show mercy to your neighbors
> always and everywhere.** (*Diary*, 742)

### *Reflection*

On an intellectual level, we know that God loves us, but sometimes we don't feel loved or even feel as if we are lovable. When we fail to recognize our lovable qualities, we also fail to show mercy to ourselves. And God wants us to treat our neighbors as we treat ourselves. How can we be more merciful toward ourselves and thus see our lovable qualities? What might we do when we feel that way? One option is to acknowledge that we probably have a hard time identifying our lovable qualities. To change that, we need to do things that make us more lovable. We can start with the easy stuff and move on from there. For instance, when we are among people we recognize but do not know we can say good morning, good afternoon, or good evening. We can compliment strangers (in safe situations). "I can tell you really like your dog." "That was so kind what you did." "What a lovely outfit you have on." Try that for a week. Then pat yourself on the back. You have been lovable to strangers and have made yourself more lovable and merciful in the process.

### *Prayer*

Help me to remember that You ask me to love others *as I love myself*.

Jesus, have mercy on us and on the whole world.

# *August 24*

## THE IMPORTANCE OF TRUST

> **When a soul approaches Me with trust, I fill it with such an abundance of graces that it cannot contain them within itself, but radiates them to other souls....** (*Diary*, 1074)

## *Reflection*

It can be hard to trust. People let us down all the time. Often, when we hear someone say, "Trust me," we automatically assume that person can't be trusted. Jesus can be trusted, however. He will never let us down. What is even more reassuring is that when we come to Jesus in trust, we not only won't get hurt, but He will give us the strength and ability to become the kind of person that others can trust. Whenever we make the smallest gesture toward Jesus, He repays us a thousandfold. Nowhere is this more apparent than when we trust Him with our lives.

## *Prayer*

Dear Jesus, I trust in You.

Jesus, have mercy on us and on the whole world.

# *August 25*

## ORDAINING AND PERMITTING WILL

... accept everything that My hand gives you. (*Diary*, 1779)

## *Reflection*

Life throws new things at us—both good and bad. But trust in God's mercy, because He'll bring good from it—if we're open to His grace. Here's some guidance from St. Faustina: "In order to purify a soul, Jesus uses whatever instruments He likes. My soul underwent a complete abandonment on the part of creatures; often my best intentions were misinterpreted by the sisters, a type of suffering which is most painful; but God allows it, and we must accept it because in this way we become more like Jesus" (38). One thing to remember is that nothing happens to us that God doesn't know about. He either actively brings it about in our lives, or He allows it to happen. But all things are under His direction.

## *Prayer*

"I accept joy or suffering, praise or humiliation with the same disposition" (485).

Jesus, have mercy on us and on the whole world.

# *August 26*
## GOD'S GOODNESS IS PERSONAL

**Write down everything that occurs to you regarding My goodness.**
I answered, "What do You mean, Lord, what if I write too much?"
And the Lord replied, **My daughter, even if you were to speak at
one and the same time in all human and angelic tongues, even
then you would not have said very much, but on the contrary,
you would have sung in only a small measure the praises of
My goodness — of My unfathomable mercy.** (*Diary*, 1605)

## *Reflection*

God could have saved us from the heights of heaven, in some "hands-off"
kind of way. But when Jesus came to save us, He rolled up His sleeves and
jumped into the trenches with us. When our Lord came into this fallen world,
He entered, as Venerable Fulton Sheen put it, "enemy-occupied territory" to
conquer death and sin — to trample upon the grave. God sent His own Son on
a personal mission to save us — a mission to reveal His unfathomable mercy.

## *Prayer*

"O Lord, eternity will hardly suffice for me to give due praise to Your unfathomable mercy and Your compassion for me" (1486).

Jesus, have mercy on us and on the whole world.

# *August 27*
## FEAR CONQUERED

**Do not fear; I will not leave you alone ... I will accomplish everything that is lacking in you. You know what is within your power to do; do that.** The Lord looked into the depth of my being with great kindness; I thought I would die for joy under that gaze. (*Diary*, 881)

## *Reflection*

St. Faustina feared the work Jesus had given her. She complained: "I am not in good health, that I have no education, that I have no money, that I am an abyss of misery, that I fear contacts with people" (881). He assured her: "I will accomplish everything that is lacking in you" (881). We struggle with feelings of inadequacy too. But remember that in doing God's work, you mustn't rely on yourself. When the Lord looked upon St. Faustina, His gaze revealed His loving-kindness. God's loving gaze filled her soul with His kindness. She nearly died of joy. St. Teresa of Calcutta taught: "Holiness grows fast where there is kindness." Christ's kindness gave St. Faustina the courage and zeal she needed to carry out the work Jesus had given and made her grow in holiness. She learned her lesson: fear, conquered by kindness, brings joy.

## *Prayer*

Lord, cast Your gaze upon me with Your kindness.

Jesus, have mercy on us and on the whole world.

# *August 28*

## MY JOY AND MY HEART'S DELIGHT

Once, when I was praying, Jesus pervaded all my soul, darkness melted away, and I heard these words within me: **You are My joy; you are My heart's delight.** (*Diary*, 27)

## *Reflection*

Jesus found such delight in the heart of St. Faustina because she had such a pure and unblemished love for Him. St. Faustina was willing to endure anything for the love of the Cross of Christ—anything for Jesus! She said: "By the grace of God, I have received such a disposition of heart that I am never so happy as when I suffer for Jesus, whom I love with every beat of my heart" (303). God delights in us. The Lord takes pleasure in His people. What Jesus said to St. Faustina, He wants to say to you: "You are My joy; you are My heart's delight."

## *Prayer*

Lord, as I enter the gates of Your Kingdom, let me hear You say: "You are My joy; you are My heart's delight."

Jesus, have mercy on us and on the whole world.

# *August 29*
## SELF-RELIANCE IS OVERRATED

When one day I resolved to practice a certain virtue, I lapsed
into the vice opposed to that virtue ten times more frequently
than on other days. In the evening, I was reflecting on why,
today, I had lapsed so extraordinarily, and I heard the words:
**You were counting too much on yourself and too little on Me.**
And I understood the cause of my lapses. (*Diary*, 1087)

## *Reflection*

How often do we learn the hard way that we are not nearly as strong as we
think we are? When it comes to the spiritual life, we are, of course, well-
intentioned in our quest to eliminate bad habits and to practice virtue. But
when we try to do so on our own, without beseeching God for His help, falling
flat on our face is a very real possibility. We are told in Scripture to not "rely
on our own strength," and that is great advice since God is always more than
willing to help us become the kind of child of His that He has desired for us
to be from the moment He created us. We can't live a spiritual life alone. We
must always lean on, rely on, and count on the Lord's help.

## *Prayer*

Your strength is all that I need, Jesus. Never allow me to think I can do it
alone, but help me to always turn to You first.

Jesus, have mercy on us and on the whole world.

# *August 30*

## AN UNEQUAL EXCHANGE

> **For you, I am mercy itself; therefore I ask you to offer
> Me your misery and this very helplessness of yours and,
> in this way, you will delight My Heart.** (*Diary*, 1775)

### *Reflection*

The word "mercy" comes from the Latin *misericordia*. It is formed from two words and literally means "having a heart for the miserable." Jesus has a heart for the miserable, as the saints attest. St. Jerome gave everything to Jesus, but Our Lord wanted more. He said, "Lord, all I have left is my misery." Jesus replied, "That's what I want—your misery." St. Faustina had a similar experience. Jesus said: "Daughter, give Me your misery, because it is your exclusive property." She remarked: "At that moment, a ray of light illumined my soul, and I saw the whole abyss of my misery. In that moment, I nestled close to the Most Sacred Heart of Jesus with so much trust that even I had the sins of all the damned weighing on my conscience, I would not have doubted God's mercy" (1318).

### *Prayer*

Lord, transform me from misery to mercy.

Jesus, have mercy on us and on the whole world.

# *August 31*

## HE LOVES US THAT MUCH!

**I have chosen you.** (*Diary*, 1605)

### *Reflection*

Wow! Sometimes it is almost mind-blowing to contemplate the depths of God's love for us. Pope Emeritus Benedict XVI states: "Our vocation is not merely to exist in the world ... nor is it solely to be creatures of God. It is something more: it is being chosen by God, even before the world's creation, in the Son, Jesus Christ. Therefore, in Him we have existed, so to speak forever." That alone should fill your heart with gladness and make you want to sing songs of praise endlessly.

### *Prayer*

Jesus, I can't comprehend that You have chosen me and loved me forever.

Give me the grace to love You even more and to do so with all the strength of my soul.

Jesus, have mercy on us and on the whole world.

CHAPTER NINE

Reflections
FOR
*September*

# September 1

## WHO IS ON YOUR THRONE OF YOUR HEART?

**Strive to make My love reign in place
of your self-love.** (*Diary*, 1488)

## Reflection

In order to love others, you need to love yourself. But if you love yourself so
much that there is little room for loving God and others, then you will never
know real love. If you want love to reign in your heart, share your love with
others. Particularly those with whom you disagree.

## Prayer

Jesus, help me risk being hurt by loving others and allowing others to love me.
Jesus, have mercy on us and on the whole world.

# *September 2*

## BUSY ABOUT THE LORD'S AFFAIRS

**Let all act as they like; you are to act as I want you to.** (*Diary*, 1760)

## *Reflection*

Mind your own business! If you don't, you might become a meddlesome tool in Satan's hands. Busybodies set aside their God-given work and nose into everyone's affairs. While we ought to be concerned for our neighbor's corporeal and spiritual welfare, we've no right to meddle. We should not take the liberty as the manager of affairs outside our circle. The job of a humble servant of God is to be busy about the Lord's affairs.

## *Prayer*

Lord, keep me focused on what You've set before me so that I might be busy about Your affairs.

Jesus, have mercy on us and on the whole world.

# September 3

## DO NOT BE DISTURBED

My child, know that the greatest obstacles to holiness are discouragement and an exaggerated anxiety. These will deprive you of the ability to practice virtue. All temptations united together ought not disturb your interior peace, not even momentarily. (*Diary*, 1488)

### Reflection

Here are two pieces of encouragement and advice from St. Faustina:

"At the beginning of my religious life, suffering and adversities frightened and disheartened me. So I prayed continuously, asking Jesus to strengthen me and to grant me the power of His Holy Spirit that I might carry out His holy will in all things, because from the beginning I have been aware of my weakness" (56).

"Oh, if souls would only be willing to listen, at least a little, to the voice of conscience and the voice—that is, the inspirations—of the Holy Spirit! I say "at least a little," because once we open ourselves to the influence of the Holy Spirit, He Himself will fulfill what is lacking in us" (359).

### Prayer

Thank you, St. Faustina, for your good advice and helping me draw closer to God.

Jesus, have mercy on us and on the whole world.

# *September 4*

## PURE AND UNADULTERATED

My child, you please Me most by suffering. In your physical as well as your mental sufferings, My daughter, do not seek sympathy from creatures. I want the fragrance of your suffering to be pure and unadulterated. I want you to detach yourself ... (*Diary*, 279)

## *Reflection*

Faustina had her share of humiliations, unjust criticism, and gossip. Some of the sisters even called her a "hysteric." But these mental sufferings gave her an opportunity to grow in virtue. And those who caused her pain actually played a role on her path toward sainthood! Without it, she would not have been credible; she would not have been a saint.

## *Prayer*

Jesus, Faustina did not complain; instead she ran to You and sought comfort. Let my strength and comfort come from You.

Jesus, have mercy on us and on the whole world.

# *September 5*

## GOD SPEAKS TO A SUFFERING SOUL

What should I do when I am ignored and rejected by people, especially by those on whom I had a right to count in times of greatest need? (*Diary*, 1487)

## *Reflection*

My child, make the resolution never to rely on people. Entrust yourself completely to My will saying, "Not as I want, but according to Your will, O God, let it be done unto me." These words, spoken from the depths of one's heart, can raise a soul to the summit of sanctity in a short time. In such a soul I delight. Such a soul gives Me glory. Such a soul fills heaven with the fragrance of her virtue. But understand that the strength by which you bear sufferings comes from frequent Communions. So approach this fountain of mercy often, to draw with the vessel of trust whatever you need (1487).

## *Prayer*

"Thank You, Lord, for Your goodness in remaining with us in this exile as the God of mercy and blessing us with the radiance of Your compassion and goodness. It is through the light of Your mercy that I have come to understand how much You love me" (1487).

Jesus, have mercy on us and on the whole world.

# *September 6*

## A WOUNDED HEART

> **But tell Me, my child, who has dared to
> wound your heart?** (*Diary*, 1487)

### *Reflection*

St. Faustina had her sorrows. She said: "Today, I experienced a great suffering during the visit of our sisters. I learned of something that hurt me terribly, but I controlled myself so that the sisters didn't notice anything. For some time, the pain was tearing my heart apart, but all that is for the sake of poor sinners ... O Jesus, for poor sinners.... Jesus, my strength, stay close to me, help me ..." (875). Jesus was her teacher. He taught her to treat trials as an opportunity to learn love of neighbor. She had grudges and took them to Jesus. He taught her not to judge others. He transformed her heart into overwhelming kindness for others.

### *Prayer*

"O Jesus, make my heart sensitive to all the sufferings of my neighbor, whether of body or of soul. O my Jesus, I know that You act toward us as we act toward our neighbor" (692).

Jesus, have mercy on us and on the whole world.

# September 7

## NO DISTANCE BETWEEN US

> Write that when they say this chaplet in the presence of the dying, I will stand between My Father and the dying person, not as the just Judge but as the merciful Savior ... and the hour of their death will be a happy one. (*Diary*, 1541)

### Reflection

St. Faustina was unable to be at the side of her dying relative to pray the Chaplet.

She wrote: "I prayed today for a soul in agony, who was dying without the Holy Sacraments, although she desired them. But it was already too late. It was a relative of mine, my uncle's wife. She was a soul pleasing to God. There was no distance between us at that moment" (207). It's never the same as being there with a loved one in person. However, St. Faustina reassures us we need not be present to say the Chaplet at the side of a dying person. We *are* there. Imagine, we have the ability to invoke mercy for the dying simply through our prayers.

If that isn't amazing, then nothing is! And what is a "happy death?" To die in the state of grace, of course.

### Prayer

Merciful Savior, I join my prayers with St. Faustina for all those who will die today without the holy sacraments.

Jesus, have mercy on us and on the whole world.

# *September 8*

## FOR MY HOMELAND IS IN HEAVEN — THIS I FIRMLY BELIEVE

> **But child, you are not yet in your homeland; so go, fortified by My grace ... and remember that the days of your exile will pass quickly.** (*Diary*, 1489)

## *Reflection*

"I see that the will of God has not yet been fulfilled in me, and that is why I must live, for I know that if I fulfill everything the Lord has planned for me in this world, He will not leave me in exile any longer, for heaven is my home. But before we go to our Homeland, we must fulfill the will of God on earth; that is, trials and struggles must run their full course in us" (897).

## *Prayer*

"Help me, happy inhabitants of the heavenly homeland, so that your sister may not falter on the way. Although the desert is fearful, I walk with lifted head and eyes fixed on the sun; that is to say, on the merciful Heart of Jesus" (886).

Jesus, have mercy on us and on the whole world.

# September 9

## NEW GRACES

> **I am looking for souls who would like to receive My grace.** (*Diary*, 1705)

### Reflection

When St. Faustina was given new duties at the convent, she asked Jesus for "a blessing and for graces to faithfully carry out the duties ..." (1267). Our Lord assured her that He'd be with her each step of the way, promising that she'd be given opportunities to do many deeds of mercy. Reflecting on this, St. Faustina was encouraged by God's goodness and that Christ had bestowed upon her a "new grace." When you have to do something new, something you've never done before, ask the Lord to guide your steps and grant you new grace to perform the actions with love.

### Prayer

Good and gracious Lord, open my heart to receive new graces.

Jesus, have mercy on us and on the whole world.

# September 10
## GOD SPEAKS WITH A PERFECT SOUL

O my merciful Lord, there are secrets in my heart which no one knows or will ever know except You because, even if I wanted to reveal them, no one would understand me. (*Diary*, 1489)

## Reflection

One of your sighs of love atones for many offenses with which the godless overwhelm Me. The smallest act of virtue has unlimited value in My eyes because of your great love for Me (1489).

## Prayer

"Jesus, I ask You, give me the strength for battle. Let it be done to me according to Your most holy will. My soul is enamored of Your most holy will" (1498).

# September 11

## A LIVING HOST

**I delight in you as in a living host.** (*Diary*, 923)

## Reflection

When St. Faustina wrote about the "host," she meant it in two ways. The first—with a capital *H*—was Our Lord in the Eucharist. The second—with a lowercase *h*—was herself. Over and over throughout the *Diary*, the young nun used the image of a host to describe what she wanted to do, what she wanted to become. It was to imitate in her own small ways, and through her own painful personal experiences, the suffering and sacrifice of Christ and join her suffering and sacrifice to His. At the same time, she wanted to praise her Savior and silently endure all hardships for the salvation of souls. This is how she became holy. This is how she became a saint.

## Prayer

Dear Faustina, "living host," pray for me and for my loved ones.

Jesus, have mercy on us and on the whole world.

# *September 12*

## AFTER RECEIVING HOLY COMMUNION

After I received Holy Communion ... (*Diary*, 757)

### *Reflection*

St. Faustina often speaks about the many revelations, insights, and conversations she had with Jesus after she received Holy Communion. During those times, she didn't use a prayer book; she spoke from her heart. By the way, it is said that the host lasts for at least 15 minutes after you consume it, so we have plenty of time to be with Jesus. Mother Gabriele Bitterlich, founder of Opus Angelorum, said: "We should do the same thing. We should hold the Lord fast in Holy Communion, as a child clings to its father and mother. Put off the obligatory prayers as long as possible and converse with the Lord fervently, and enthusiastically like a child. For when you turn away from Him and turn again to the bulletin, customary prayer, you pass from being a child to being a servant, a handmaid. Make good use of these precious minutes after Holy Communion and forget everything around you, so that nothing may distract you. Immerse yourself in His sight, His majesty, and grandeur, now that this Divine Majesty makes Himself the prisoner of your Love."

### *Prayer*

Most holy Jesus, I welcome You into my heart. I am a prisoner of Your love. Jesus, have mercy on us and on the whole world.

# *September 13*

## PERSEVERANCE IS A GRACE

> Both the sinner and the righteous person have need of My mercy. Conversion, as well as perseverance, is a grace of My mercy. (*Diary*, 1577)

## *Reflection*

Jesus taught St. Faustina the importance of persevering in praying for the conversion of sinners. He told her not to grow weary of praying for sinners. Here are his directives: "Let the soul be aware that, in order to pray and persevere in prayer, one must arm oneself with patience and cope bravely with exterior and interior difficulties. The interior difficulties are discouragement, dryness, heaviness of spirit and temptations. The exterior difficulties are human respect and time; one must observe the time set apart for prayer" (147). "Let every soul remember these words: '*And being in anguish, He prayed longer.*' I always prolong such prayer as much as is in my power ..." (872).

## *Prayer*

Today, dear Lord, accept my heartaches, my anxieties and my pain for the conversion of my family.

Jesus, have mercy on us and on the whole world.

# September 14

## MERCY IS OUR DEFENSE

> ... tell souls that I am giving them My mercy as a
> defense. I Myself am fighting for them and am bearing
> the just anger of My Father. (*Diary*, 1516)

## *Reflection*

God loved us so much, that He sent Jesus as our Savior. Our Lord is a God of
love and of mercy. He's patient with each of us. In His goodness God extends
us graces countless times. What is even more amazing, Jesus is there, defending
us against the just anger of God for our sins. St. Faustina tells us that when
we pray the Divine Mercy Chaplet, the righteous anger of God is placated.
The voice of our Heavenly Father told her that "the very depths of My tender
mercy are moved for the sake of the sorrowful Passion of My Son" (811). He
hears the voice of His pleading children. God's Heart is not made of stone.
We are wrapped in the arms of Mercy.

## *Prayer*

Lord, forever I will remember Your unfathomable mercy toward me.

Jesus, have mercy on us and on the whole world.

# September 15

## THE ESSENCE OF TEARS

After these words, my love made great efforts to express to him what he was to me, but I was at a loss for words and burst into tears in my helplessness. And Jesus said, **For you, I am mercy itself; therefore I ask you to offer Me your misery and this very helplessness of yours and, in this way, you will delight My heart.** (*Diary*, 1775)

## *Reflection*

Scientists have looked at tears under extreme magnification and have learned that, depending on the emotion that causes the tears, they have very different appearances. Tears of grief and sorrow look like shards of broken glass, tears of joy and happiness look like beautiful landscapes, and tears from onions look like pressed ferns. When we, like St. Faustina, cry, Jesus sees the very essence of our tears. When we cry from helplessness, He responds with mercy because we have entrusted His deepest essence to His care. And in doing so, we delight His Heart.

## *Prayer*

Dear Lord, You know me, even to the kind of tears I shed.
  Jesus, have mercy on us and on the whole world.

# *September 16*

## PROTECT THE CHILDREN

As I walked about, inspecting everything, I suddenly saw a crowd of children who seemed to be no older than five to eleven years of age. When they saw me they surrounded me and began to cry out, "Defend us from evil," (179) and they led me into the chapel which was in this convent. When I entered the chapel, I saw the distressful Lord Jesus. Jesus looked at me graciously and said that He was gravely offended by children: **You are to defend them from evil.** From that moment, I have been praying for children, but I feel that prayer alone is not enough. (*Diary*, 765)

### *Reflection*

St. Faustina makes an important point when it comes to protecting children, a topic that dominates the news in our own time. Yes, we need to keep them in our prayers, but "that alone is not enough." We're also called to take action to keep them safe from those who would harm them.

### *Prayer*

Dear Lord Jesus, bless the children. Help all of us protect them with our prayers and our actions.

Jesus, have mercy on us and on the whole world.

# *September 17*

## SIMPLE DOES IT

> **Know ... that the simpler your speech is, the more you attract Me to yourself.** (*Diary*, 797)

## *Reflection*

Mark Twain, the great American writer, said: "Don't use a five-dollar word when a fifty-cent one will do." Apparently, his words apply to prayer as well as novels. Jesus tells us not to try to make our prayers wordy and pretentious. Instead, He tells us it is more pleasing to Him when we speak simply and straightforwardly. What does that mean? Instead of saying, "Lord, render Your assistance with the financial constraints that result from my current monetary tribulation," say, "Lord, help me pay my bills this month." A good rule in prayer is to say what you mean and mean what you say. Nothing more and nothing less.

## *Prayer*

Jesus, help me to come to You with simple faith.

Jesus, have mercy on us and on the whole world.

# *September 18*
## CHOOSE WISELY

**I cannot help such a soul because it scorns Me; having a free will, it can spurn Me or love Me.** (*Diary*, 580)

## *Reflection*

God has given each of us free will. That means that everything relies on our choice. We can choose good or evil. Life or death. Hope or despair. While it might seem that it would be easier if we didn't have free will, Jesus does not want us to have to love Him like a robot that has no options. He wants us to desire to love Him. He wants us to choose Him. And because we get to choose, we can either spurn Jesus' love or accept it. It's your choice. Choose wisely, for all eternity depends on it.

## *Prayer*

Jesus, I choose You.

Jesus, have mercy on us and on the whole world.

# September 19

## THE BEST FOR GOD

**They have time for everything, but they have no time to come to Me for graces.** (*Diary*, 367)

### Reflection

St. Faustina saw this problem in the convent. She shared this: "The conversations that I hear in this place about worldly matters makes me so tired that I nearly faint" (1788). The same holds true for us. Even more so. Our world is loud, fast, non-stop. Our time is consumed with chatter from 24-hour news to social and (sometimes anti-social) media. Our schedules are packed. We run out of time at the end of the day. It makes us tired and faint. Jesus is waiting for you to stop, slow down, and unite your heart with His. In it is new love, new consolations, new graces. When we give God our time, He returns to us immeasurable graces, because God can't be outdone in generosity. When it comes to making time for the Lord each day, give the best for God. Plus a bonus! You will find that you have *more* time in the day than if you started without Him!

### Prayer

Thank you, Lord, for the intimate conversations with You. Keep me close to You when my days get hectic and to focus on what really matters to my eternal soul.

Jesus, have mercy on us and on the whole world.

# *September 20*

## EASIER THAN YOU THINK

At noon, during the examination of conscience, I complained to God about my weakness. Then I heard the following words in my soul. **From today on you will do this easily; I shall strengthen you.** (*Diary*, 65)

### *Reflection*

Life is hard. There's no doubt about it. But life doesn't have to be as hard as we sometimes think it has to be. St. Faustina had difficulty handling heavy pots of boiled potatoes. At first she tried to avoid the work, but then she heard Jesus tell her that He would help make the task easy. And so He did. Often we think that something is going to be more difficult than it really is. Is there something facing you that feels almost impossible? Are you avoiding some difficult task? Ask the Lord to give you strength ... and then trust that He will.

### *Prayer*

Dear Jesus, give me the grace of Your strength for my daily tasks.

Jesus, have mercy on us and on the whole world.

# *September 21*
## SAY THE CHAPLET!

The Lord said to me, **My daughter, help Me to save a certain dying sinner. Say the chaplet that I have taught you for him.** (*Diary*, 1565)

## *Reflection*

Once, when St. Faustina began to pray the Chaplet of Divine Mercy, she saw a multitude of devils waiting for a dying man's soul. As she continued to pray, she saw the rays from Jesus' merciful heart banish the powers of darkness, and the man died in peace. She realized then that the Chaplet was particularly powerful when prayed for someone at the moment of death. Right now, someone in the world is dying and in need of your prayer. You don't need to know who that person is. God knows. You don't even need to be present. Just say the Chaplet for that person, asking that, through your intercession, the anger of God might be appeased and the power of the devils be conquered.

## *Prayer*

Lord Jesus, save the soul most in need of Your mercy.
Jesus, have mercy on us and on the whole world.

# *September 22*

## POWER GIVEN TO PRIESTS

Once, when a certain doubt rose within me shortly before Holy Communion, the Seraph with the Lord Jesus stood before me again. I asked the Lord Jesus, and not receiving an answer, I said to the Seraph, "Could you perhaps hear my confession?" And he answered me, "No spirit in heaven has that power." (*Diary*, 1677)

## *Reflection*

Priests receive a power from God that He has given to neither angels nor archangels — the power to hear confessions and forgive sins. God above confirms what priests do here below. "The Lord wills that his disciples possess a tremendous power: that his lowly servants accomplish in his name all that he did when he was on earth" (CCC 983). What a great honor He has given to priests, but what a great gift He has given to us! Through the physical presence and words of the priest, we can have absolute assurance that our sins are forgiven. We don't need to wonder and worry if God has heard our confession. We can know it for sure. When was the last time you went to Confession?

## *Prayer*

Lord Jesus, I am most heartily sorry for my sins.

Jesus, have mercy on us and on the whole world.

# *September 23*

## PRAY, HOPE, AND DON'T WORRY

I went to the Lord and said, "Jesus, don't You see how they are hindering Your work?" And I heard a voice in my soul: **Do as much as is in your power, and don't worry about the rest. These difficulties prove that this work is Mine. Be at peace so long as you do all that is in your power.** (*Diary*, 1295)

## *Reflection*

One of the hardest commands for us to follow is, "Don't worry." As humans, we fall into worry with great ease. We worry about ourselves, our families, our friends and some, like St. Faustina, even worry for Jesus! The Lord tells us that we aren't required to solve everything. We are supposed to do only what is in our power and leave the rest to Him. The next time you are tempted to worry, take all the practical steps you can and trust the outcome to Him.

## *Prayer*

Dear Jesus, help me to let go of worry and be at peace.

Jesus, have mercy on us and on the whole world.

# *September 24*

**This prayer will serve to appease My wrath.** (*Diary*, 476)

## *Reflection*

What is God's wrath? Pastor and author Monsignor Charles Pope offers this explanation: "God's wrath is His passion to set things right. We see an example of this right at the beginning, in Genesis, when God cursed Satan and uttered the protoevangelium: *I will make you and the woman enemies . . . one of her seed will crush your head while you strike at his heel* (Gen 3:15). God is clearly angered at what sin has done to Adam and Eve. He has a passion for our holiness. He wants what is best for us and is angered by what hinders this. All sins provoke His wrath, but there are five that especially cry out to heaven for vengeance: willful murder (Gen 4:10), the sin of the Sodomites (Gen 18:20, 19:13), the cry of the oppressed (Ex 3:7-10); the cry of the foreigner, the widow, and the orphan (Ex 20:20-22), and injustice to the wage earner (Deut 24:14-5, Jas 5:4, CCC 1867). In terms of sin, injustice, and anything that hinders the possibility of salvation, God has a wrathful indignation and a passion to set things right. This is part of His love for us. His wrath may be manifested through punishment, disturbance of our conscience, or simply by allowing us to experience the consequences of our sin." What then shall we do? God offers us the powerful Chaplet of Divine Mercy to appease His wrath. You can find it in the Appendix on page 405.

## *Prayer*

Jesus, I trust in You.

Jesus, have mercy on us and on the whole world.

# *September 25*

## PROLONGING THE TIME OF MERCY

When once I asked the Lord Jesus how he could tolerate so many sins and crimes and not punish them, the Lord answered me, **I have eternity for punishing [these], and so I am prolonging the time of mercy for the sake of [sinners].** (*Diary*, 1160)

## *Reflection*

Imagine for a moment that you have a very close friend. Now imagine that this friend has betrayed something you told them in confidence. You learn about the betrayal from another friend. What is your reaction? Do you call up the first friend and give them a piece of your mind? Do you end the friendship? Now consider how Jesus treats you when you sin. Can you extend some of the forgiveness Jesus gives you to the person who has offended you? While you don't need to accept mistreatment or open yourself up to additional hurt, you can express how you feel without falling into anger or judgment. Perhaps the person had a reason for talking that you didn't know about. Or perhaps they are truly sorry for their betrayal. St. Faustina reminds us: "We resemble God most when we forgive our neighbors" (1148). Extend mercy and see what happens.

## *Prayer*

Dear Jesus, help me to grant mercy as You grant mercy.
Jesus, have mercy on us and on the whole world.

# *September 26*
## VALE OF TEARS

**Join your sufferings to My Passion and offer them to the heavenly Father for sinners.** (*Diary*, 1032)

### *Reflection*

Everyone experiences some kind of suffering in this life. That's why the world is called the "vale of tears." However, the purpose of our suffering isn't merely to experience sadness and pain; it is to use our sorrow and hurt to transform and renew the earth. When we unite our suffering to Jesus' suffering on the Cross as an offering for sinners, we do our part in bringing about the "new heaven and the new earth" Jesus spoke of. While we may not always understand how it works, we can be sure that it does work, for Jesus has given us that promise.

### *Prayer*

Dear Jesus, take my sorrow and my pain. Use it as You will to bring healing to a hurting world.

Jesus, have mercy on us and on the whole world.

# September 27
## NO LIMIT TO GOD'S MERCY

At the hour of their death, I defend as My own glory every soul that will say this chaplet; or when others say it for a dying person, the indulgence is the same. When this chaplet is said by the bedside of a dying person, God's anger is placated, unfathomable mercy envelops the soul, and the very depths of My tender mercy are moved for the sake of the sorrowful Passion of My Son. (*Diary*, 811)

### Reflection

The power of intercessory prayer for the dying is seen in the Divine Mercy Chaplet. On numerous occasions Jesus urged Faustina to pray the Chaplet. When offered for the dying, even the worst sinners are embraced by the loving and merciful arms of God. When a woman was writhing in her last agony, St. Faustina came to her bedside and prayed. St. Faustina recounts: "Suddenly the dying person opened her eyes and looked at me; I had not managed to finish the entire Chaplet when she died, with extraordinary peace ... I could feel the power of mercy envelop that soul" (810). Whatever we're wrestling with, we obtain everything we need through the Chaplet. In this prayer Jesus gave to St. Faustina and you, there's no limit to God's mercy.

### Prayer

Jesus, grant me fervor in praying the Chaplet for the dying.
Jesus, have mercy on us and on the whole world.

# *September 28*
## LOVING OUR ENEMIES

... pray for those who have made you suffer
and wish them well. (*Diary*, 1628)

## *Reflection*

Loving our enemies is one of the toughest challenges of the Christian life. Much of the time we don't feel much like loving those who hurt us. In fact, with human strength alone it would be impossible to love people who cause us suffering. But Jesus gives us the answer: Pray for them and wish them well. When we do this, He will make the impossible possible.

## *Prayer*

Lord, help me to bless my enemies and those who afflict me. Let me draw upon Your example of forgiving those who crucified You.

Jesus, have mercy on us and on the whole world.

# *September 29*

*Feast of Sts. Michael, Gabriel, and Raphael, Archangels*

## FLYING BLIND WITH ST. MICHAEL

I asked Jesus why the Angels had been punished as soon as they had sinned. I heard a voice: **Because of their profound knowledge of God....** (*Diary*, 1332)

## *Reflection*

Statues of St Michael the Archangel were in all the houses of St. Faustina's Congregation. He was ordered by God to take special care of St. Faustina. St. Michael revealed to St. Eutropius that he is the Guardian of the Most Blessed Sacrament. St. Faustina had a great devotion to and admiration for St. Michael because of his virtues. "I have great reverence for St. Michael the Archangel; he had no example to follow in doing the will of God, and yet he fulfilled God's will faithfully" (667). He was in a sense ... flying blind. He is the perfect example of showing us what it means to faithfully follow God's will.

## *Prayer*

St. Michael, help me and pray for me!
    Jesus, have mercy on us and on the whole world.

# *September 30*
## THINKING OF YOU!

When I received Holy Communion, I said to Him, "Jesus, I thought about You so many times last night," and Jesus answered me, **And I thought of you before I called you into being.** "Jesus, in what way were You thinking about me?" **In terms of admitting you to My eternal happiness.** After these words, my soul was flooded with the love of God. I could not stop marveling at how much God loves us. (*Diary*, 1292)

## *Reflection*

God does not need us. He is self-sufficient. But because we are made in His image and likeness, we all have a spark of Him in us and He can't live without us! God never had to create you.

Billions of possible human beings God saw, but He created YOU! They might have been holier, smarter, far more interesting. But He did not create them. There was something about you that attracted Him to you. That drew Him to create you!

St. Catherine of Siena said in *The Dialogue*, "You absolutely do not need us but You act as if You can't get along without us!" He loves us more than anybody else and more than anybody can. And He thinks about you day and night, waiting to admit you to His eternal happiness!

## *Prayer*

O my Lord, let my marveling for Your love of me never cease.

Jesus, have mercy on us and on the whole world.

CHAPTER TEN

# Reflections
FOR
*October*

# *October 1*

## GOD'S MERCY IS OUR LAST REFUGE

> **Do all you possibly can for this work of My mercy. I desire that My mercy be worshipped, and I am giving mankind the last hope of salvation; that is, recourse to My mercy.** (*Diary*, 998)

## *Reflection*

Do you desire holiness? Learn to rely on God's mercy, because sinners who humbly approach Jesus "experience the unspeakable effects of [His] mercy" (1680). Even the lukewarm can find refuge in God's mercy—their last hope. But the redeemed in heaven "worship the mercy of the Lord" (745). Forever blessed are self-centered souls who've been crushed and reshaped by the Master's hand to be full of mercy. St. Faustina teaches us to glorify God's mercy, because "His mercy is without limit or end. And although evil will attain its measure, in mercy, there is no measure" (423). With St. Faustina, let us be apostles of mercy, teaching all people that God's Mercy is our last refuge.

## *Prayer*

"God of unfathomable mercy, embrace the whole world and pour Yourself out upon us through the merciful Heart of Jesus" (1183).

Jesus, have mercy on us and on the whole world.

# *October 2*

## LOVE OF THE ANGELS

His gaze was like lightning, and I understood how the fire
of God's love burned in that look.... (*Diary*, 1271)

## *Reflection*

St. Faustina's order, The Congregation of Our Lady of Mercy, had a special
devotion to the guardian angels, designating them as one of its patrons. Daily
prayers and meditations were offered to the angels to protect the sisters against
the enemy. Faustina had a very close relationship to her Guardian Angel.
She says she often thanked God that He gave us angels for companions.
She reminds us that our Guardian Angel's great mission is to see us home in
heaven. They pray for us with great love before the throne of God. They are
intent on obtaining every grace and favor for our eternal welfare. We must
ask their help every day to purify us here on earth so as to avoid purgatory. If
we invoke our Guardian Angels, they will strengthen us against temptation,
and they will be a most powerful help at the hour of our death. Call on them.
Develop a relationship with them. They burn for love of God and you.

## *Prayer*

Dear Guardian Angel, take me by the hand so that I may obey Your guidance,
and attain eternal happiness.

Jesus, have mercy on us and on the whole world.

# October 3

## YOUR HEROIC SACRIFICES

> You will save more souls through prayer and suffering than will a missionary through his teachings and sermons alone. (*Diary*, 1767)

## Reflection

When we think about heroes and heroines of the faith, we are tempted to remember those who have literally put their lives on the line—missionaries and martyrs. However, Jesus tells us that we can save souls, not only by acts of courage or dying for the faith but through ordinary prayer and suffering. Faustina was called the "Dump" because everyone dumped their problems on her. St. Thérèse of Lisieux showed a smile and only kindness to a cranky nun. The children of Fatima gave up their lunch to poor children along the roadside, and for a penance they wore a rope around their waist, which caused discomfort all day. The sacrifices of these saints were constant and heroic, but they aren't beyond our abilities. Our daily trials can be heroic sacrifices too.

## Prayer

Dear Lord, let me not measure my sacrifices by their difficulty, but by how much I offer them to You.

Jesus, have mercy on us and on the whole world.

# *October 4*

## HOW TO DEAL WITH HURT FEELINGS

... I went for five-minute adoration, when suddenly I saw the crucifix I have on my breast come alive. Jesus said to me, **My daughter, suffering will be a sign to you that I am with you.** My soul was greatly moved by these words. (*Diary*, 669)

### *Reflection*

There's an old saying, "Sticks and stones may break my bones, but names will never hurt me." We now know that simply isn't true. Hurtful words can cut deeper and last longer than physical blows. Little wonder that St. Faustina called hurt feelings real suffering. So what did St. Faustina do when someone hurt her feelings? Here's her response: "I am learning how to be good from Jesus, from Him who is goodness itself, so that I may be called a daughter of the heavenly Father. This morning, when someone hurt my feelings, I tried, in that suffering, to unite my will to the will of God, and praised God by my silence" (669).

Jesus answered Faustina (although our crucifix may not come alive!) that suffering was a sign that He was with her. We can unite and praise God in our suffering. He is with us, too!

### *Prayer*

Jesus, when my feelings are hurt, use my suffering on behalf of the souls in purgatory.

Jesus, have mercy on us and on the whole world.

# *October 5*

## TO REIGN IS TO SERVE

**Your love and your humility make Me leave the heavenly throne and unite Myself with you.** (*Diary*, 512)

## *Reflection*

The Lord promises that our humility draws Him close to us. But we must learn to practice humility by putting ourselves in the service of others. Here's a wonderful example that shows us how. Cardinal Merry del Val, Secretary of State to Pope Pius X, offered Mass one day in the Vatican. He realized there was no altar server. He proceeded to vest for Mass but then turned around and saw Pope Pius X himself dressed in altar server garb. Pope Pius X told him he was going to be his altar server from that point on. To reign is to serve!

## *Prayer*

Lord, I humble myself before You as Your servant. And I ask Your grace to help me dedicate my life in service to others.

Jesus, have mercy on us and on the whole world.

# October 6

## SUPPORTED BY DAILY ADORATION

> Go to the Superior and ask her to allow you to make a
> daily hour of adoration for nine days. (*Diary*, 32)

### Reflection

What do St. John Paul II, St. Mother Teresa, and St. Faustina have in common? Adoration! They relied on it. They drew strength, consolation, and support from it. Adoration is part of the spiritual life of every saint because it transforms lives and transforms the world. St. Faustina shared her joys with Him. She asked for healing. She wept in front of Jesus. She thanked Him, loved Him, and rested in Him.

She came to know herself and God. It was Adoration that called her forth to go out and help others. It was Adoration that empowered her to share Jesus' compassion with everyone she encountered. She became the one she befriended. In a special way she offered her adoration for her parents and her whole family.

What if you are unable to go to an Adoration chapel? Many times Faustina was too frail and sick to leave her room. On those occasions, she would spiritually "take flight." You can make spiritual adoration at any time. From your sofa or wheelchair. In your car. At work. On a walk. Even waiting in line! From your own heart. "I adore You." Just as long as you turn your heart and mind toward the Lord.

### Prayer

Jesus, I adore You. Let my adoration never cease.

Jesus, have mercy on us and on the whole world.

# *October 7*

... for the many souls who are often worried because they do not have the material means with which to carry out an act of mercy. Yet spiritual mercy, which requires neither permission nor storehouses, is much more meritorious and is within the grasp of every soul. If a soul does not exercise mercy somehow or other, it will not obtain My mercy on the day of judgment. (*Diary*, 1317)

## *Reflection*

If you ask a person what they would do if they won the lottery, most say that they would give at least some of it away in acts of mercy and charity. Unfortunately, that good intention often goes by the wayside, and the lottery winner is swept up in the lure of riches. If you aren't a lottery winner and you don't have the material means to carry out acts of mercy, never fear. Jesus tells us that spiritual mercy far exceed material mercy. To start, Jesus says to pray! He repeatedly requests the Chaplet. The spiritual and corporal works of mercy are also an excellent way to exercise mercy. These acts are unquestionable proof of your love of God and neighbor.

## *Prayer*

Jesus, may the mercy I extend to others be extended to me.
    Jesus, have mercy on us and on the whole world.

# *October 8*

## THE RESPONSIBILITY OF
## THE LAITY TO PRIESTS

**Speak to priests about this inconceivable mercy of Mine.** (*Diary*, 177)

## *Reflection*

We have been taught that we, all of us, are the Body of Christ, the Church. That means that while priests have responsibilities toward the laity, the laity have responsibilities toward priests as well. One of those responsibilities is to remind priests (and bishops) about the mercy of God and encourage them to speak often about it in their homilies. God wants everyone to know about His mercy. It is only with the laity and clergy working together that the message can be shared with the entire world.

## *Prayer*

Lord, give me the courage to talk to my priest about the mercy of God.

Jesus, have mercy on us and on the whole world.

# *October 9*

## DON'T BE AFRAID

Do not be afraid of what will happen to you. I will give you nothing beyond your strength. You know the power of My grace; let that be enough. (*Diary*, 1491)

### *Reflection*

As Jesus tells St. Faustina, "I will give you nothing beyond your strength." Every life is peppered with a lot of "somethings" that make it challenging, and frightening, but none of them will be beyond what we can handle.

### *Prayer*

Dear Lord, it's reassuring to know that You will give me nothing beyond my strength. Your grace will be enough.

Jesus, have mercy on us and on the whole world.

# *October 10*

## GOD SPEAKS TO A SUFFERING SOUL

My Lord, I am also discouraged because neither my superiors nor my confessor understand my interior trials. A darkness clouds my mind. How can I advance? All this discourages me from striving for the heights of sanctity. (*Diary*, 1487)

### *Reflection*

Well, My child, this time you have told Me a good deal. I realize how painful it is not to be understood, and especially by those whom one loves and with whom one has been very open. But suffice it to know that I understand all your troubles and misery. I am pleased by the deep faith you have, despite everything, in My representatives. Learn from this that no one will understand a soul entirely—that is beyond human ability. Therefore, I have remained on earth to comfort your aching heart and to fortify your soul, so that you will not falter on the way.... Know, too, that the darkness about which you complain I first endured in the Garden of Olives when My Soul was crushed in mortal anguish. I am giving you a share in those sufferings because of My special love for you and in view of the high degree of holiness I am intending for you in heaven. A suffering soul is closest to My Heart (1487).

### *Prayer*

Lord Jesus, thank you for giving me comfort only You can give. Hold me close to Your Heart.

Jesus, have mercy on us and on the whole world.

# *October 11*

## BRIEF MOMENTS OF ADORATION

I entered the chapel for a moment ... (*Diary*, 527)

## *Reflection*

In her free moments from work, St. Faustina frequently ran to the chapel. "For a moment." For a minute. Eucharistic Adoration—and spiritual Eucharistic Adoration—have no requirement on how long they must last. Throughout the day, follow St. Faustina's example. Not necessarily rushing to the chapel but slowing down to spend a moment or two in simple adoration. Sometimes before the tabernacle or monstrance—and other times wherever you may be. Just as Jesus in the Blessed Sacrament waited for Faustina, join Faustina in one of her tender moments of prayer. He waits for you!

## *Prayer*

"Adore my soul, the mercy of the Lord."

"I adore You, O Living Bread."

"Praise and glory be to You, O Indivisible Trinity, One God, unto ages of ages!" (1623, 195, 278).

Jesus, have mercy on us and on the whole world.

# *October 12*

## BUSY HANDS INVITE JESUS

This morning after completing my spiritual exercises, I began at once to crochet. I sensed a stillness in my heart; I sensed that Jesus was resting in it. (*Diary*, 961)

### *Reflection*

There is something about keeping our hands busy with repetitive manual activities like crocheting or knitting or even doing the dishes that quiets the mind. St. Faustina used her handiwork as a way to integrate her faith into her menial work, In fact, she even had the audacity to ask Jesus to "grant the grace of conversion to as many souls as the [number of] stitches that I will make today with this crochet hook." While Jesus first said that her demand was "too great," He soon agreed that since St. Faustina couldn't do greater penances because her spiritual advisor forbade them, her "mere nothings" would do for the conversion of souls. When we keep our hearts still and our hands busy, we, too, can help convert souls.

### *Prayer*

Lord, accept the "mere nothings" of my life as a sacrifice for the conversion of souls.

Jesus, have mercy on us and on the whole world.

# *October 13*

## A CROWN OF CROWNS

I saw that God himself seemed to be opposing [him], and I asked the Lord why He was acting in this way toward him, as though He were placing obstacles in the way of his doing what He himself had asked him to do. And the Lord said, **I am acting thus with him to give testimony that this work is Mine. Tell him not to fear anything; My gaze is on him day and night. There will be as many crowns to form his crown as there will be souls saved by this work. It is not for the success of a work, but for the suffering that I give reward.** (*Diary*, 90)

### *Reflection*

Jesus values our faithfulness more than our success. He allows us to suffer in order to expand our trust in Him. Our suffering engages God's love. And He rewards us by showering grace on all of our concerns.

### *Prayer*

Blessed Sopocko, thank you for your perseverance and faithfulness in the work of promoting Divine Mercy. Intercede for me to complete my mission that the Lord is asking me to do.

Jesus, have mercy on us and on the whole world.

# October 14

## CONVERTED BY PRAYER AND SUFFERING

From the ciborium came a voice: **These hosts have been received by souls converted through your prayer and suffering.** (*Diary*, 709)

### Reflection

Through St. Faustina's prayer and suffering, souls were converted. This theme runs throughout St. Faustina's *Diary*. But what does conversion mean?

It means to change one's way of life—to forsake sin, selfishness, arrogance, pride—and to open ourselves to humility, love, and to never give up. Conversion has two elements: one whereby we are called to forsake sin; and another whereby we are called to open ourselves to love. None of us will be able to say "I love enough" or "I can't love more." This is conversion: to try and love more, to try and get to be fully aware of sin, to pray for the spirit of love, and to go forward. It requires hard work. Don't grow weary. Conversion lasts the whole of one's life. Our Lord understands this. St. Faustina wrote: "My sanctity and perfection consist in the close union of my will with the will of God. God never violates our free will. It is up to us whether we want to receive God's grace or not. It is up to us whether we will cooperate with it or waste it" (1107).

### Prayer

Dear Lord, give me the graces I am in most need of to do Your will. I don't want to waste any graces You give me.

Jesus, have mercy on us and on the whole world.

# *October 15*

## TO BE A SAINT — TAKE BABY STEPS

> **This firm resolution to become a saint is
> extremely pleasing to Me.** (*Diary*, 1361)

### *Reflection*

God's resolved to make you a saint. It seems impossible. Sin's always at our doorstep. But holiness isn't a mysterious spiritual state that only an elite few can reach. The call to holiness is for everyone. Jesus told St. Faustina: "Be watchful that you lose no opportunity that My providence offers you for sanctification. If you do not succeed in taking advantage of an opportunity, do not lose your peace, but humble yourself profoundly before Me and, with great trust, immerse yourself completely in My mercy" (1361). Follow God one step at a time. He'll bless your efforts. Growth in holiness doesn't happen by leaps and bounds but by baby steps.

### *Prayer*

Lord, teach me to humbly follow You one step at a time.

Jesus, have mercy on us and on the whole world.

# *October 16*

## NEVER GIVE UP

There are souls who thwart My efforts, but I have not given up on them; as often as they turn to Me, I hurry to their aid, shielding them with My Mercy, and I give them the first place in My compassionate Heart. (*Diary*, 1682)

## *Reflection*

Sometimes we give up on other people, writing them off as worthless or unsalvageable. Sometimes we even give up on ourselves, especially when we commit the same sin over and over. Jesus tells us that He never gives up on anyone. The moment we turn to Him, asking His aid and grace, He is instantly there. What a great gift to be able to start over at any moment! No matter what we have done, we have an unlimited number of second chances. All we have to do is ask.

## *Prayer*

My Lord, never let me forget that I can always have a fresh start in Your love. Jesus, have mercy on us and on the whole world.

# October 17

## DO NOT BE DISCOURAGED

Apostle of My mercy, proclaim to the whole world My unfathomable mercy. Do not be discouraged by the difficulties you encounter in proclaiming My mercy. These difficulties that affect you so painfully are needed for your sanctification and as evidence that this work is Mine. (*Diary*, 1142)

## Reflection

St. Faustina knew that bringing God's message of mercy to the world would come at a great personal price. But she was willing to pay it, because not only was it God's will that she do so, but she knew that, through affliction, her soul would be sanctified. Think about some of the toughest times in your life. Chances are, they probably also taught you some of the most important lessons that you needed to learn in order to grow spiritually. "No pain no gain" is a famous buzz phrase for physical fitness, but it is certainly applicable for spiritual growth as well.

## Prayer

Lord, let me always acknowledge that any suffering is for my ultimate good. Jesus, have mercy on us and on the whole world.

# *October 18*

## A POWERFUL LITTLE WORD

> **He who trusts in My mercy will not perish, for all his affairs are mine, and his enemies will be shattered at the base of My footstool.** (*Diary*, 723)

### *Reflection*

*Trust.* That one small word is used so consistently throughout St. Faustina's *Diary.* Jesus is letting her, and us, know that the road to eternal life is paved with trust in His unfailing mercy. He promises He will take care of everything else for us, so that we can stop living in a state of anxiety. Just trust Him. There are many things in this life that will let you down, but God never will. Remember, all your affairs are His.

### *Prayer*

Jesus, I trust in You, for You are all good and all-powerful. I have nothing to fear when I put my faith in You and You alone.

Jesus, have mercy on us and on the whole world.

# *October 19*

## ANGELS AT THE GATE

When I heard how dangerous it was to be at the gate these days … I went in and had a talk with the Lord and asked Him to so arrange it that no evil person would dare come to the gate. Then I heard these words: **My daughter, the moment you went to the gate I set a Cherub over it to guard it. Be at peace.** After returning from my conversation with the Lord, I saw a little white cloud and, in it, a Cherub with his hands joined…. (*Diary*, 1271)

### Reflection

St. Faustina prayed daily to her Guardian Angel. She had no doubt that he protected her and helped her in everyday life. She also wrote how he showed her purgatory. The angels play an important role in purgatory. They console the holy souls. They inspire friends and relatives to offer a Mass and practice good deeds for a speedy release. They inform the holy souls who are assisting them and to pray for those who help them. Her Guardian Angel asked her to pray the Chaplet for the dying and assisted her in spiritual battles.

Today, remember to thank the holy angels that God has sent into your life.

### Prayer

Holy Angels, ever watch over me, help guide my steps, protect my soul from the barbs of the evil one.

Jesus, have mercy on us and on the whole world.

# *October 20*

## SAVING SOULS

> **Know, my child, that Satan hates you; he hates every soul, but he burns with a particular hatred for you, because you have snatched so many souls from his dominion.** (*Diary*, 412)

### *Reflection*

St. Faustina was a mighty warrior for God. Living a consecrated life, dedicated to prayer and to making God's mercy known to the whole world, she dealt Satan one defeat after another. She snatched so many souls away from him, it is little wonder that he seethed with hatred toward her. In fact, the enemy's bitterness extends to all who tear down the kingdom of darkness and build up the Kingdom of God.

### *Prayer*

Dear Lord, give me the courage of St. Faustina. Help me to do my part to stand against evil and to promote Your great mercy to all souls. Especially those who need Your grace this very moment.

Have mercy on us and on the whole world.

# *October 21*

## BE ONE OF THE FEW

Although I was ill, I made up my mind to make a Holy Hour today as usual. During that hour, I saw the Lord Jesus being scourged at the pillar. In the midst of this frightful torture, Jesus was praying. After a while, He said to me, **There are few souls who contemplate My Passion with true feeling; I give great graces to souls who meditate devoutly on My Passion.** (*Diary*, 737)

## *Reflection*

To contemplate the terrible ordeal that Jesus underwent, leading to His death, is something we may instinctively want to avoid. It is heartbreaking to imagine how horribly He must have suffered. Yet, we are encouraged to be among the "few souls" to do so with "true feeling." This means we must do our best to try to empathize with the Lord in His ordeal. Only then, can we perhaps begin to, at least in some small measure, grasp the depth of His love for us.

## *Prayer*

Let me never forget, O Lord, that You were willing to undergo the most severe torture for the love of me. If I had a million ways to say "Thank you," it still would not be enough.

Jesus, have mercy on us and on the whole world.

# *October 22*

## CLOTHE US IN COURAGE

**Do not fear struggle; courage itself intimidates temptations, and they dare not attack us.** (*Diary*, 1760)

### *Reflection*

Temptation assails us and we experience inner struggles. We're weak and prone to consent to temptations daily. Calling upon Jesus, we find grace to wrestle with temptation courageously. Scripture encourages us: "Be strong and of good courage; be not frightened, neither be dismayed; for the Lord your God is with you wherever you go" (Josh 1:9). When we succumb to temptation, we feed a beast that intimidates us even more the next time the temptation returns. On the other hand, the more we starve our temptations, the more power we gain over them. With Christ-like courage, we'll be victorious in the battle against temptation. St. Faustina explains: "How often You have poured into my soul courage and perseverance to go forward. It is You Yourself who removed obstacles from my road, intervening directly in the actions of people" (1489). On our own we're weak and helpless to defeat our temptations. But when Jesus feeds us in the Holy Eucharist, we're clothed in courage.

### *Prayer*

Lord, when fear makes our knees tremble, wrap us in a love stronger than death. Make us brave and clothe us in courage. Amen.

Jesus, have mercy on us and on the whole world.

# *October 23*

## WHAT IS YOUR MOTIVE?

... the Lord gave me an understanding of God's incomprehensible love for people. He lifts us up to His very Godhead. His only motives are love and fathomless mercy... (*Diary*, 1172)

### *Reflection*

We always have a motive for the things we do. Sometimes we act out of good and uplifting motives—like when we donate to a good cause because we believe in the mission of the cause. But other times we act out of less honorable motives—like cutting someone off in traffic because we are running late. God's only motives are love and mercy. Think how amazing that is. God never does anything except for love or mercy. How would your life be different if everything you did was based on God's motives? How would the world be changed if everyone did that?

### *Prayer*

Jesus, give me the courage to examine the motives for my behavior.

Jesus, have mercy on us and on the whole world.

# *October 24*

## LET GO AND LET GOD

> **Why are you afraid? Do you think that I will not have enough omnipotence to support you?** (*Diary*, 527)

### *Reflection*

God can do anything. He's all-powerful. But our loving God does only what's best for us. When we block God from our lives, we foolishly trust in our own "strengths" instead of relying on His omnipotence. But whatever strengths we have come from Him. So, in our weaknesses, Jesus teaches us to rely totally on Him. St. Faustina says: "As the soul continues to immerse itself more deeply into the abyss of its nothingness and need, God uses His omnipotence to exalt it" (593). Opening our hearts to him, God "is able to accomplish abundantly far more than all we can ask or imagine" (Eph 3:20). Think of Joshua. At the walls of Jericho, he stood helpless until he learned to trust the Lord's battle plan. Or consider the disciples trying to feed the five thousand; all remained hungry until they brought Jesus the five loaves and two fishes. Once we rely on our all-powerful God, His power is unleashed in our lives—things change.

### *Prayer*

"For the sake of His sorrowful Passion, show us Your mercy, that we may praise the omnipotence of Your mercy forever and ever. Amen" (1211).

Jesus, have mercy on us and on the whole world.

# *October 25*

## STRENGTHEN THEIR HEARTS

Once when I was having a long talk with Jesus about our student, encouraged by His kindness, I asked Him, "Do You have among our students any who are a comfort to Your Heart?" The Lord answered [that] He has, **but their love is weak, and so I put them in your special care—pray for them.** (*Diary*, 288)

## *Reflection*

"Carpe diem!" That's the world's motto—"Seize the day!" Being virtuous today isn't easy—especially for youth, because the world's mindset says, "Living large" and "Follow your own conscience." The secular worldview is immoral and unchristian—"You're only young once." But St. Paul exhorts young people to be an example "in speech and conduct, in love, in faith, in purity" (1 Tim 4:12). St. Faustina learned that her students were precious to Jesus—a comfort to His Heart. Assaulted by temptations, youth struggle to follow Him. To help St. Faustina understand, Christ let her experience a student's temptation—suicidal thoughts. She wrote: "For seven days I suffered; and after the seven days Jesus granted her [the student] the grace which was being asked ..." (192). Join with St. Faustina. Let us have special care for our young people.

## *Prayer*

Lord, fill our youth will love for You and strengthen their hearts.

Jesus, have mercy on us and on the whole world.

# *October 26*

## I AM YOURS

> **Now you shall consider My love in the Blessed Sacrament. Here, I am entirely yours, soul, body and divinity, as your Bridegroom....** (*Diary*, 1770)

### *Reflection*

There is a reason why Adoration of the Blessed Sacrament is such an important and beautiful time. It gives us an ideal opportunity to reflect on just how closely Jesus wants to unite with us and to tell us in no uncertain terms how much He loves us. He remains mysteriously in our midst as the one who loved us and gave Himself up for us. Our response? To love Him back! He patiently waited for St. Faustina. And she immersed herself in the fire of His love and the abyss of His mercy. Our Lord in the Blessed Sacrament waits for you! He wants to transform you and the world. God gives all of Himself to us, and the Blessed Sacrament helps us to further the lifelong and ultimately eternal process of giving ourselves, fully and with a joyful heart, right back to Him.

### *Prayer*

Jesus in the Most Blessed Sacrament, I praise You, I thank You, I adore You. Jesus, have mercy on us and on the whole world.

# *October 27*

## LIMITS VS. NO LIMITS

Listen ... although all the works that come into being by My will are exposed to great sufferings, consider whether any of them has been subject to greater difficulties than that work which is directly Mine—the work of Redemption. You should not worry too much about adversities. The world is not as powerful as it seems to be; its strength is strictly limited. (*Diary*, 1643)

### *Reflection*

"The world is not as powerful as it seems to be; its strength is strictly limited." Could there be any more encouraging words—especially when it feels like the pressures of life are just too much to bear? God assures us that what He has endured for us on the Cross was far more severe, so we must put it all into perspective. The world's power is "strictly limited," while the power of God is infinite. The power of His divine love can never fail, it triumphs over all of our suffering.

### *Prayer*

You are there for me, Lord, stronger than all adversity. Let me feel Your power. Jesus, have mercy on us and on the whole world.

# *October 28*

## JUSTICE AND GOODNESS

**Even the devils glorify My Justice but do not believe in My Goodness.** (*Diary*, 300)

## *Reflection*

Isn't it interesting that even the devils know and understand God's justice, but they don't believe in God's goodness? Ironically, many people are more inclined to believe in God's goodness than they are in His justice. They figure they can skate on into heaven no matter what they have done because God is good and merciful. The reality is that God is both good and merciful as well as just. That is hard for us to understand because all too often in this life, mercy and goodness are at odds with justice.

## *Prayer*

My God, I know You are just, but I trust in Your mercy.

Jesus, have mercy on us and on the whole world.

# *October 29*

**For you I descended from heaven to earth; for you I allowed myself to be nailed to the cross; for you I let my Sacred Heart be pierced with a lance, thus opening wide the source of mercy for you. Come, then, with trust to draw graces from this fountain ...** (*Diary*, 1485)

## *Reflection*

Jesus invites us to receive the graces flowing from His pierced side. To grasp God's grace, we must be first willing to let go of our little treasures. Like a man sinking in the ocean, tightly grasping bars of gold in his fists. He must first lose these, before he's free to swim towards a lifeboat and obtain the greater gift—life. While he fears financial loss, wisdom teaches him to treasure his own life more. Servant of God Father John Hardon, S.J., once said that "pain is the proof of love, pain is the price of love. That's why God became Man: that He might be able to endure pain, especially pouring of His Blood out of love for us." A price paid in pain and in love.

## *Prayer*

Blood of Christ, save us.

Jesus, have mercy on us and on the whole world.

# *October 30*

> **Oh, if only souls knew how to gather eternal treasure
> for themselves, they would not be judged, for they would
> forestall My judgment with their mercy.** (*Diary*, 1317)

## *Reflection*

How can we be sure that we will not be judged harshly for our sins? Jesus
gave St. Faustina the answer when He said that the key is to "gather eternal
treasure." What He means is that rather than striving to obtain material possessions and to live "the good life," we should focus our attention on acts of
charity, prayer, forgiveness ... the things that rust cannot tarnish and time
cannot destroy. If we do so, Jesus promises that we will not be judged and that
His mercy will forestall His judgment.

## *Prayer*

My Lord, show me what You would have me do today to "gather eternal
treasure." Do not let the things of the world lure me away from You.

Jesus, have mercy on us and on the whole world.

# *October 31*

## THE FATHER'S LOVE

When I entered the chapel, once again the majesty of God overwhelmed me. I felt that I was immersed in God, totally immersed in Him and penetrated by Him, being aware of how much the heavenly Father loves us. Oh, what great happiness fills my heart from knowing God and the divine life! It is my desire to share this happiness with all people. (*Diary*, 491)

## *Reflection*

What force in heaven or earth is more potent than the Father's love for us? His love moves mountains, calms the roaring sea, heals wounded hearts, and liberates those in the shackles of sin. We see the depths of God's love in the life of Jonah. After Jonah sinned, he hid from God—even in the belly of the whale. Because of the shame of sin, He believed that God had no more love for him. There in the depths, the Father's love touched him. There's nowhere we can hide from God because His love pursues us always. We're wrapped in His love. Oh, the depth of the Father's love!

## *Prayer*

Eternal Father, from the depths of my heart, fill me with Your love.

Jesus, have mercy on us and on the whole world.

CHAPTER ELEVEN

Reflections
FOR
*November*

# November 1

## BECOMING A SAINT FOR OUR TIME

**You are that saint.** (*Diary*, 1650)

### Reflection

We're called to be saints. We say, "Impossible!" Reading the lives of the saints, we think, "I can't do that!" We're overwhelmed at the thought of imitating holiness. One asks, "How can I live the poverty of St. Francis or sacrifice my life like St. Maximilian Kolbe at Auschwitz?" There's good news! You don't ever have to be someone else. God doesn't want that. Sanctity's goal is living the virtuous life—the life of grace—in our own skin. We strive for holiness in our own circumstances one day at a time. It simply begins with humility. Jesus said to St. Faustina: "You are that saint." He says that to us too. He's calling us to holiness. We start fresh each day with acts of faith, hope, and charity done in humility. Each day we've got spiritual homework. We're enrolled in the school of sanctity and, as EWTN foundress Mother Angelica once remarked: "Where most men work for degrees after their names, we work for one before our names: 'St.' It's a much more difficult degree to attain. It takes a lifetime, and you don't get your diploma until you're dead."

### Prayer

Make me holy as You are holy.

Jesus, have mercy on us and on the whole world.

# November 2

## THEY NEED YOU!

> The Lord said to me, **Enter into purgatory often, because they need you there.** (*Diary*, 1738)

## *Reflection*

The souls in purgatory, "the masterpiece of God's mercy," have already learned a truly invaluable lesson: how interdependent we all are upon one another. God in His wisdom has set things up this way; that those who are seeking their final purification will ultimately achieve it through the prayerful intercession of others. Just as we help one another on this earth, it is of utmost importance to enter into purgatory for those who desperately need the offering of our Masses. They can no longer earn any merit on their own; they are helpless. They are entirely dependent on our prayers, but they can intercede for us while they are in purgatory, making it a win-win situation!

## *Prayer*

Today, I pray for that soul in purgatory most in need of Your mercy. May Your mercy, O Lord, rest upon them!

Jesus, have mercy on us and on the whole world.

# November 3
## GREEDY FOR GRACE

**Draw all the indulgences from the treasury of My Church and offer them on their behalf. Oh, if you only knew the torments they suffer, you would continually offer for them the alms of the spirit and pay off their debt to My justice.** (*Diary*, 1226)

## Reflection

Why do we have indulgences? Their purpose is to make up for penances omitted, poorly done, or too light in comparison with the enormity of the sins. Venerable Fulton J. Sheen explained: "It is like a nail in a board. Once you remove the nail—the sin—with Confession, the hole which is the punishment remains to be filled by penance and reparation." Indulgences arise from the mercy of Jesus; with them we can satisfy our debts and the debts of the holy souls. They are an aid for growth toward spiritual perfection, inner change, or a deeper conversion of heart. We can do this "repair work" here on earth or in purgatory. By going to Confession regularly, we can gain many plenary indulgences for the holy souls, healing all the effects of their sins.

## Prayer

Dear Lord, light a spark of love in my soul on behalf of the souls in purgatory. Jesus, have mercy on us and on the whole world.

# *November 4*

## PURGATORY — THE MASTERPIECE
## OF GOD'S MERCY

**You are guilty of one day of fire in purgatory.** (*Diary*, 36)

### *Reflection*

When Jesus permitted St. Faustina to see her soul through His eyes, she remarked, "I could clearly see all that is displeasing to God. I did not know that even the smallest transgressions will have to be accounted for" (36). "Life is like a cash register, in that every account, every thought, every deed, like every sale, is registered and recorded," said Venerable Fulton J. Sheen. Our lives aren't all bad, because we perform many good deeds too. But, in all honesty, we've got some work to do, because we struggle with sin daily. When Christ told Faustina she needed deeper purification, He asked her, "Which do you prefer, suffer now for one day in purgatory or for a short while on earth?" Because she deeply loved Christ, she asked for both. But Jesus said: "One [of the two] is enough; you will go back to earth, and there you will suffer much, but not for long; you will accomplish My will and My desires...." The Lord is purifying us for His Kingdom. Remember, this is not punishment but a purification. Jesus tells us, "[D]on't let this frighten you; I am with you" (36).

### *Prayer*

Purify me, Lord, of all that's displeasing to You.

Jesus, have mercy on us and on the whole world.

# *November 5*

## HOLY PRISONERS

**Today bring to Me the souls who are in the prison of Purgatory, and immerse them in the abyss of My mercy. Let the torrents of My Blood cool down their scorching flames. All these souls are greatly loved by Me. They are making retribution to My justice. It is in your power to bring them relief.** (*Diary*, 1226)

### *Reflection*

We need purification and healing because of our sin and selfishness. Purgatory exists because of God's love and His incomprehensible holiness. It is God's love that cleanses and purifies us to be able to stand before His presence. Pope Francis imagined that someone might say to him, "But, Father, I do not have any [faults]!" To which he would respond: "Ah, congratulations! I assure you that if you do not realize here that you have them, you will find them in purgatory! Better to see them here." (March 3, 2019, homily, Rome, Italy.)

### *Prayer*

"Oh, my God, allow my sinful soul the contact of your infinite purity" (*St. Gertrude*).

Jesus, have mercy on us and on the whole world.

# *November 6*

## CHEERING US ON

> **Know that you are on a great stage where all heaven
> and earth are watching you.** (*Diary*, 1760)

### *Reflection*

Shakespeare said, "All the world's a stage." If that's true, the actors are in a mad dash called the "race of life." As we run, we grow weary. Those running ahead finish first. Their success gives us courage. My finish line is marked at a different place than yours because the finish line is the moment of one's own death. As we run, the saints stand on the sidelines to cheer us on. They encourage us to trust in God and to persevere, so that life's obstacles don't overcome us. When each of us crosses the finish line at the end of the race, may we say with the saints: "I have fought the good fight, I have finished the race, I have kept the faith" (2 Tim 4:7).

### *Prayer*

Lord, may I faithfully run life's race, as the saints cheer me on!
Jesus, have mercy on us and on the whole world.

# *November 7*

## OVERCOMING EVIL WITH GOOD

**If someone causes you trouble, think what good you can do for the person who caused you to suffer.** (*Diary*, 1760)

## *Reflection*

Jesus desires that we live in peace. Jesus encouraged St. Faustina to do good to those who caused her to suffer. Christ told her she should not be concerned with the actions of others, but instead, she should be a reflection of His love and mercy. Faustina wasn't so sure about this and said that people take advantage of her goodness. Jesus lovingly answered her: "That is no concern of yours. As for you, be always merciful toward other people, and especially toward sinners" (1446). Jesus doesn't want us to worry about getting even with those who cause us trouble. Rather, He wants to teach us how to be a reflection of His loving-kindness: "Do not be overcome by evil, but overcome evil with good" (Rom 12:21).

## *Prayer*

My sweet Lord, You have taught us to love our enemies and to do good to them, expecting nothing in return. Grant that when someone causes me to suffer, I may think what good I can do for them in return.

Jesus, have mercy on us and on the whole world.

# *November 8*

## FASTING FOR THE HOLY SOULS IN PURGATORY

> This evening, one of the deceased sisters came and asked me for one day of fasting and to offer all my [spiritual] exercises on that day for her. I answered that I would. (*Diary*, 1185)

### *Reflection*

What good does fasting do? While fasting is a traditional means to conversion, it does more than that. It can eliminate excesses so that we have more time for God. It can help us develop self-control, which is one of the gifts of the Holy Spirit. It helps us recognize our weakness and dependence on God. But it has another benefit. Fasting can help free the souls in purgatory. The sister who asked for a day of fasting was in purgatory. St. Faustina had a brief experience of her torment. She said: "I experienced such an intense hunger for God that I seemed to be dying of the desire to become united with Him ... I understood what the longing of the souls in purgatory was like" (1186). The souls long for God. This is their greatest suffering. They desperately need our fasting.

### *Prayer*

Dear Lord, thank you for this way for me to move closer to You today as You gently transform my heart, my mind and my soul through the small sacrifices I make.

Jesus, have mercy on us and on the whole world.

# *November 9*
## PRUDENCE

**Do not pour out your feelings.** (*Diary*, 1760)

## *Reflection*

"A moment on the lips, a lifetime on the hips!" That's the dieter's motto.
The motto of those who pour out their feelings haphazardly is: "A moment of
telling brings a lifetime of regretting!" Be prudent when you open your heart,
lest someone betray your confidence. Talking to a gossiper, you feed a beast.
In an age of talk-shows, reality TV, and social media, where people foolishly
chatter, Catholics have an advantage — the sacrament of Confession. Under
the sacramental seal, we can safely pour out our hearts before the Lord. We tell
our sins, unveil our emotional fragility, and experience Christ's healing touch.

## *Prayer*

Lord, make me prudent in speech with my neighbor, and let me pour out my
heart to You who loves me with an indescribable love.

Jesus, have mercy on us and on the whole world.

# *November 10*

## MARKED BY THE CROSS

**My daughter, try your best to make the Stations of the Cross in this hour, provided that your duties permit it.** (*Diary*, 1572)

## *Reflection*

The Stations of the Cross was Faustina's favorite daily devotion and powerful for the holy souls. Praying the Stations of the Cross greatly pleased Jesus. St. Leonard of Port Maurice also loved this devotion and was known as the Preacher of the Way of the Cross. He wrote: "What salutary insights will the continual meditation on the bitter passion of the Son of God stir up on the soul! Daily experience has taught me that by this devout form of prayer men's lives are quickly changed for the better. For the antidote for vice, the cleansing of unbridled desires, and an effective incentive to virtue and holiness of life. If we set the excruciating sufferings of the Son of God portrayed in so many vivid pictures before the eyes of the soul we can hardly refrain from abhorring the defilements of our own life because of the abundant light that fills our souls. Nay, I should rather say that we will be urged to repay such great love with our own love or at least to bear willingly the misfortunes that from time to time in every walk of life fall to our lot" (*St. Leonard of Port Maurice in Proper Offices of Franciscan Saints, IV, 197*).

## *Prayer*

Lord, You are the Alpha and the Omega. In Your mercy we were created, and it is by Your mercy we are redeemed.

Jesus, have mercy on us and on the whole world.

# *November 11*

## PURE IN HEART

I saw my Guardian Angel, who ordered me to follow him.
In a moment I was in a misty place full of fire in which
there was a great crowd of suffering souls. (*Diary*, 20)

## *Reflection*

When his wife died, C.S. Lewis remarked how his beloved was "a splendid thing, a soul straight, bright, and tempered like a sword. But not a perfect saint ... I know there are not only tears to be dried, but stains to be scoured. The sword will be made even brighter ... But O God, tenderly, tenderly." Souls in purgatory are on the way to heaven. But just as a bride won't process down the aisle with a stained dress, souls won't dare enter heaven's gates until perfect. Bridal attendants prepare the bride: so, too, we help suffering souls through the prayers, sacrifices, and Masses we offer for them. Purgatory is a place where God prepares his unprepared children to be able to stand before His presence. It's *not* a punishment. It's the place where mercy and justice meet. More than we can imagine, the holy souls long to be cleansed of every stain because the pure in heart shall see God.

## *Prayer*

Eternal rest grant unto them, O Lord, and let perpetual light shine upon them. Amen.

Jesus, have mercy on us and on the whole world.

# *November 12*

## NO GUARDS AT THE DOOR

> **I am not surrounded by a retinue or guards. You can
> come to me at any moment, at any time; I want to speak
> to you and desire to grant you grace.** (*Diary*, 1485)

### *Reflection*

Unlike earthly rulers, God is not surrounded by guards. He doesn't have a
divine appointment secretary. You don't need an appointment to speak to
Him. The King of kings is waiting. Jesus wants to speak to *you*! What are
you waiting for?

### *Prayer*

Lord, speak to me.

Jesus, have mercy on us and on the whole world.

# November 13
## GOD'S EXPECTATION

**I expect from you, My child, a great number of souls who will glorify My mercy for all eternity.** (*Diary*, 1489)

### Reflection

What does God expect from us? We can all list a dozen or more things, but one might surprise you. He expects each of us to bring souls to Him. As Jesus tells His disciples: "The harvest is plentiful but the workers are few" (Mt 9:37). He expects each of us to be a worker in the harvest.

### Prayer

Show me, Lord, those souls who are prepared to listen to Your message of mercy and grant me the courage to tell them about it.

Jesus, have mercy on us and on the whole world.

# *November 14*

## SOLACE IN MY DYING HOUR

> **I am giving you a share in the redemption of mankind.**
> **You are solace in My dying hour.** (*Diary*, 310)

### *Reflection*

What does Jesus mean when He says that St. Faustina was "solace" in his dying hour? What does that have to do with us? Theologians can argue about it for centuries. For St. Faustina, perhaps it was quite simple. Her numerous hours praying before the crucifix were a loving meditation on the Divine Passion. As you would console a friend who is in pain, it was her presence, her "being there with the Lord" that gave Him solace. We can do the same thing. Hang a crucifix somewhere in your home and, each time you pass, say a silent prayer of thanksgiving for Jesus' love and great sacrifice. We share in Christ's redemption when we give our "yes" to Him.

### *Prayer*

My suffering Jesus, as I see how You are much offended by sin, I contemplate Your love and mercy that You showed sinners on the Cross.

Jesus, have mercy on us and on the whole world.

# *November 15*

## PRAY, PRAY, AND PRAY SOME MORE

> Say the Chaplet. (714) Make a novena, recite the
> Litany of Saints. (59) Through your prayers, you
> shall mediate between heaven and earth. (438)

### *Reflection*

The Catechism of the Catholic Church says: "Prayer is the raising of one's mind and heart to God or the requesting of good things from God" (CCC 2559). Prayer is our salvation. It opens the key to God's Heart. Without prayer, we are lost. But what kind of prayer did Jesus want? Jesus gave St. Faustina specific prayers and novenas to pray: Our Lord expressed his desire for St. Faustina to offer a Novena of Masses. The highest act of prayer is the Mass. She prayed the daily Rosary, is the most powerful Marian prayer on earth. In a special way, he told her say the Chaplet "unceasingly." To pray the Litany of Saints. To offer her adoration for special intentions. Jesus directed St. Faustina to meditate on His Passion. He gave her a conversion prayer. St. Faustina even made her work a prayer. "O Most Holy Trinity dwelling in my heart, I beg You: grant the grace of conversion to as many souls as the [number of] stitches that I will make today with this crochet hook" (961). She became a powerful mediator between heaven and earth. He is asking us to do the same.

### *Prayer*

Jesus, make me faithful in prayer. Without it I lose the meaning of life.

Jesus, have mercy on us and on the whole world.

# November 16

Know, My daughter, that you caused Me more sorrow by not uniting yourself with Me in Holy Communion than you did by that small transgression. (*Diary*, 612)

## Reflection

One time St. Faustina was worried that she might have seriously offended Jesus, so she refrained from receiving Communion before going to Confession, even though she had made an act of contrition at the time. When she no longer felt God's presence, she assumed it was punishment for her sin. When she was confessing, her confessor told her that her sin was not an obstacle to receiving Holy Communion. Later, Jesus Himself said the same thing. Remember the only thing that bars you from Communion is mortal sin. Receive Holy Communion as often as you can. It's the key to holiness.

## Prayer

God, do not let my scruples about sin prevent me from being united with You. Help me to understand when Confession before Communion is needed.

Jesus, have mercy on us and on the whole world.

# *November 17*

## LOVE COMPENSATES FOR COLDNESS

When I received Him into my heart, the veil of faith was torn away. I saw Jesus who said to me, **My daughter, your love compensates Me for the coldness of many souls.** (*Diary*, 1816)

### *Reflection*

It is said that it takes more muscles to frown than it does to smile. While scientists can't agree on the exact number, they do agree that a smile is easier to make than a frown. And they agree that the muscles we use to smile are stronger than the muscles we use to frown. The same is true for love. Jesus told Faustina that her love, and her love alone, could compensate for the coldness of many souls. So love … and smile … as much as you can!

### *Prayer*

Lord, I love You. The thought of You brings a smile to my face and song to my heart.

Jesus, have mercy on us and on the whole world.

# *November 18*

## WE ALL CAN BE SAINTS

**The greatest sinners would achieve great sanctity,
if only they would trust in My mercy.** (*Diary*, 1784)

## *Reflection*

The difference between a saint and a sinner is not as vast as we might think. Yes, sinners do harmful and evil things, and saints do holy and blessed things, but the real difference is that saints have learned to trust in God's mercy. Some of the greatest sinners, once they have truly understood what it means to be under the mercy of God, have become our greatest saints. There's an old saying about a man falling off a horse to his death: "Twix the saddle and the ground, mercy sought and mercy found." Don't wait until you are falling off the horse before seeking God's mercy.

## *Prayer*

My Lord, I trust in You. Help me to overcome my sinful nature and find sanctity in Your mercy.

Jesus, have mercy on us and on the whole world.

# *November 19*

## CONVERSION

Conversion The Lord said to me, **The loss of each soul plunges Me into mortal sadness. You always console Me when you pray for sinners.** (*Diary*, 1397)

### *Reflection*

Did you know that the most calls that EWTN Global Catholic Network gets for prayer "worldwide" are prayers for conversion? (Not health or finances.) Conversions of families, of friends. And children calling in for the conversion of their parents! Catholic Radio and pastors have shared the same response. How many times do you pray for the conversion of sinners? Remember these prayers always console the Heart of Jesus.

### *Prayer*

O my Jesus, lead all souls to heaven, especially those who are in most need of Your mercy today.

Jesus, have mercy on us and on the whole world.

# *November 20*

## ADMIT IT — YOU SOMETIMES PUT OFF CONFESSION

**Daughter, every time you go to confession, immerse yourself entirely in My mercy, with great trust, so that I may pour the bounty of My grace upon your soul. When you go to confession, to this fountain of My mercy, the Blood and Water which came forth from My Heart always flows down upon your soul and ennobles it.** (*Diary*, 1602).

## *Reflection*

Jesus call the sacrament of Reconciliation the "fountain of mercy." The key to opening this fountain of mercy is incredibly simple: go regularly to Confession. It sounds too easy, but that's really all it takes. No secrets. No hard labor. Jesus understands that it isn't easy to go to Confession. We don't like to admit our faults. It's hard to acknowledge our failures and sins. We can feel ashamed, embarrassed, or even unworthy of God's mercy. If you find yourself staying away from Confession, remember that Confession isn't a punishment; it's a grace. Be humble and trust Him. It's the way that we experience the unlimited mercy of God. Confess your sins and rest in God's forgiveness for your sake, and the sake of the entire world.

## *Prayer*

Dear Jesus, I am sorry for all the times I have failed to take advantage of the grace of Confession.

Jesus, have mercy on us and on the whole world.

# *November 21*
## ETERNAL LIVES

**Pray as much as you can for the dying.** (*Diary*, 1777)

## *Reflection*

Praying the Chaplet for the dying is constantly repeated throughout the *Diary*. Obviously, this is important to Jesus. We have this great honor to play a role in changing ... eternal ... lives.

## *Prayer for a Happy Death by St. John Henry Newman*

O my Lord and Savior, support me in my last hour by the strong arms of Your sacraments and the fragrance of Your consolations. Let Your absolving words be said over me, and the holy oil sign and seal me. Let Your own body be my food and Your blood my sprinkling. Let my Mother Mary come to me, and my angel whisper peace to me, and Your glorious saints and my own dear patrons smile on me; that, in and through them all, I may die as I desire to live, in Your Church, in Your faith, and in Your love. Amen.

Jesus, have mercy on us and on the whole world.

# *November 22*

## PREPARED BY JOY

When Jesus came, I threw myself into His arms like a little child. I told Him of my joy... When I asked pardon of Jesus for not preparing myself for Holy Communion, but for continually thinking of sharing in this joy as soon as possible, He answered that **Most pleasing to Me is this preparation with which you have received Me into your heart**. (*Diary*, 1824)

### *Reflection*

St. Maximilian Kolbe once said, "If angels could be jealous of men, they would be so for one reason: Holy Communion." Receiving the Body, Blood, Soul, and Divinity of Jesus Christ in Holy Communion, our hearts should be filled with joy. There's no greater gift we can receive. St. Faustina remarked: "All the good that is in me is due to Holy Communion. I owe everything to it. I feel that this holy fire has transformed me completely" (1392). When we approach Holy Communion with special devotion, we experience "how great is the value of communing with Christ ... for there is nothing more effective for advancing on the road to holiness" (St. Paul VI, *Mysterium Fidei*, September 1965). Never take preparation for Holy Communion lightly, for it is far more important than you may have ever realized.

### *Prayer*

Lord Jesus, I would like to receive You with the same joy and purity of Our Lady, the zeal of the saints, the love of the angels, and the same fervor of the holy souls in purgatory if they could return.

Jesus, have mercy on us and on the whole world.

# *November 23*

## HELPING HAND

On one occasion, after a person had asked me for prayer, when I met the Lord I said to Him, "Jesus, I especially love those souls whom You love." And Jesus answered, **And as for Me, I bestow special graces on those souls for whom you intercede.** (*Diary*, 599)

## *Reflection*

Think you can't make a difference in the lives of others? Try praying for them! Jesus told St. Faustina that we are all a part of one body as the Church has always taught. Faustina faithfully interceded for souls by praying the Rosary, the Chaplet of Divine Mercy, novenas, and litanies. She also interceded for the lost through her fasting and suffering. She demonstrated the power of intercession when she prayed for her younger sister Wanda, claiming that her constant prayer "forced" God to grant her sister grace. "Now I can see how much power intercessory prayer has before God" (202).

## *Prayer*

Heavenly Father, show me at least one person today who is in need of my prayers.

Jesus, have mercy on us and on the whole world.

# *November 24*

## A MERCIFUL DEATH

**With souls that have recourse to My mercy and with those that glorify and proclaim My great mercy to others, I will deal according to My infinite mercy at the hour of their death.** (*Diary*, 379)

## *Reflection*

We don't like thinking about death. Our sins make us reluctant to go to Confession. Frozen by fear, we imagine our sins too great to be forgiven. However, we ought to have confidence in our recourse to the Mercy of God. "One thing alone is necessary; that the sinner set ajar the door of his heart, be it ever so little, to let in a ray of God's merciful grace, and then God will do the rest" (1507). The Divine Physician heals us of our sins and saves us from the power of hell. St. Faustina proclaims God's mercy, reminding us that "even if a person's sins were as dark as night God's mercy is stronger than our misery" (1507). When we proclaim God's mercy we have nothing to fear at the hour of death.

## *Prayer*

My sweet Jesus, grant me the grace of a humble and contrite heart at the hour of my death so that I might approach Your throne at the hour of my judgment bathed in the ocean of your unfathomable Mercy.

Jesus, have mercy on us and on the whole world.

# *November 25*
## SPIRITUAL EYES

They were praying fervently, but to no avail, for themselves;
only we can come to their aid ... **My mercy does not
want this, but justice demands it.** (*Diary*, 20)

## *Reflection*

For a long time now in the modern Church, many people seem to have forgotten about the suffering souls in purgatory. God forbid! Purgatory exists because of God's love and His incomprehensible holiness. We need purification and healing because of our sin and selfishness. It is God's love that cleanses and purifies us to be able to stand before His presence. God's justice demands it. These people desperately need our assistance. Only we have the power and privilege to assist and deliver them through our Mass, Rosary, and Stations of the Cross. And we gain powerful intercessors when we do! If you saw someone suffering right before your physical eyes, surely you would come to their aid. Today, see the suffering souls in purgatory through spiritual eyes. Let us, therefore, pray for the holy souls and ourselves.

## *Prayer*

Lord, I beg You on behalf of the suffering souls in purgatory, speed their time of purification through our intercession and graciously show them the unspeakable beauty of the Beatific Vision. May they rest in peace. Amen.

Jesus, have mercy on us and on the whole world.

# *November 26*

## SPIRITUAL GIANTS

I remained in prayer for a whole hour and united myself in spirit with those souls who are already worshipping God in the perfect way. But toward the end of the hour, I suddenly saw Jesus, who looked at me penetratingly and said with ineffable sweetness, **Your prayer is extremely pleasing to Me.** (*Diary*, 691)

### *Reflection*

Those worshipping God "in the perfect way" would be Our Lady and all of God's saints. When we engage with the adoration of the saints, "a cloud of witnesses" (Heb 12:1) join us, intercede for us and brings us so much closer to God Himself. Our Lady offers our prayers to Jesus. She embellishes them. She knows how to make gold out of our dross. She supplies that which they lack, making them "extremely pleasing" to Jesus. It is like we are apprentices, and they are the pros. So, learn from the best! As you commune with God, you will be doing so in great company.

### *Prayer*

Lord, through the communion of saints, may I humble myself before spiritual giants, learning the way of holiness and uniting with them in worshipping You more completely.

Jesus, have mercy on us and on the whole world.

# *November 27*

## FOR ALL SOULS WHO DIE TODAY

And the Lord looked at me with love and said,
**And what is it that you desire to tell Me?**
"Jesus, I beg You, by the inconceivable power of Your mercy, that all the souls who will die today escape the fire of hell, even if they have been the greatest sinners. Today is Friday, the memorial of Your bitter agony on the Cross; because Your mercy is inconceivable, the Angels will not be surprised at this." Jesus pressed me to His Heart and said, **My beloved daughter, you have come to know well the depths of My Mercy. I will do what you ask, but unite yourself continually with My agonizing Heart and make reparation to My justice.** (*Diary*, 873)

### Reflection

We should never be satisfied with just our own salvation—what about everyone else? Our prayers must not be focused just on ourselves, but, like St. Faustina, we should pray that all people, especially those in greatest need, turn to the Lord. We should offer our own suffering to Him for the benefit of others. Praying the Divine Mercy Chaplet is a powerful way to make reparation to His justice. Jesus never wants to lose a soul.

### Prayer

Jesus, unite my suffering to Yours, in reparation for my sins and that of all mankind.

Jesus, have mercy on us and on the whole world.

# *November 28*
## SUFFERING RESCUES SOULS

Today the Lord said to me, **I have need of your suffering to rescue souls**. (*Diary*, 1612)

### *Reflection*

Do we love others enough to be willing to suffer for their redemption as well? How does Jesus make use of our suffering? He uses it, in fact, to help rescue souls! One way is by using suffering to draw us closer to Him. We oftentimes only come to the Lord when we are in great need. He humbles us through suffering so that we learn to understand that we are powerless without Him. When we acknowledge that profound truth, and join our suffering to His, others take notice, which can lead to their salvation as well. Faustina adds that if we only knew how we are loved by God when we are suffering, we would die of joy and excess of happiness!

### *Prayer*

Lord, help me to willingly join my sorrows to Yours and those of Your Blessed Mother.

Jesus, have mercy on us and on the whole world.

# *November 29*

## ALL IS NOT YET LOST

O soul steeped in darkness, do not despair. All is not yet lost. Come and confide in your God, who is love and mercy. (*Diary*, 1486)

### *Reflection*

When we despair, our world shrinks, we see few choices, and the choices we see we don't believe will help. There are times when we have to acknowledge that life is bleak. We know that if this despair continues, we will lose all hope. But if we share our despair with another, life becomes more tolerable. That can make us feel more hopeful. All is not lost. With Jesus, who is our hope, our world expands.

### *Prayer*

Lord, in moments when I feel steeped in darkness, remind me of Your words, "All is not yet lost."

Jesus, have mercy on us and on the whole world.

# *November 30*

## MEETING THE LORD FACE TO FACE

Oh, what happens to a soul that meets the Lord face to face,
no pen has ever expressed or ever will express! (*Diary*, 691)

## *Reflection*

St. Faustina had visions of heaven. "Today I was in heaven in spirit, and I saw its inconceivable beauties and the happiness that awaits us" (777). In Michael Brown's book *The Other Side*, people who have had near death experiences share this: "I am a very visual person, being an artist, yet there was nothing visual, just the sense of leaving my body ... as I was rising I felt the most peaceful, joyful, loving fatherly Presence, which to this day is impossible for me to describe or explain." Another woman adds: "When I first saw Him the light and the glory and the surging of power was so tremendous.... I just don't feel that I have found a way to describe what it was like—an indescribable contentment and uplifting, a tremendous ecstasy of feeling on all realms ... an unusually vivid knowledge of the intense, sympathetic love around you—the warmth of it, the light of it—something that not external but is *part of you*." "Everything there was full of life. Something drew my eyes to the light ... and there was Christ. He was full of light and his hands were out to receive me. He *was* light. His arms were outstretched and I knew I was home and I was ecstatic!"

## *Prayer*

Jesus, I look forward to coming home!

Jesus, have mercy on us and on the whole world.

# CHAPTER TWELVE

# Reflections

FOR

*December*

# December 1

## JOY IS OUR REWARD

> **May your heart be joyful.** (*Diary*, 415)

### *Reflection*

Joy is essential to the spiritual life. St. Francis de Sales said: "A sad saint would be a sorry saint." To carry our crosses all the way to heaven's door, we need joy—it's a fruit of the Holy Spirit. Earthly happiness is an emotional roller-coaster with its ups and downs. But Christian joy is a rock. It's the joy of calling God *Abba*, "Father." When Christ's joy fills our hearts, we're formed by it. It's infectious, and we spread that joy to others. In Confession, St. Faustina was told: "Act in such a way that all those who come in contact with you will go away joyful. Sow happiness about you because you have received much from God; give, then, give generously to others. They should take leave of you with their hearts filled with joy, even if they have no more than touched the hem of your garment" (55). American author Mark Twain put it this way: "To get the full value of joy you must have somebody to divide it with." When we give joy, joy is our reward.

### *Prayer*

"O incomprehensible God, my heart dissolves in joy that You have allowed me to penetrate the mysteries of Your mercy!" (109).

Jesus, have mercy on us and on the whole world.

# *December 2*
## DISCOVERING GOD

And from this light came a voice which said, **Who God is in His Essence, no one will fathom, neither the mind of Angels nor of man.** Jesus said to me, **Get to know God by contemplating His attributes**. (*Diary*, 30)

## *Reflection*

There's an old Spiritual that says: "My God is so high; you can't get over Him. He's so low; you can't get under Him. He's so wide; you can't get around Him. You must come in, by and through the Lamb." This is a simple way of stating the perennial truth that our weak minds can't comprehend God. But the wonders of His creation proclaim His greatness. Modern scientists agree that we've but scratched the surface of our understanding of the universe that God has created. Even if we understood God's creation, God Himself is mysterious—beyond our understanding. Nonetheless, when we seek God, He teaches us something about Himself. As we learn about God by contemplating His attributes, we discover God—His holiness, His justice, His love and mercy.

## *Prayer*

God from God, Light from Light, true God from true God, I adore You.
Jesus, have mercy on us and on the whole world.

# *December 3*

## SIMPLICITY OF HEART

I heard a voice in my soul: **Meditate on the mystery of the Incarnation**. And suddenly the Infant Jesus appeared before me, radiant with beauty. He told me how much God is pleased with simplicity in a soul. (*Diary*, 332)

## *Reflection*

Consider what the French archbishop François Fénelon writes: "Contemplate the single-hearted love of Mary at Christ's Incarnation and behold how the Virgin's heart has been formed by the Lord. Mary's heart beats for God alone. But we live in an age of complexity, where simplicity of heart is a rare quality. Steeped in the shallowness of our trendiness, people today are in a frantic pursuit of happiness. But the nervous activities that occupy our attention don't satisfy the longing of our hearts. If we would only come to Christ with simplicity of soul, He could disentangle them from the worldly pursuits that leave us empty. We ought to instead seek simplicity of heart—that sincere love of the pure and simple truth. How desirable is this simplicity … it is the pearl of great price."

## *Prayer*

"With the trust and simplicity of a small child, I give myself to You today, O Lord Jesus, my Master" (228).

Jesus, have mercy on us and on the whole world.

# December 4

## I AM YOUR CHILD

> **You see how weak you are, so when shall I be able to count on you?** Jesus, be always with me, for I am your little child. Jesus. You know what little children do. (*Diary*, 722)

## Reflection

When St. Faustina was praying one day, she was planning to meditate on Christ's agony in the Garden of Gethsemane. Jesus inspired her to meditate on His Incarnation instead. The Holy Infant appeared and said: "Although My greatness is beyond understanding, I commune only with those who are little. I demand of you a childlike spirit" (332). If we have a childlike faith, we take God at His word, without doubting. We see this perfectly in the Virgin Mary, when, at the Annunciation, she showed perfect childlike trust in God. Jesus told His disciples, "Unless you turn and become like children, you will never enter the kingdom of heaven" (Mt 18:3). King David understood the need for childlike humility before God when he wrote, "I do not occupy myself with things too great and too marvelous for me. But I have calmed and quieted my soul, like a child quieted at its mother's breast ..." (Ps 131:2).

## Prayer

Lord, deliver me from a childish faith that is easy, comfortable, and self-centered, and grant that I have a childlike love that is joyful and pure of heart.

Jesus, have mercy on us and on the whole world.

# *December 5*

> I saw the little Infant Jesus, who told me that I was to
> depend on him for everything. (*Diary*, 659)

## *Reflection*

We Americans pride ourselves on our independence. But as children of God, we need to declare our utter dependence upon the Lord. Because every good thing we have comes from Him, God expects us to use the good things He's given with wisdom and prudence. A sick person with strep throat who "piously" whispers, "I depend on God alone to heal me," is filled with pride, because they refuse to go to the doctor. Relying upon God doesn't lead to foolishness, because God wants us to use good common sense and act wisely. There's a world of difference between depending on God and putting Him to the test. Jesus didn't jump off the pinnacle of the Temple when Satan tempted Him to see if angels of God would come to the rescue. Venerable Fulton J. Sheen explained: "Humility is dependence on God as pride is independence of Him." With Faustina, depend on Jesus, "because he is found by those who do not put him to the test, and manifests himself to those who do not distrust him" (Wis 1:2).

## *Prayer*

"O my Jesus, You Yourself must help me in everything, because You see how very little I am, and so I depend solely on Your goodness, O God" (742).

Jesus, have mercy on us and on the whole world.

# *December 6*

> **Why do you not tell Me about everything that concerns you, even the smallest details? Tell Me about everything, and know that this will give Me great joy ...** "But You know about everything, Lord." And Jesus replied, **Yes, I do know; but you should not excuse yourself with the fact that I know, but with childlike simplicity talk to Me about everything, for My ears and heart are inclined towards you, and your words are dear to Me.** (*Diary*, 921)

## *Reflection*

When a small child tells their parent about their "great discovery," for example, that ice cubes are frozen water, a good mom or dad will listen intently, sharing their excitement as if it were worthy of a Nobel Prize. It doesn't matter that the parents already knew what happens when water gets below 32 degrees. Out of love, they enjoy hearing their children talk to them, and it's an intimate union. So it is with God. He never tires of hearing from us, and nothing we can say is ever trivial to His ears.

## *Prayer*

Jesus, with the trust and simplicity of a child, I know that I can tell You anything, and in Your great love, You are happy to hear whatever it is that I have to say.

Jesus, have mercy on us and on the whole world.

# *December 7*

## GOD'S LITTLE CHILDREN

> **Today bring to me the meek and humble souls and the souls of little children ...** (*Diary*, 1220)

### *Reflection*

As parents comfort little ones, so God lifts us out of poverty and gives us the riches of His love. When the world leaves us hungry, God feeds us with Himself—the "Living Bread." When the world leaves us out in the cold, God warms us with His Spirit. Once, when Jesus was trying to explain the depths of His love to St. Faustina, He asked her to imagine what it'd be like to have God's sovereign power. Jesus asked her how she'd respond to a poor, starving child crying at her doorstep for a morsel of food. St. Faustina replied: "Jesus, I would give the child all it asked and a thousand times more" (229). We're precious to the Lord. His love is as the love a mother has for her children. Faustina expresses her sentiment: "You are always a most tender mother to me, and You surpass all mothers" (1490). We're God's little children.

### *Prayer*

Lord, the world has left me hungry and cold. I knock on the door of Your heart, because I want to be Your little child.

Jesus, have mercy on us and on the whole world.

# *December 8*

*Solemnity of the Immaculate Conception
of the Blessed Virgin Mary*

## THE POWER OF A PURE SOUL

**A pure soul has inconceivable power before God.** (*Diary*, 534)

## *Reflection*

After David committed adultery, he fasted and prayed, crying out: "Create in me a clean heart, O God …" (Ps 51:10). Whatever our state in life, God calls us to live as pure souls in His sight. Try to reject temptation by sheer willpower, and you'll fail. To be a pure soul we need God's grace. To help us, Jesus gives us Mary, whom St. Faustina describes as "a shield and protection for a weak heart" (161). The purity St. Faustina sought was resplendent in Mary. Perhaps, because she worked as a gardener in the convent in Vilnius, Faustina described virtues as flowers. She saw the lily as a symbol of purity. She addressed Our Lady: "O my Mother, cover my soul with your virginal mantle and grant me the grace of purity of heart, soul and body.… O lovely lily!" (79).

## *Prayer*

Oh, Mary, I give you the lily of my heart. Be thou its guardian forever.
    Jesus, have mercy on us and on the whole world.

# December 9

## TRUE GREATNESS

I asked the child, "How do you know that true greatness of the soul is in loving God and in humility? Only theologians know about such things and you haven't even learned the catechism. So how do you know?" To this He answered, **I know; I know all things.** (*Diary*, 427)

### Reflection

If I try to consciously train myself to be humble, I'm straining to grasp something—to win a coveted prize. Humility achieved is no humility at all, because it's a spiritual trophy one polishes with pride. One who boasts of his humility is puffed up with pride. If we're honest, we've done little purely for God. Oftentimes, our good deeds seek the spotlight. Our vices put on masks and parade as virtues. We need to do deeds out of humble love; otherwise vainglory can spoil our best works. St. Teresa of Calcutta revealed the unbreakable link between love and humility when she remarked: "To forgive takes love, to forget takes humility." Humility opens the soul and prepares the way for love.

### Prayer

Lord, sow in me the seed of humility.

Jesus, have mercy on us and on the whole world.

# December 10

### KEEP IT SIMPLE

> Jesus said to me, **My child, do not be afraid of the house of your Father. Leave these vain inquiries to the wise of this world. I want to see you always as a little child.** (*Diary*, 290)

## Reflection

Once Faustina was fearful and troubled by doubts. Jesus assured her that all eternity and everything in it belongs to the Father. Recall when you were a little child and how exciting it was when your parents took you somewhere different. All you wanted to do was have fun exploring your new surroundings, and you happily welcomed new experiences. Your curiosity brought with it no apprehension—especially when you knew your parents were nearby. Our eternal Father is always right there for us, so when we accept the wonders of eternity with childlike simplicity and awe, our fears are replaced with indescribable joy.

## Prayer

Heavenly Father, let me contemplate Your eternal mysteries with childlike simplicity. I don't understand all that You have in store for me, but I trust in You.

Jesus, have mercy on us and on the whole world.

# *December 11*

## BEG FOR ACTUAL GRACES

**Do not fear. I am watching you this very moment and am helping yo ... I will send two sisters ... and then you will find it easy to continue the conversation.** (*Diary*, 1494)

## *Reflection*

"Oh, how good it is to call on Jesus for help during a conversation. Oh, how good it is, during a moment of peace, to beg for actual graces. I fear most of all this sort of confidential conversation; there is need of much divine light at times like this, in order to speak with profit, both for the other person's soul, and for one's own as well. God, however, comes to our aid; but we have to ask Him for it. Let no one trust too much in his own self" (1495).

## *Prayer*

Lord, let my conversations be only words of kindness.
Jesus, have mercy on us and on the whole world.

# December 12

*Feast of Our Lady of Guadalupe*

HEART OF MERCY

**Be always merciful as I am merciful. Love everyone out of love for Me, even your greatest enemies, so that My mercy may be fully reflected in your heart.** (*Diary*, 1695)

## Reflection

Our Father tells us to love. To love everyone, including those who are difficult for us to love.

Loving those who are difficult does not mean we like what they do; it means we love the sparks of God's love that exist in all of us. St. Faustina reminds us: "We resemble God most when we forgive our neighbors" (1148).

## Prayer

I hear You, O my God, and I listen to what You are telling me.

Jesus, have mercy on us and on the whole world.

# *December 13*
## HOUR OF MERCY

As often as you hear the clock strike the third hour, immerse yourself completely in My mercy, adoring and glorifying it; invoke its omnipotence for the whole world, and particularly for poor sinners; for at that moment mercy was opened wide for every soul. In this hour, you can obtain everything for yourself and for others for the asking; it was the hour of grace for the whole world—mercy triumphed over justice. (*Diary*, 1572)

## *Reflection*

Some times of the day and night seem to be more significant than others. Think about the implications of "high noon" or the "midnight hour." While we assign meaning to certain times, God has assigned meaning to one time in particular—3 p.m.—the hour when Our Lord died. Every day, at that hour, the communication lines to heaven are opened especially wide. When we pray then, Jesus tells us that we can obtain everything for ourselves and others, as long as it is the divine will of God. What is it that you most desire? What is it that you most want from God? Today, set an alarm for 3 p.m., immersing yourself in His mercy, adoring and glorifying it. Trust that your prayer will be heard.

## *Prayer*

Jesus, You know the deepest desire of my heart. If it is Your will, grant it to me this day.

Jesus, have mercy on us and on the whole world.

# *December 14*

## A MIRROR OF JESUS

**Look into My Merciful Heart and reflect its compassion in your own heart and in your deeds.** (*Diary*, 1688)

## *Reflection*

St. Faustina teaches us that "Whatever Jesus did, He did well. He went along, doing good. His manner was full of goodness and mercy. His steps were guided by compassion. Toward His enemies He showed goodness, kindness, and understanding, and to those in need help and consolation" (1175). As she considered the merciful and compassionate Heart of Christ, she resolved to "mirror faithfully these traits of Jesus" (1175) despite the cost. To grow in virtue costs us. But if we've the courage to do this, we can proclaim His mercy to the world and mirror the virtues we see so resplendent in Him. If your compassion for others remains an intellectual exercise, it's not the compassion Jesus wants.

## *Prayer*

Lord, give me Your Heart. And let my heart reflect the compassion in Yours. Jesus, have mercy on us and on the whole world.

# *December 15*

## SIMPLER IS BETTER

After Holy Communion today, I spoke at length to the Lord Jesus about people who are special to me. Then I heard these words: **My daughter, don't be exerting yourself so much with words.** (*Diary*, 739)

## *Reflection*

When we pray, we sometimes have a tendency to "go overboard" a bit, forgetting that Jesus completely understands us. It is different than when you are speaking with someone who may not "get it." God knows you better than you know yourself. Pour out your heart to Him and move on. He will take care of the rest.

## *Prayer*

Lord, let my prayer be as humble as it is simple.

Jesus, have mercy on us and on the whole world.

# *December 16*

## DEEDS OF LOVE

> **Put your self-love in the last place, so that it does not taint your deeds.** (*Diary*, 1760)

## *Reflection*

St. Paul says: "If I give away all I have … but have not love, I gain nothing" (1 Cor 13:3). In God's eyes, small deeds done with love excel great deeds devoid of love. Religious people can fall into the temptation of doing good deeds for wrong reasons. Consider the showy scribes and Pharisees. Jesus rebuked them. They considered themselves superior because they followed religion strictly. Their pride stinks just like ours whenever we do good deeds seeking praise. Instead, we ought to help our neighbor secretly (Mt 6:3-4). St. Faustina asked: "How can one be pleasing to God when one is inflated with pride and self-love under the pretense of striving for Gods glory, while in fact one is seeking one's own glory?" (1139). When we hoard our time, money, or possessions, the antidote is generosity. St. Faustina taught, "I see that the smallest things done by a soul that loves God sincerely have an enormous value in His Holy eyes" (340).

## *Prayer*

"Jesus, King of Mercy, again the time has come when I am alone with You. Therefore, I beg You, by all the love with which Your Heart burns, to destroy completely within me my self-love and, on the other hand, to enkindle in my heart the fire of Your purest love" (371).

Jesus, have mercy on us and on the whole world.

# December 17

## CAN GOD COMPLAIN?

During Holy Hour today, Jesus complained to me about the ingratitude of souls: **In return for My blessings, I get ingratitude. In return for My love, I get forgetfulness and indifference. My Heart cannot bear this.** (*Diary*, 1537)

## Reflection

Is it possible for God to complain? St. Faustina says it is. She says that Jesus complained about ingratitude for blessings. What an interesting concept—that God can be saddened, not just by our sin, but by our ingratitude as well. We all have at least one blessing in our lives that we take for granted, that we forgot, or are indifferent to. As you go about your day, remember, it isn't just sin that hurts Jesus. Ingratitude is one thing the Heart of Jesus cannot bear. Before the day ends, tell Jesus how very grateful you are.

## Prayer

Thank you, Lord, for all the blessings You have given me. Forgive my lack of gratitude.

Jesus, have mercy on us and on the whole world.

# December 18
## BE OBEDIENT

**My daughter, I have not released you from taking action.** I
answered, "Lord, my hand is too feeble for such work." **Yes, I know;
but joined with My right hand you will accomplish everything.
Nevertheless, be obedient, be obedient to the confessors. I
will give them light on how to direct you.** (*Diary*, 1374)

### Reflection

Here is spiritual counsel from St. Faustina's confessor, Father Andrasz. "Go
through life doing good, so that I could write on its pages: 'She spent her life
doing good.' May God bring this about in you" (55).

"Another time the confessor said to me, 'Comport yourself before God
like the widow in the Gospel; although the coin she dropped into the box
was of little value, it counted far more before God than all the big offerings
of others'" (55).

"Still another time he gave me the following recommendation: "Let God
push your boat out into the deep waters, toward the unfathomable depths of
the interior life'" (21).

### Prayer

Holy Spirit, I pray for all confessors, and especially for N.

Jesus, have mercy on us and on the whole world.

# *December 19*

## CHARITY BEGINS AT HOME!

> ... you will ask your superiors only for penances. (*Diary*, 169)

### *Reflection*

The priest gives us a "penance" to perform after Confession. It could be three Hail Marys or a prayer, or spending a few minutes meditating on a passage from the Bible. But what does it really do for you? This is how the glossary of the Catechism of the Catholic Church defines penance:

*Interior* penance: a conversion of heart toward God and away from sin, which implies the intention to change one's life because of hope in divine mercy (1431). *External* acts of penance include fasting, prayer, and almsgiving (1434). (Emphasis in original).

Penance is something we can do for the conversion of others or for ourselves. Opportunities abound every day, and we don't even have to leave home! Because that's where it begins. St. Faustina knew this well. Charity begins at home—kind, patient, forgiving, to those closest to us. Then it will spill over to those outside our home and to the world. This is the spirit of penance and avoiding purgatory.

### *Prayer*

Jesus, take my penances for the conversion of my dear ones.

Jesus, have mercy on us and on the whole world.

# *December 20*

## THE SMALLEST SACRIFICE

> **The smallest sacrifice finds great value in My eyes...** (*Diary*, 639)

### Reflection

Of all the small sacrifices we can make, fasting is one of the most powerful. Asterius of Amasea, a fifth-century evangelist who lived in modern-day Turkey, had at least seventeen of his sermons survive the test of time. In one sermon Asterius makes an extraordinary claim about the power surrounding fasting. He writes: "Angels are close guardians and keepers of the homes that fast." When it comes to protecting and healing our families, few actions are more effective than fasting.

### Prayer

Thank you for this way for me to be more open to Your grace and to better serve You.

Jesus, have mercy on us and on the whole world.

# December 21

## WORDS AND INTENTIONS

Before Holy Communion, Jesus gave me to understand that I should pay absolutely no attention to what a certain sister would say, because her cunning and malice were displeasing to Him. **My daughter, do not speak to this person about either your views or your opinions.** I begged the Lord's pardon for what in that soul was displeasing to Him, and I begged Him to strengthen me with His grace when she would come to talk with me again. She has asked me about many things, to which I gave answer with all my sisterly love and, as evidence that I have spoken to her from the bottom of my heart, I have told her some things that came from my own experience. But her intentions were something quite different from the words on her lips.... (*Diary*, 1492)

### Reflection

Most people are kind, and respond to kindness with kindness. Some people are deceptive and use words to mislead and to manipulate us in harmful ways. Can we be fooled? Yes. But once we learn that a person is deceitful, we need to remember to avoid them—not hate them, just avoid them. We can pray for them. Indeed we should pray for them.

### Prayer

Lord, protect me from the harm of cunning people.

Jesus, have mercy on us and on the whole world.

# *December 22*

## SAVOR JOY

**Heart of My Heart, be filled with joy.** (*Diary*, 1669)

### *Reflection*

Throughout the *Diary*, Jesus talks to Faustina about joy. We all have experienced joy, but unfortunately, we sometimes don't savor those joyful moments. We get uncomfortable and want to move on. How can we experience joy on a practical level? Instead of passing over our joy, we can acknowledge it to ourselves and to others. For example, someone says: "You look cheerful today," instead of nodding and moving on, say: "I appreciate your saying that. It makes me feel good to know. Thank you, you just added to my cheerfulness." The formula for abiding in joy is simple: Recognize the feeling of joy when you feel it (even if it's difficult). Acknowledge when someone does or says something nice. Let the person know how it makes you feel that they said or did that. Then tell them they added to making your day even more joyful. You will need to practice this, as it is more difficult to do than it may seem at first blush. Once you get the hang of it, it becomes easier to savor and share your joyful moments.

### *Prayer*

Lord, help me to see and acknowledge the moments of joy in my life.

Jesus, have mercy on us and on the whole world.

# *December 23*

## MAKE MY GOODNESS KNOWN

> **I am very pleased that you had not been talking with Me, but were making My goodness known to souls and rousing them to love Me.** (*Diary*, 404)

### *Reflection*

As St. Faustina was preparing to leave her family to join the convent, twenty-five or more family members gathered to say goodbye. She kissed the sick children, asking God to heal them. Her parents and godmother blessed her as they cried, so joyful that their daughter was entering religious life. As she departed, one of her relatives, Stanley, walked her to the car. St. Faustina talked to him about Jesus. She describes the scene: "When I was telling him about the goodness of God ... he burst out crying like a little child, and I was not surprised, for this was a pure soul and, as such, more capable of recognizing God" (402). Reaching the Warsaw convent, she visited the chapel to greet Jesus in the tabernacle. She apologized for not talking to Him more while she was home. St. Faustina feared she was neglecting her Lord by spending so much time conversing with her family. But Christ gently assured her how pleased He was with her, by encouraging her family in the spiritual life, rousing them to love God, and sharing with them in the fellowship of Christ.

### *Prayer*

Lord, help me to rouse my family to love of You, so that You may be the center of our lives.

Jesus, have mercy on us and on the whole world

# December 24

**I shall strengthen you.** (*Diary*, 65)

## Reflection

God the Father gave us a gift — Jesus! "He saved us, not because of any works of righteousness that we had done, but according to his mercy … " Because of this, St. John Paul II said that mercy is "love's second name" (*Dives in Misericordia*, 7). Oftentimes, we want to reflect Jesus' love. But we feel unable to meet love's demands. St. Faustina instructs us: "When I see that the burden is beyond my strength, I do not consider or analyze it or probe into it, but I run like a child to the Heart of Jesus and say only one word to Him: 'You can do all things.' And then I keep silent, because I know that Jesus Himself will intervene in the matter, and as for me, instead of tormenting myself, I use that time to love Him" (1033).

## Prayer

My Lord, there is no other gift that I long for except Your presence.

Jesus, have mercy on us and on the whole world.

# *December 25*

**Through the Word Incarnate, I make known the bottomless depth of My mercy.** (*Diary*, 88)

## *Reflection*

St. Faustina tells us that the "immense love and abyss of mercy are made known in the Incarnation of the Word and in the Redemption …" adding, "it is here that I saw this as the greatest of all God's attributes" (180). God's mercy embraces us when we repent of our sins. Those who claim they're without sin and don't need God's mercy call God a liar. But for those who seek it, there's no limit to His mercy. St. Faustina exclaims: "How great is the mercy of God contained in the Mystery of the Incarnation of the Son of God" (1433). For God to take on human flesh reveals His mercy for us. He could have come in glory and power. But that we might not cower in fear of Almighty God, He came as a tender, little Babe. By Christ's Incarnation, God brought forth Mercy—"in the flesh."

## *Prayer*

Word made flesh, I adore You.

Jesus, have mercy on us and on the whole world.

# *December 26*

**Do not be unduly fearful, because you are not alone.** (*Diary*, 1760)

## *Reflection*

Each Christmas we read the Nativity story: "In that region there were shepherds living in the fields, keeping watch over their flock by night. Then an angel of the Lord stood before them, and the glory of the Lord shone around them, and they were terrified. And the angel said to them: 'Be not be afraid; I bring you good news of great joy which will come to all the people; for to you is born this day in the city of David a Savior, who is Christ the Lord'" (Lk 2:8-12). When the angel appeared, the shepherds had mud on their boots. They weren't dressed in their Christmas finest. Even so, the angel invited them to enter the stable and worship the newborn King. The angel first calmed them, saying: "Do not be afraid." In the original Greek, he said: "No Fear." It's like telling a baby "Stop crying!" Perhaps the shepherds were fearing the wrong things. When we're told "No fear," perhaps God is releasing us from fear of things we can't control, so that we can serve Him without fear.

## *Prayer*

Lord, deliver me of the spirit of fear and fill me with Your Holy Spirit.

Jesus, have mercy on us and on the whole world.

# December 27

## CHILDLIKE, NOT CHILDISH

"Jesus, You are so little, and yet I know that you are my Creator and Lord." And Jesus answered me, **I am, and I keep company with you as a child to teach you humility and simplicity.** (*Diary*, 184)

### Reflection

Jesus appears as a child many times to St. Faustina in order to teach her humility and simplicity. Children are filled with joy, love, kindness, and trust. He wants us to be childlike in our heart. Jesus also taught her the secret to happiness ... simplicity.

### Prayer

Jesus, make my heart like unto Yours.

Jesus, have mercy on us and on the whole world.

# December 28

## CHILDREN'S TEARS UPHOLD THE WORLD

I beg You, Jesus, look not on our sins, but on the tears of little children, on the hunger and cold they suffer ... At that moment, I saw the Lord Jesus, His eyes filled with tears, and He said to me, **You see ... what great compassion I have for them. Know that it is they who uphold the world.** (*Diary*, 286)

### Reflection

An old spiritual reminds us: "He's got the whole world in his hands. He's got the wind and the rain in his hands. He's got the itsy-bitsy baby in his hands ... He's got the whole world in his hands." The daily news reports the suffering of children through the ravages of war, hunger, political unrest, hatred, and poverty. St. John Paul II said: "It is this suffering which burns and consumes evil with the flame of love and draws forth even from sin a great flowering of good." There's no tear shed by a child that God doesn't bottle. The heart-strings of God are tugged by the power of their tears—these little ones who uphold the world.

### Prayer

"Eternal Father, turn Your merciful gaze upon meek and humble souls, and upon the souls of little children who are enfolded in the abode which is the Most Compassionate Heart of Jesus" (1223).

Jesus, have mercy on us and on the whole world.

# December 29

*Solemnity of the Holy Family
of Jesus, Mary, and Joseph*

## HEALING OF THE FAMILY

**I am granting them not only necessary graces, but special graces as well.**
I understood that the Lord would call them to a greater union with Him.
I rejoice immensely that such great love reigns in our family. (*Diary*, 401)

## Reflection

On the day that St. Faustina was leaving home to join the convent, her family and friends gathered to say farewell. Amidst the joy and love of that gathering, a profound sorrow crept through the door. Faustina describes: "I was very sorry not to have seen two of my sisters. I felt interiorly that their souls were in great danger. Pain gripped my heart at the thought of them" (401). When Faustina sensed that some temptation or trial was placing the souls of her sisters in danger, she turned to Jesus to beg graces for them. Our Lord then told her: "I am granting them not only necessary graces, but special graces as well" (401). St. Faustina teaches us to pray for our loved ones, so that Jesus might bring our families His grace. Placing perfect trust in Jesus, let us never give up hope on our loved ones, because Jesus brings healing to families who open their doors to Him.

## Prayer

Lord, as You call my loved ones to greater union with You, grant the healing of my family, so that You may reign in our hearts and homes.

Jesus, have mercy on us and on the whole world.

# *December 30*

## BE FAITHFUL TO YOUR MISSION

**Your duty is to be faithful to My grace ...** (*Diary*, 1650)

## *Reflection*

"God has created me to do Him some definite service. He has committed some work to me which He has not committed to another. I have my mission. I may never know it in this life, but I shall be told it in the next. I am a link in a chain, a bond of connection between persons.

"He has not created me for naught. I shall do good; I shall do His work. I shall be an angel of peace, a preacher of truth in my own place, while not intending it if I do but keep His commandments.

"Therefore, I will trust Him, whatever I am, I can never be thrown away. If I am in sickness, my sickness may serve Him, in perplexity, my perplexity may serve Him. If I am in sorrow, my sorrow may serve Him. He does nothing in vain. He knows what He is about. He may take away my friends. He may throw me among strangers. He may make me feel desolate, make my spirits sink, hide my future from me. Still, He knows what He is about." (*St. John Henry Newman*)

## *Prayer*

"... [M]y Guardian Angel said to me: 'Here is your throne, for your faithfulness in fulfilling the will of God'" (633). Lord, Your will be done

Jesus, have mercy on us and on the whole world.

# *December 31*

## FOR LOVE OF YOU

> **I too came down from heaven out of love for you; I lived for you, I died for you, and I created the heavens for you.** (*Diary*, 853)

### *Reflection*

"Love is a mystery," St. Faustina remarked, that "transforms everything it touches into things beautiful and pleasing to God" (890). To reveal the mystery of His love, God paints the picture of His love. The humility of Christ paints a beautiful image at His Nativity. Leaving heaven's grandeur, Christ came down to earth and was born of a Virgin in the lowly stable of Bethlehem. Christ's meekness paints a portrait of His tenderness as He lived among us—healing the sick, feeding the hungry, and preaching the Good News. The beauty of God's creation paints a portrait of Him who made the blue skies and the mountains topped in snow. But the most convincing portrait of love ever known was painted in Jesus' Blood. The portrait of God's love is proof of His love—for you!

### *Prayer*

Open my eyes to see the portrait of love You have painted for me and let me dwell forever in the depths of Your love. Amen.

Jesus, have mercy on us and on the whole world.

# Appendices

# The Divine Mercy Promises

Throughout her *Diary*, St. Faustina recorded promises Jesus made *not only to her but to those who would pray to, promote, and trust in Divine Mercy.*

### *To those souls who venerate the image of Divine Mercy*

"I promise that the soul that will venerate this image will not perish. I also promise victory over [its] enemies already here on earth, especially at the hour of death. I Myself will defend it as My own glory." (*Diary*, 48)

### *To those souls who pray the Chaplet of Divine Mercy*

"The souls that say this chaplet will be embraced by My mercy during their lifetime and especially at the hour of their death." (*Diary*, 754)

"When hardened sinners say it, I will fill their souls with peace, and the hour of their death will be a happy one." (*Diary*, 1541)

"… [W]hen they say this chaplet in the presence of the dying, I will stand between My Father and the dying person, not as the just Judge but as the merciful Savior." (*Diary*, 1541)

"Whoever will recite it will receive great mercy at the hour of death.... Even if there were a sinner most hardened, if he were to recite this chaplet only once, he would receive grace from My infinite mercy." (*Diary*, 687)

### To those souls who honor and spread the worship of Divine Mercy

"I Myself will defend as My own glory, during their lifetime, and especially at the hour of their death, those souls who will venerate My fathomless mercy." (*Diary*, 1225)

"... All those souls who will glorify My mercy and spread its worship, encouraging others to trust in My mercy, will not experience terror at the hour of death. My mercy will shield them in that final battle." (*Diary*, 1540)

"Souls who spread the honor of My mercy I shield through their entire lives as a tender mother her infant, and at the hour of death I will not be a Judge for them, but the merciful Savior.... Happy is the soul that during its lifetime immersed itself in the Fountain of Mercy, because justice will have no hold on it." (*Diary*, 1075)

### To those souls who put their trust in Divine Mercy

"He who trusts in My mercy will not perish, for all his affairs are Mine, and his enemies will be shattered at the base of My footstool." (*Diary*, 723)

"Souls that make an appeal to My mercy delight Me. To such souls I grant even more graces than they ask." (*Diary*, 1146)

"Every soul believing and trusting in My mercy will obtain it." (*Diary*, 420)

### *To those souls who honor the Hour of Mercy*

"This is the hour of great mercy for the whole world. I will allow you to enter into My mortal sorrow. In this hour, I will refuse nothing to the soul that makes a request of Me in virtue of My Passion ..." (*Diary*, 1320)

### *To priests who proclaim and extol the Divine Mercy*

"To priests who proclaim and extol My mercy, I will give wondrous power; I will anoint their words and touch the hearts of those to whom they will speak." (*Diary*, 1521)

### *Our Lord's Promises Attached to the Praying of the Chaplet of Divine Mercy as Revealed to St. Faustina*

In addition to verses shared with the Divine Mercy Promises (*Diary*, 48, 754, 1541, 687, 1521, and 1387), the Promises Attached to the Praying of the Chaplet also include:

"At three o'clock, implore My mercy, especially for sinners; and, if only for a brief moment, immerse yourself in My Passion, particularly in My abandonment at the moment of agony. This is the hour of great mercy for the whole world. I will allow you to enter into My mortal sorrow. In this hour, I will refuse nothing to the soul that makes a request of me in virtue of My Passion...." (*Diary*, 1320; also cf. 1572)

"Souls who spread the honor of My mercy ... at the hour of death I will not be a Judge for them, but the Merciful Savior." (*Diary*, 1075)

"The two rays denote Blood and Water.... These two rays issued from the very depths of My tender mercy when My agonized Heart was opened by a lance on the Cross. These rays shield souls from the wrath of My Father.... I desire that the first Sunday after Easter be the Feast of Mercy.... [W]hoever approaches the Fount of Life on this day will be granted complete remission of sins and punishment. Mankind will not have peace until it turns with trust to My mercy." (*Diary*, 299–300)

"I desire that the Feast of Mercy be a refuge and shelter for all souls.... The soul that will go to Confession and receive Holy Communion (in a state of grace on this day) shall obtain complete forgiveness of sins and punishment.... It is My desire that [the Feast] be solemnly celebrated on the first Sunday after Easter...." (*Diary*, 699)

"Through this chaplet you will obtain everything, if what you ask for is compatible with My will." (*Diary*, 1731)

"My mercy is greater than your sins and those of the entire world." (*Diary*, 1485)

# The Chaplet of Divine Mercy

[Jesus said to St. Faustina:] **Say unceasingly the chaplet that I have taught you. Whoever will recite it will receive great mercy at the hour of death.** *(Diary, 687)*

Traditionally, a five-decade rosary is used for praying the Divine Mercy Chaplet.

1. Begin with the Sign of the Cross, one Our Father, one Hail Mary, and the Apostles' Creed.

2. On the Our Father bead pray:

   *Eternal Father, I offer You the Body and Blood, Soul and Divinity of Your dearly beloved Son, Our Lord Jesus Christ, in atonement for our sins and those of the whole world.*

3. On the ten Hail Mary beads pray:

   *For the sake of His sorrowful Passion, have mercy on us and on the whole world.*

(Repeat steps 2 and 3 for all five decades).

4. After the fifth decade, conclude the chaplet by praying three times:

*Holy God, Holy Mighty One, Holy Immortal One, have mercy on us and on the whole world.*

### A Prayer Jesus Taught to St. Faustina

"[Jesus said to St. Faustina:] I desire that you know more profoundly the love that burns in My Heart for souls, and you will understand this when you meditate upon My Passion. Call upon My mercy on behalf of sinners; I desire their salvation. When you say this prayer, with a contrite heart and with faith on behalf of some sinner, I will give him the grace of conversion. This is the prayer:

"O Blood and Water, which gushed forth from the Heart of Jesus as a fount of Mercy for us, I trust in You." (*Diary*, 186–187)

# Promises of the Chaplet for Special Graces

### *For Those Who Are Devoted to the Chaplet*

St. Faustina lamented to Jesus how greatly concerned she was for all mankind. He told her to say the chaplet to bring humankind closer to Him. Here are ways you can pray the chaplet for various needs. Pray it unceasingly.

**The souls that say this chaplet will be embraced by My mercy during their lifetime and especially at the hour of their death.** (*Diary*, 754)

While I was saying the chaplet, I heard a voice which said, **Oh, what great graces I will grant to souls who say this chaplet; the very depths of My tender mercy are stirred for the sake of those who say the chaplet.** O what a great multitude of souls I see! They worshiped the Divine Mercy and will be singing the hymn of praise for all eternity. (*Diary*, 848)

### *To Appease His Anger*

**This prayer will serve to appease My wrath.** (*Diary*, 476)

When this chaplet is said by the bedside of a dying person, God's anger is placated. (*Diary*, 811)

This chaplet mitigates God's anger, as He Himself told me. (*Diary*, 1036)

It [the chaplet] appeases the anger of God. (*Diary*, 1565)

## *For the Dying*

**At the hour of their death, I defend as My own glory every soul that will say this chaplet; or when others say it for a dying person, the pardon is the same. When this chaplet is said by the bedside of a dying person, God's anger is placated, unfathomable mercy envelops the soul, and the very depths of My tender mercy are moved for the sake of the sorrowful Passion of My Son. (*Diary*, 811)**

I realize more and more how much every soul needs God's mercy throughout life and particularly at the hour of death. This chaplet mitigates God's anger, as He Himself told me. (*Diary*, 1036)

**Pray as much as you can for the dying. By your entreaties, obtain for them trust in My mercy, because they have most need of trust, and have it the least. Be assured that the grace of eternal salvation for certain souls in their final moment depends on your prayer.** (*Diary*, 1777)

## *Dying in Peace*

The sick man peacefully breathed his last. When I came to myself, I understood how very important the chaplet was for the dying. It appeases the anger of God. (*Diary*, 1565)

### For the Conversion of Sinners

**Priests will recommend it to sinners as their last hope of salvation. Even if there were a sinner most hardened, if he were to recite this chaplet only once, he would receive grace from My infinite mercy.** (*Diary*, 687)

**When hardened sinners say it, I will fill their souls with peace, and the hour of their death will be a happy one.** (*Diary*, 1541)

### For Souls in Despair

Today, the Lord came to me and said, **My daughter, help Me to save souls. You will go to a dying sinner, and you will continue to recite the chaplet, and in this way you will obtain for him trust in My mercy, for he is already in despair.** (*Diary*, 1797)

Suddenly, I found myself in a strange cottage where an elderly man was dying amidst great torments. All about the bed was a multitude of demons and the family, who were crying. When I began to pray, the spirits of darkness fled, with hissing and threats directed at me. The soul became calm and, filled with trust, rested in the Lord. At the same moment, I found myself again in my own room. How this happens ... I do not know. (*Diary*, 1798)

### Demons Flee in Panic

When I entered the chapel for a moment, the Lord said to me, **My daughter, help Me to save a certain dying sinner. Say the chaplet that I have taught you for him.** When I began to say the chaplet, I saw the man dying in the midst of terrible torment and struggle. His

Guardian Angel was defending him, but he was, as it were, powerless against the enormity of the soul's misery. A multitude of devils was waiting for the soul. But while I was saying the chaplet, I saw Jesus just as He is depicted in the image. The rays which issued from Jesus' Heart enveloped the sick man, and the powers of darkness fled in panic. The sick man peacefully breathed his last. (*Diary*, 1565)

## *Against Storms*

Today I was awakened by a great storm. The wind was raging, and it was raining in torrents, thunderbolts striking again and again. I began to pray that the storm would do no harm, when I heard the words: **Say the chaplet I have taught you, and the storm will cease.** I began immediately to say the chaplet and hadn't even finished it when the storm suddenly ceased, and I heard the words: **Through the chaplet you will obtain everything, if what you ask for is compatible with My will.** (*Diary*, 1731)

When a great storm was approaching, I began to say the chaplet. Suddenly I heard the voice of an angel: "I cannot approach in this storm, because the light which comes from her mouth drives back both me and the storm." Such was the angel's complaint to God. I then recognized how much havoc he was to have made through this storm; but I also recognized that this prayer was pleasing to God, and that this chaplet was most powerful. (*Diary*, 1791)

# A Novena to the Divine Mercy for the Conversion of the World

O n Good Friday, 1937, Jesus requested that St. Faustina make a special novena. " … I am to begin it for the conversion of the whole world and for the recognition of The Divine Mercy … [Jesus tells St. Faustina] … **so that every soul will praise My goodness. I desire trust from My creatures. Encourage souls to place great trust in My fathomless mercy. Let the weak, sinful soul have no fear to approach Me, for even if it had more sins than there are grains of sand in the world, all would be drowned in the unmeasurable depths of My mercy.** (*Diary*, 1059)

The Lord dictated the intentions for each day. Faustina was to bring to His heart a different group of souls each day and immerse them in the ocean of His mercy.

[Jesus to St. Faustina]: **I desire that during these nine days you bring souls to the fountain of My mercy, that they may draw therefrom strength and refreshment and whatever grace they need in the hardships of life, and especially at the hour of death.** (*Diary*, 1209)

### First Day

**Today, bring to Me all mankind, especially all sinners....** (*Diary*, 1210)

Most Merciful Jesus, whose very nature it is to have compassion on us and to forgive us, do not look upon our sins but upon our trust which we place in Your infinite goodness. Receive us all into the abode of Your Most Compassionate Heart, and never let us escape from it. We beg this of You by Your love which unites You to the Father and the Holy Spirit....

Eternal Father, turn Your merciful gaze upon all mankind and especially upon poor sinners, all enfolded in the Most Compassionate Heart of Jesus. For the sake of His sorrowful Passion, show us Your mercy, that we may praise the omnipotence of Your mercy forever and ever. Amen. (*Diary*, 1211)

### Second Day

**Today bring to Me the souls of priests and religious....** (*Diary*, 1212)

Most merciful Jesus, from whom comes all that is good, increase Your grace in us, that we may perform worthy works of mercy, and that all who see them may glorify the Father of Mercy who is in heaven....

Eternal Father, turn your merciful gaze upon the company [of chosen ones] in Your vineyard—upon the souls of priests and religious; and endow them with the strength of Your blessing. For the love of the Heart of Your Son in which they are enfolded, impart to them Your power and light, that they may be able to guide others in the way of salvation, and with one voice sing praise to Your boundless mercy for ages without end. Amen. (*Diary*, 1213)

### Third Day

**Today bring to Me all devout and faithful souls....** (*Diary*, 1214)

Most Merciful Jesus, from the treasury of Your mercy You impart Your graces in great abundance to each and all. Receive us into the abode of Your Most Compassionate Heart and never let us escape from it. We beg this of

You by that most wondrous love for the heavenly Father with which Your Heart burns so fiercely....

Eternal Father, turn Your merciful gaze upon faithful souls, as upon the inheritance of Your Son. For the sake of His sorrowful Passion, grant them Your blessing and surround them with Your constant protection. Thus may they never fail in love or lose the treasure of the holy faith, but rather, with all the hosts of Angels and Saints, may they glorify Your boundless mercy for endless ages. Amen. (*Diary*, 1215)

### Fourth Day

**Today bring to Me the pagans and those who do not yet know Me....** (*Diary*, 1216)

Most Compassionate Jesus, You are the Light of the whole world. Receive into the abode of Your Most Compassionate Heart the souls of pagans who as yet do not know You. Let the rays of Your grace enlighten them that they, too, together with us, may extol Your wonderful mercy; and do not let them escape from the abode which is Your Most Compassionate Heart....

Eternal Father, turn Your merciful gaze upon the souls of pagans and of those who as yet do not know You, but who are enclosed in the Most Compassionate Heart of Jesus. Draw them to the light of the Gospel. These souls do not know what great happiness it is to love You. Grant that they, too, may extol the generosity of Your mercy for endless ages. Amen. (*Diary*, 1217)

### Fifth Day

**Today bring to Me the souls of the heretics and schismatics....** (*Diary*, 1218)

Most Merciful Jesus, Goodness Itself, You do not refuse light to those who seek it of You. Receive into the abode of Your Most Compassionate Heart the souls of heretics and schismatics. Draw them by Your light into the unity of the Church, and do not let them escape from the abode of Your Most

Compassionate Heart; but bring it about that they, too, come to extol the generosity of Your mercy....

Eternal Father, turn Your merciful gaze upon the souls of heretics and schismatics, who have squandered Your blessings and misused Your graces by obstinately persisting in their errors. Do not look upon their errors, but upon the love of Your own Son and upon His bitter Passion, which He underwent for their sake, since they, too, are enclosed in the Most Compassionate Heart of Jesus. Bring it about that they also may glorify Your great mercy for endless ages. Amen. (*Diary*, 1219)

## *Sixth Day*

**Today bring to Me the meek and humble souls and the souls of little children....** (*Diary*, 1220)

Most Merciful Jesus, You Yourself have said, "Learn from Me for I am meek and humble of heart." Receive into the abode of Your Most Compassionate Heart all meek and humble souls and the souls of little children. These souls send all heaven into ecstasy and they are the heavenly Father's favorites. They are a sweet-smelling bouquet before the throne of God; God Himself takes delight in their fragrance. These souls have a permanent abode in Your Most Compassionate Heart, O Jesus, and they unceasingly sing out a hymn of love and mercy.... (*Diary*, 1221)

Eternal Father, turn Your merciful gaze upon meek souls and humble souls, and upon the souls of little children who are enfolded in the abode which is the Most Compassionate Heart of Jesus. These souls bear the closest resemblance to Your Son. Their fragrance rises from the earth and reaches Your very throne. Father of mercy and of all goodness, I beg You by the love You bear these souls and by the delight You take in them: Bless the whole world, that all souls together may sing out the praises of Your mercy for endless ages. Amen. (*Diary*, 1223)

## *Seventh Day*

**Today bring to Me the souls who especially venerate and glorify My mercy....** (*Diary*, 1224)

Most Merciful Jesus, whose Heart is Love Itself, receive into the abode of Your Most Compassionate Heart the souls of those who particularly extol and venerate the greatness of Your mercy. These souls are mighty with the very power of God Himself. In the midst of all afflictions and adversities they go forward, confident of Your mercy. These souls are united to Jesus and carry all mankind on their shoulders. These souls will not be judged severely, but Your mercy will embrace them as they depart from this life....

Eternal Father, turn your merciful gaze upon the souls who glorify and venerate Your greatest attribute, that of Your fathomless mercy, and who are enclosed in the Most Compassionate Heart of Jesus. These souls are a living Gospel; their hands are full of deeds of mercy, and their spirit, overflowing with joy, sing a canticle of mercy to You, O Most High! I beg You, O God: Show them Your mercy according to the hope and trust they have placed in You. Let there be accomplished in them the promise of Jesus, who said to them, I Myself will defend as My own glory, during their lifetime, and especially at the hour of their death, those souls who will venerate My fathomless mercy. (*Diary*, 1225)


## *Eighth Day*

**Today bring to Me the souls who are in the prison of Purgatory....** (*Diary*, 1226)

Most Merciful Jesus, Your Yourself have said that You desire mercy; so I bring into the abode of Your Most Compassionate Heart the souls in Purgatory, souls who are very dear to You, and yet, who must make retribution to Your justice. May the streams of Blood and Water which gushed forth from Your Heart put out the flames of purifying fire, that in that place, too, the power of Your mercy may be praised....

Eternal Father, turn Your merciful gaze upon the souls suffering in Purgatory, who are enfolded in the Most Compassionate Heart of Jesus. I beg You, by the sorrowful Passion of Jesus Your Son, and by all the bitterness with which His most sacred Soul was flooded, manifest Your mercy to the souls who are under Your just scrutiny. Look upon them in no other way than through the Wounds of Jesus, Your dearly beloved Son; for we firmly believe that there is no limit to Your goodness and compassion. (*Diary*, 1227)

## *Ninth Day*

**Today bring to Me souls who have become lukewarm....** (*Diary*, 1228)

Most compassionate Jesus, You are Compassion Itself. I bring lukewarm souls into the abode of Your Most Compassionate Heart. In this fire of Your pure love let these tepid souls, who, like corpses, filled You with such deep loathing, be once again set aflame. O Most Compassionate Jesus, exercise the omnipotence of Your mercy and draw them into the very ardor of Your love; and bestow upon them the gift of holy love, for nothing is beyond Your power....

Eternal Father, turn Your merciful gaze upon lukewarm souls, who are nonetheless enfolded in the Most Compassionate Heart of Jesus. Father of Mercy, I beg You by the bitter Passion of Your Son and by His three-hour agony on the Cross: Let them, too, glorify the abyss of Your mercy.... (*Diary*, 1229)

# Indulgences

What is an indulgence?

"An indulgence is a remission before God of the temporal punishment due to sins whose guilt has already been forgiven, which the faithful Christian who is duly disposed gains under certain prescribed conditions through the action of the Church which, as the minister of redemption, dispenses and applies with authority the treasury of the satisfactions of Christ and the saints."

"An indulgence is partial or plenary according as it removes either part or all of the temporal punishment due to sin." The faithful can gain indulgences for themselves or apply them to the dead. (CCC 1471)

An indulgence is granted to the Christian faithful who devoutly visit a cemetery and pray, if only silently, for the dead. This indulgence is applicable only to the souls in purgatory. This indulgence is a plenary one, from November 1 through November 8. On other days of the year, it is a partial indulgence.

This indulgence also calls for:

- Reception of sacramental confession.

- Reception of Holy Communion.

- Performance of the prescribed work, such as Stations of the Cross, the Rosary, etc.

- Praying for the pope's intentions—for example, the Our Father, Hail Mary, or any pious prayer.

- That all conditions are met within eight days prior to or after the prescribed work.

### *What Are Other Devotions That Grant Indulgences?*

- Nine First Fridays: For the practice of the Nine First Fridays devotion, Our Lord promises the grace of final repentance.

- Five First Saturdays: For the practice of the Five First Saturdays devotion, Our Lady promises to assist at the hour of death with the graces necessary for salvation.

# Moveable Feasts

Holy Thursday

Good Friday

Holy Saturday

Easter Sunday

Solemnity of the Ascension of Our Lord

Solemnity of Pentecost

Solemnity of the Most Holy Trinity

Feast of Corpus Christi or
the Most Holy Body and Blood of Christ

Feast of the Sacred Heart

Feast of the Immaculate Heart

Feast of Christ the King

Feast of the Holy Family

# Bibliography and Acknowledgments

Brown, Michael H. *The Other Side*. Palm Coast, Florida: Spirit Daily Publishing, 2008.

Czaczkowska, Ewa K. *Faustina: The Mystic and Her Message*. Stockbridge, MA: Marian Press, 2014.

Kieninger, Father Titus, O.R.C. *The Angels in the Diary of Saint Faustina Kowalska*. Carrollton, OH: Order of the Holy Cross, Inc., 2014.

Kosicki, George, W., C.S.B. *Thematic Concordance to the Diary of St. Maria Faustina Kowalska*. Stockbridge, MA: Marian Press, 2015.

———. *Mercy Minutes: Daily Gems of St. Faustina to Transform Your Prayer Life*. Stockbridge, MA: Marian Press, 2006.

Kowalska, St. Maria Faustina. *Diary of Saint Maria Faustina Kowalska*. Stockbridge, MA: Marian Press, 1987.

Lawson, James Gilchrist (ed.). *Cyclopedia of Religious Anecdotes*. New York: Fleming H. Revell, 1923.

Lewis, C. S., *The Complete C. S. Lewis Signature Classics*. Grand Rapids, MI: Zondervan, 2002.

Siepak, Sister M. Elzbieta, O.L.M., and Sister M. Nazaria Dlubak, O.L.M. *The Spirituality of St. Faustina*. Krakow, Poland: Misericordia Publications, 2000.

Tarnawska, Maria. *Sister Faustina Kowalska: Her Life and Mission*. Stockbridge, MA: Marian Press, 2000.

—— ⟡ ——

# Resources

For information about the National Shrine of The Divine Mercy and to become a Friend of Mercy, go to www.thedivinemercy.org.

Association of Marian Helpers
Eden Hill
Stockbridge, MA 01263

Holy Souls Sodality
c/o Association of Marian Helpers
Eden Hill
Stockbridge, MA 01263
www.prayforsouls.org

For memberships and to obtain Masses and Gregorian Masses:

Pious Union of St. Joseph
953 East Michigan Avenue
Grass Lake, MI 49249
(517) 522-8017
www.pusj.org

# About the Author

S usan Tassone has long been a passionate champion for the holy souls in purgatory and is recognized as leading a worldwide "purgatory movement."

The award-winning author of twelve best-sellers, including *Day by Day with Saint Faustina, St. Faustina Prayer Book for Adoration, St. Faustina Prayer Book for the Conversion of Sinners, St. Faustina Prayer Book for the Holy Souls in Purgatory*, and *Day by Day for the Holy Souls in Purgatory*, Susan shares her passion for saving souls through innumerable speaking engagements throughout the country. More than a dozen cardinals and bishops around the world have endorsed her works.

She is a frequent, popular guest on national radio and television programs, as well as having a major impact through social media. In 2017, she appeared on the cover of *Catholic Digest* magazine. In 2013, she was featured in the groundbreaking documentary *Purgatory: The Forgotten Church*, bringing her unique style and penetrating message to a new generation.

Through her tireless work, she raises awareness of purgatory as well as donations for Masses for the holy souls.

Susan holds a master's degree in religious education from Loyola University Chicago and is the recipient of numerous awards. She has had the privilege and honor of being granted two private audiences with St. John Paul II, who bestowed a special blessing on her and her ministry for the holy souls.

Learn more at: susantassone.com.

# Sophia Institute

Sophia Institute is a nonprofit institution that seeks to nurture the spiritual, moral, and cultural life of souls and to spread the Gospel of Christ in conformity with the authentic teachings of the Roman Catholic Church.

Sophia Institute Press fulfills this mission by offering translations, reprints, and new publications that afford readers a rich source of the enduring wisdom of mankind.

Sophia Institute also operates the popular online resource CatholicExchange.com. *Catholic Exchange* provides world news from a Catholic perspective as well as daily devotionals and articles that will help readers to grow in holiness and live a life consistent with the teachings of the Church.

In 2013, Sophia Institute launched Sophia Institute for Teachers to renew and rebuild Catholic culture through service to Catholic education. With the goal of nurturing the spiritual, moral, and cultural life of souls, and an abiding respect for the role and work of teachers, we strive to provide materials and programs that are at once enlightening to the mind and ennobling to the heart; faithful and complete, as well as useful and practical.

Sophia Institute gratefully recognizes the Solidarity Association for preserving and encouraging the growth of our apostolate over the course of many years. Without their generous and timely support, this book would not be in your hands.

www.SophiaInstitute.com
www.CatholicExchange.com
www.SophiaInstituteforTeachers.org